ROBERT PENN WARREN'S

All the King's Men

THREE STAGE VERSIONS

ROBERT PENN WARREN'S

All the King's Men

THREE STAGE VERSIONS

EDITED BY

James A. Grimshaw Jr.

AND

James A. Perkins

THE UNIVERSITY OF GEORGIA PRESS

ATHENS

Published by the University of Georgia Press
Athens, Georgia 30602

Designed by Betty Palmer McDaniel
Set in 10/13 Electra by G & S Typesetters
Printed and bound by McNaughton & Gunn
The paper in this book meets the guidelines for
permanence and durability of the Committee on
Production Guidelines for Book Longevity of the
Council on Library Resources.

Printed in the United States of America
04 03 02 01 00 C 5 4 3 2 1

Library of Congress Cataloging-in-Publication Data
Warren, Robert Penn, 1905–
Robert Penn Warren's All the king's men : three stage versions / edited by James A. Grimshaw Jr.
and James A. Perkins.
p. cm.
Includes bibliographical references.
ISBN 0-8203-2097-8 (alk. paper)
1. Warren, Robert Penn, 1905– All the king's men—Adaptations.   2. Politicians—Southern States—Drama.
3. Political plays, American.   I. Title: All the king's men.   II. Grimshaw, James A.
III. Perkins, James A., 1941– IV. Title.

PS3545.A748 A6 2000
812'.52—dc21   99-040043

To the memory
of
Cleanth and Tinkum Brooks

Contents

Foreword

JOHN BURT

When an author first begins to think through an ambitious work, it presents itself in a penumbra of hints, intuitions, and possibilities, each capable of being developed in a bewildering variety of ways. The author may laboriously plan the work or may, as Robert Penn Warren says he did, merely follow his or her nose, eager to see where it leads, but no matter how careful the preparation, the author always ultimately must examine a concept that can be seen only in the half-darkness of latency; the author, like the reader, is curious to see what this thing that itches him into writing is, is curious to see, when he feels the pressure of urgent meaningfulness, what the meaning ultimately will turn out to be. Realizing these possibilities in a concrete and completed work of art requires the author to sacrifice many possibilities, to choose one way (or a few ways) over others through the Garden of Forking Paths. No matter how many byways the author explores, there will always be roads not traveled, roads that burden him with the sense that they might have made all the difference.

The completed text never fully exhausts the potential of the latent concept, because the latent concept contains strains of implication and development that may band together inwardly but that cannot always be made consistent with one another. Writing a book is a complex attempt to keep articulate faith with a set of motivating intuitions that articulation always at least partly betrays. But if the articulation of the work has a price, it also rewards the author and reader alike with a compensating value, for as the author works his or her way through the possible developments of a literary intuition, discarding some courses in favor of others, connecting events in a scheme of motivation and plausibility, constructing situations that put the governing themes and moral insights of the work to the test, each choice, while excluding a hundred possibilities, yields a hundred new possibilities that the author could not have seen clearly before making that choice. Each turn opens up new turns; each solution presents a new set of problems; each moment of closure presents new ways to alter the conditions or raise the stakes of the thought-experiment the author is performing; each tightening of the nuts and bolts of the story enables the author to make a new turn of the screw, transforming the developing work in ways that cast an intense and unexpected light on its deepest aims.

It is this sense of the losses and the gains that attends every articulation of a literary work that underlies one of the great inventions of the fiction of the last two centuries, multiple point of view narration. Multiple conflicting points of view offer the author not the opportunity to present some thesis about the reliability and unreliability of human witnesses or to give play to skepticism about the reality of the external world (both are ultimately rather sophomoric pursuits) but rather the opportunity to live out several of the alternative lives that presented themselves to him or her in that moment of literary possibility. Something similar motivates the view in current literary criticism that a text is all of its versions: keeping all of the different versions and states of a text somehow before the mind might give one some insight into the matrix of intuitions from which the text arises.

The tension between the work and its generative matrix of intuitions is something every student of Robert Penn Warren's work must feel. Warren was a notoriously restless writer, not merely revising his texts as his style or views changed, as James or Auden did, but continuously rethinking them. Poems Warren published in the 1930s were still under active revision in the 1980s, by which time they might have appeared in as many as six different states. The book-length *Brother to Dragons*, itself the product of laborious rewriting and reenvisioning at the time of its original publication in 1953, was overhauled from stem to stern to make a two-act play in 1976 and another book-length poem in 1979. Warren was at work on a third version of *Brother to Dragons* as late as the summer of 1987. But *All the King's Men* is in a class by itself; the rich textual materials collected in the Beinecke Rare Book and Manuscript Library provide an unparalleled opportunity to trace the author's visions and revisions of a major work both before and after its publication.

With scrupulous care and scholarship, James A. Grimshaw and James A. Perkins have put together three of the very different ways Warren attempted to think through the material of *All the King's Men* in dramatic form. The 1960 play version has seen publication before, but it has been out of print for some time. The 1955 *Willie Stark: His Rise and Fall* is little known, although it did enjoy a brief run on stage; Grimshaw and Perkins present it here in print for the general reader for the first time, and the text is a startling departure from the novel on which it is based — more startling even than the 1960 play, which itself handles the novel's material with a freedom only the author himself would have dared. Warren provided in interviews and essays a great deal of information about *Proud Flesh*, the verse-tragedy in which he first worked out his thoughts about the Long regime, and scholars have had access to its many versions in the Beinecke Rare Book and Manuscript Library; but for the first time Grimshaw and Perkins have sorted out those versions to produce a reliable text. *Proud Flesh* occupied Warren's mind for at least five years between 1935 and 1940; and its several versions, differing somewhat in structure and in such things as the names of the principal characters, indicate painstaking processes of composition and revision. Grimshaw and Perkins argue persuasively, and against the received wisdom about the text, that the versions in which the principal character is named Willie Strong predate the versions in which the character is named Willie Talos (after the mechanical man who attends Artegall, Spenser's Knight of Justice in *The Faerie Queene*).

Proud Flesh is not merely a first draft of *All the King's Men* but an entirely different work, a work that shares some characters and scenes with its successors but that also has a different focus and presents some of the action in a profoundly different way. It also presents some possibilities that Warren foreclosed in later versions; and although the play shines with its own light, it casts considerable illumination on the novel and on the other versions.

Verse tragedy might have seemed a less outlandish genre in the late 1930s than it does now. Certainly it was a genre with enough popular life that Maxwell Anderson could use it with success in *Winterset*, and there was also the example of Expressionist playwrights like Federico García Lorca. Writing in verse enables the characters to speak with a dreamlike, crystalline intensity that modern prose, even Jack Burden's prose, intoxicated with its own toughness and the posture of plainness it so often affects, cannot manage. Much of this verse would be hard to manage on the stage of the present day, but it does place one in the inwardness of the play as prose could not do. The choice of verse interspersed with prose motivates the Expressionist aspects of the play as well — the visionary and hyperreal quality of the choral speeches by the different groups of masked persons that open each act, for instance, or the seething and coiling of the rage and life-hatred of Keith Amos (*Proud Flesh*'s version of Adam Stanton). The moment when a radio speech about Willie changes from businesslike reportorial prose to charged verse — right after Willie rips the plug of the radio out of the wall — captures something of how verse is used to heighten the action by placing it in an absolute light unconstrained by verisimilitude. The sinister crooning of "I Can't Give You Anything but Love, Baby" at the climax of the dancing scene and Tiny Harper's vaudeville song as Willie tries to break off the deal with Gummy Satterfield are also moments drawn from the repertory of Expressionist drama.

However, as Grimshaw and Perkins point out, the major influence on this play is not Expressionist verse tragedy but Shakespearean verse tragedy, in which Warren was soaked during the years he was composing *Proud Flesh*. Warren draws his five-act structure here from Shakespeare's reading of Plutarch. Even Warren's contemporary sense of the Long regime in Louisiana is Shakespearean: Long is a kind of Caesar to Warren, and Warren has the kind of mixed feelings about Long that Shakespeare did about Caesar. When in Warren's Shakespeare lecture course at Louisiana State University during the Long regime the syllabus came to *Julius Caesar*, Warren for once enjoyed a perfectly rapt and silently attentive class: those students, who included Rose Long, the governor's daughter, knew clearly how that play related to their own lives.

Some of *Proud Flesh* will be familiar to readers of *All the King's Men*. The plot swirls around the hospital project, which is also the focus of the crisis of the novel's last half. Tiny Harper, the railroad commissioner (in the 1920s the second most powerful member of Southern state governments), is as sebaceous and as supine and as ultimately treacherous as Tiny Duffy, Willie's lieutenant governor in the novel. And Willie Strong, if somewhat less gleeful and less in command of telling extended metaphors than Willie Stark, nevertheless has his brooding intelligence, his tense impatience with the niceties of due process and with the corruption of his own means.

The principal thing that readers of *All the King's Men* will miss in *Proud Flesh* is the story—and the tone of voice—of Jack Burden. Jack has at best a cameo role, making small talk with Keith Amos in the moments before the assassination of Governor Strong. Without Jack's judgment, and without his entanglement in his own different moral drama, we see the other characters very differently. This version is Willie's play, and the only character who really shares the stage with him is Keith Amos, who is given a much richer development than Adam Stanton is given in the novel.

Consider the brilliant opening scene, in which Keith and Dr. Shipworth are stopped by a motorcycle policeman as Keith rushes to his first meeting with Governor Strong, who will ask him to head up the grand new hospital he is planning. When the trooper realizes who they are (and that, as Keith's snide and oily passenger reminds him, ticketing them will lose him his job), his swagger evaporates, and he is reduced to begging to be allowed to do them favors to save his neck. Keith will have none of it; he never lets the trooper off the hook, demanding that the trooper do his duty and give him the ticket, and he promises the trooper nothing. Perhaps Keith sees this as playing by the rules. But he also takes a bit too much pleasure in making the trooper writhe. Nothing in the novel shows so clearly that close kinship in his nature between rigid devotion to principle and naked sadism that makes him ultimately such a frightening alternative to Willie.

Keith is already in a rage when he is stopped, and it is only partly a rage against having to meet with the governor, whose corruption (alleged corruption—we never see him doing anything that is corrupt in the sense Keith means) offends his nostrils. Keith thinks he is enraged about political corruption. But what he is really enraged about is having a human body, subject to desire and to decay, a porous bag of foul-smelling fluids:

> A stink, and on a man's fingers,
> Whatever he lays hands to, it's there,
> And the stink climbs the multitudinous sweetness of air,
> Lovingly lingers, a kiss upon the tongue,
> And fouls the nostril's secret stair—
> Smell it, it's there
> On your fingers, and mine—Whatever you touch,
> The cup lifted familiarly, morningly, to the lips,
> The friend's hand—that delicate
> Film of moisture slick upon the palm
> There, there it will live, proliferate,
> Swelling like algae spored upon a pond—
> The flower you pluck, and the door-knob
> Kind to your fingers, accustomed, the door
> Which opens to the innermost room where love lies.

This is not just priggishness; there is something sexually charged, even positively kinky, about Keith's disgust here. These are not the accents of a rejecter of sexual life but of a sexual sadist whose rejection of sexuality is a kind of erotic cruelty. He has a natural cousin in the Thomas Jefferson of Warren's *Brother to Dragons*, whose speeches likewise often drip with sexually charged disgust, and he has a natural ancestor in Angelo of *Measure for Measure*, perhaps the original of all of those characters who link Puritanism and sadism. His later tirade in which he compares the male genitalia to "a sly purse of pleasure" sounds like Angelo at his most revolted and mesmerized. It is not for nothing that it is Keith's sister Anne's sexual involvement with Willie, rather than anything political, that drives him over the edge. Something of this view of Adam is plausible even in the novel, but we do not focus on it there in the way we do here, because there it is obscured by Jack's own moral drama and by his inability, so strange in a narrator proud of his toughness, to see his friends with perfect clarity.

Anne Amos also cuts a different figure from the novel's Anne Stanton. Jack Burden blames himself for everything Anne does and for everything that happens to her. His own sexual cowardice, he believes, practically threw her, years later, into Willie Strong's arms. But it is clear even in the novel that Anne has her own reasons for her connection with Willie: she is struggling with an attraction to him as early as the impeachment rally scene. Anne Stanton sees Willie as someone who is able to cut through illusion and inhibition in the service of justice; his roughness, relative to the priggish and self-serving Good Government types who complain about Willie back in Burden's Landing, is a sign to her of his deeper knowledge of the world and his more intense commitment to do good in it. But her moral passion has an unmistakable sexual edge, sharpened both by the sexual thrill of power and by the sexual thrill of her own class transgression. Lucy Ferriss, in *Sleeping with the Boss*, her study of Warren's female characters, argues that the novelist has a grittier vision of Anne than the narrator does, because Jack Burden sees Anne only in terms of his story, not in terms of her own. Ferriss's views are richly borne out by Anne Amos, who is a firmer and more frankly sexual character.

When we first see her—Keith Amos, leaving his first meeting with Willie, bumps into her on her own way in to see him—she is a woman of the world who knows what you have to do to get something done and is not shy about doing it. It is Anne's own persuasiveness, not the Irwin scandal that Jack Burden uses against him in the novel and in the other dramatic versions, that moves Keith to take the job as director of the hospital in the play. (There is no Judge Irwin in *Proud Flesh*, although Willie alludes early on to having driven a Senator Crosby to suicide by revealing a corrupt bargain in his distant past.) And it is Anne Amos Willie feels he has to explain himself to when he first makes the bargain Tiny Harper proposes with Gummy Satterfield (Gummy Larsen in the novel).

In *All the King's Men* we never see Anne and Willie together; we do not have a sense of the quality of their relationship. But in *Proud Flesh* we see them dancing together, and we see the sexual hunger and desperate need on both sides. The scene occurs at a vulnerable moment for Willie. He has just, in the scene before, made his corrupt bargain with Satterfield, in which he will gain control of the Fourth and Fifth Districts in exchange for the hospital construction contract. He makes this bargain not, as in the novel, to evade political pressure put on him by his son Tom's carryings on and not, as in *Willie Stark: His Rise and Fall*, to outflank a threatened impeachment but simply because it gives him an advantage. At the very moment he closed the deal (Tiny Harper had sprung Satterfield on him as he was watching his son's heroics at a football game), Tom was injured on the field, so in the scene with Anne that follows he has both political and familial problems in mind. Willie is uneasy about the deal he has just made, but when he explains himself to Anne she not only is persuaded, she is even a little turned on by his realism:

ANNE. I know, I know—but isn't there some other way? Does it have to be like this? And the medical center contract.

STRONG. Buck up! It's no news. You know how things are.

ANNE. No. No news.—*(She faces him directly.)*—I know how things are. I'm not a child. What has to be done, has to be done. Oh, Willie—(*She hesitates, then reaches out to touch him on the lapel.*)—I love you.

STRONG. (*Apparently paying no attention to her declaration.*) I wanted you to know. Before I told you what I have to tell you. I want you to marry me.

It is not Willie's realism here that bothers Anne—she announces, rather formidably, that she is "not biddy hearted to brook / And fluff on opportunities like eggs"—but his self-doubt. Willie has been brooding on a remark by his estranged wife, Clara (Lucy Stark in *All the King's Men*), that he has become fragmentary and unstrung, that he has lost his way. When he wonders aloud whether Clara had it right, Anne not only gives him no help but begins to wonder whether he is man enough for her or whether he is instead fool enough to think that love will somehow give him back his sense of a transforming moral purpose. From the novel one imagines Anne's feelings for Willie as clingy and dependent, and one thinks of her as not fully aware that her romantic feelings for Willie are sexual feelings; it is a surprise to see Anne in *Proud Flesh* as having the emotional upper hand and as being the more forthrightly sexual of the two. Certainly Tiny Harper understands this, for when Willie is called to the hospital, Tom's having taken a surprising turn for the worst, he too presses himself upon Anne with the air of one who knows what kind of woman she is.

Much of what the novel dramatizes is not dramatized in the play. And much of what is presented directly in the play is presented indirectly in the novel. We actually see Willie's attempted reconciliation with Clara—a tougher customer in *Proud Flesh* than Lucy in *All the King's Men*—as well as the conspiracy between Sue Parsons (Sadie Burke in the novel) and Tiny Harper to push Keith Amos into murdering Willie (in the novel Jack Burden learns about Sadie Burke's role almost by accident from Sadie herself long afterward). We even see Tiny Harper, in person, working Keith Amos up to the murder. (In the novel, even Adam's murderous rage is presented indirectly, through Anne's frantic search for him after he abuses her.) At the same time, we do not see anything of Willie's early career. Sue Parsons tells us that she "put [Willie] in the big time," but there is no trace of the story of the schoolhouse contract or of Willie's first race for governor that is so important to establishing Willie's good faith in the novel.

That in *Proud Flesh* we never see Willie as the idealistic Cousin Willie from the country may be an advantage, for the story of Willie's early career motivates a particularly common misreading of the novel, a misreading that sees it as a story of how the political system corrupts decent men—as if it were "Mr. Stark Goes to Baton Rouge" rather than *All the King's Men*. It is a mistake to think of Willie as a man who loses sight of his moral aims once he comes to power; his problem is that his seriousness about his moral aims blinds him to the amorality of his means, and he only really understands those moral aims once he comes to power. His difficulty is not that he suddenly becomes mad for power once he has some of it, but, having torn the law down around him to serve his vision of justice, he can no longer tell whether it is justice or power that he was ultimately all about. Willie does not lose his moral interest once he comes to power; it is in taking a bold if wrongheaded position as a kind of armed prophet that he has his moral interest in the first place. In presenting him only at the height of his power, *Proud Flesh* keeps its focus on what really matters about Willie, and it is not tempted into the morally simpler but also morally shallower view of Willie that the Robert Rossen film adopts. *Proud Flesh* also, unlike the novel, never learns the lesson Jack Burden learns, that History is blind but Man is not, for the play's conclusions are unremittingly dark, and the final scene leaves Tiny Harper and his like in complete control.

Willie Stark: His Rise and Fall includes much more of the novel's plot than *Proud Flesh* does, but as the title indicates it is focused on Willie Stark, not on Jack Burden. Most crucially, Judge Irwin is Anne and Adam Stanton's uncle rather than Jack Burden's father, and the whole story of Jack's fall and redemption and his role in the death of the man who turns out to be his father are, startlingly, not factors in this play. *All the King's Men* may well have too complicated a plot to stage in any but the most stylized way, and on stage even *Willie Stark: His Rise and Fall* ran too long to be a successful drama. But Jack's responsibility for his father's death is a very curious thing to decide to cut, as if it were a side issue.

Willie Stark: His Rise and Fall does, however, condense the novel in a few interesting particulars. Rather than covering several different political crises (about Byram White, about the impeachment, about the hospital, about Tom Stark's sexual peccadilloes), *Willie Stark: His Rise and Fall* superimposes them. The whole action takes place under the shadow of an impeachment proceeding that arises from Tiny Duffy's corruption (not from Byram White's). The hospital project is not only Willie's attempt to prove to himself that not all of his work is corrupt, but it is also his attempt to prove the same thing to the electorate. And the deal with Gummy Larsen is not designed as a counterstroke to answer a blackmail attempt against Tom but to turn a few crucial votes during the impeachment hearings. There is, indeed, no blackmail plot against Tom in this play, although he is the same churl in this version as in every version, and here as everywhere it is Willie's guilt in the face of Tom's death that motivates his final revulsion against the Larsen deal and against his affair with Anne.

The most daring revisions of the novel's plot turn on Judge Irwin. One wonders whether anybody but the author himself would have had the daring to decide that Jack Burden's responsibility for the death of his own father was after all so minor an issue that it could be totally dropped from a stage version of *All the King's Men*. The play conflates Judge Irwin and Hugh Miller, so that it is

Judge Irwin who is present during Willie's grilling and humiliation of Tiny Duffy after his kickback scheme is revealed, and it is Judge Irwin who resigns as attorney general when Willie decides not to throw Tiny Duffy to the wolves. (Carlisle Floyd did the same thing in the libretto to his 1980 opera *Willie Stark*.) Superimposing Judge Irwin and Hugh Miller makes Judge Irwin's relationship with Willie a far more complicated issue than in the novel (and in some ways makes him a slightly more attractive figure).

Warren also combines elements of the scene where Jack and Willie attempt to bully Judge Irwin early in the novel with the later scene where Jack presents him with the evidence he has against him. Indeed, Willie charges into the room in the midst of Jack's revelations about Irwin's role in the American Electric Power Company (Gummy Larsen's company, by coincidence), and most of the really dirty work of the blackmail attempt, and all the keen perception about what kind of man Irwin really is, is given to Willie, not to Jack, who indeed nearly comes to blows with Willie over his interference. Jack—even more incredibly for readers of the novel—encourages Irwin to lie about the past and promises to back him up. Willie tells Jack both before and after this scene that he suspects that Jack will somehow scheme to get Judge Irwin off, so Jack's gesture here is especially fatuous and seems the work of a far more lightweight character than the Jack Burden of the novel, who at least faces the Judge for what he is. All of this serves, I think, to make Irwin's chief relationship not his relationship with Jack but his relationship with Willie, a relationship that does not exist at all in the novel.

Willie is an edgier figure in *Willie Stark: His Rise and Fall* than in either the novel or *Proud Flesh*. We never see in him the self-knowing happy warrior we sometimes see in the novel, and there is an element of desperation in his deal with Gummy Larsen. In *Proud Flesh* he entered into that deal with his eyes open. In the novel he entered into the bargain to deflate the blackmail attempt by MacMurfee's boys against his son, and even then only when his attempt to squeeze MacMurfee by pressuring Judge Irwin was thwarted by Irwin's suicide. Here, despite the pressure of the looming impeachment and despite the failure of his attempt to thwart the impeachment by turning on Judge Irwin, Willie still refuses to deal with Larsen, and in the scene that closely parallels the football game scene in *Proud Flesh* in which the deal with Larsen is struck, Willie leaves Larsen hanging instead. He deals with Larsen not before his son's injury, as in *Proud Flesh*, but immediately after it, in a moment of inebriated panic brought on by the threat to his son's life.

As in every retelling of this story, it is Tom's death that pushes Willie into breaking the bargain he has just made. *Proud Flesh* and *Willie Stark: His Rise and Fall* both dramatize Willie's attempted reconciliation with his wife, which *All the King's Men* reported only at second hand, and in both dramatic versions it is far from clear that she will accept him back. Again as in *Proud Flesh* (and not the novel), Willie's breaking of the bargain and Sadie's conspiracy with Tiny Duffy are dramatized directly. But *Willie Stark: His Rise and Fall* goes further than this, having Willie even attempt to square his accounts publicly with the electorate. When Willie beats down the impeachment attempt midway through *All the King's Men*, the speech he gives is an example of Willie Stark at his greatest persuasiveness and gusto. Here, at the very end of the play, stung by his son's death, Willie instead confesses everything he has done and makes a rather flabby plea for forgiveness or justification, so that when Adam Stanton shoots him, seconds later, he shoots a man who has just stopped being the man he has come to shoot. It is a puzzling conclusion, and Jack's and Anne's concluding speeches are, without the development of Jack that the novel but not this play gave him, more puzzling still.

The 1960 play version (performed in 1959) follows the novel somewhat more closely than the previous versions do. The story of Willie's early career—the schoolhouse construction project, the first run for governor, the Upton speech, even the scene in Slade's speakeasy—is presented, either directly or indirectly, as it is not in the other dramatic versions. Jack Burden also plays somewhat closer to the role he plays in the novel. His complicated relationship with his mother—who does not appear in the 1955 play at all—is dramatized, for instance (down to her silvery soprano scream after Judge Irwin's death), and Judge Irwin, who has no relationship with Willie (and is in other ways more like the figure in the novel than in the 1955 play), does in fact turn out to be Jack's father.

Judge Irwin has the power to get under Willie's skin in the play as he does not in the novel: Willie's immediate motivation for undertaking the hospital project is not, as in the novel, the desire to prove to himself that despite protecting Byram White he is still a moral person but his desire to answer the moral discomfort Judge Irwin's disapproval (which Willie explicitly compares with Lucy's disapproval) has raised in his mind. Willie's demand that Jack find out what dirt there is on Irwin is partly motivated by the same thing: although there is an impeachment process under way (we are not given details of it in this version — it is not because of Byram White, as in the novel, or because of Tiny Duffy, as in *Willie Stark: His Rise and Fall*), and although Irwin is supporting it (which is why Jack and Willie have come to bully him in the first place), the local context of Willie's demand on Jack suggests that it is not just an attempt to force Judge Irwin to change sides but is also given special urgency by the doubts about himself that Willie is beginning to feel in the aftermath of having been rebuked by both Irwin and, offstage, by Lucy. Discrediting Irwin is a way of beating down the self-doubt Irwin causes in him. Willie's desire to have Adam direct the hospital arises from similar doubts. Willie hits on the idea in the immediate aftermath of rejecting Tiny Duffy's initial proposal of the Larsen deal; it is a way of washing the taste of that proposal out of his mouth.

Anne and Adam Stanton are closer here to their portrayals in the novel. In the 1960 play we know that Anne and Jack are former lovers. (In *Willie Stark: His Rise and Fall* even Willie knows this, which makes his own desire to pursue a relationship with her a little stronger medicine.) Like the 1955 text, the 1960 version takes from the novel the scene in which Anne begs Jack to pressure Adam into taking the directorship of the hospital. Jack provides her with the evidence against Judge Irwin, and she turns against Jack in consequence. But in the 1960 play it is Anne herself, not Jack, who actually "changes the picture in Adam's head" by presenting him with the evidence of Judge Irwin's misdeeds, so that when Adam takes the directorship as a kind of expression of despair he is not merely adopting a more embittered version of Jack's own cynicism but is also engaged in a complicated moral dance with Anne. Anne's role in Adam's entanglement with Willie is foregrounded here, making what Adam takes to be her betrayal of him (by her affair with Stark) all the more stinging. In both the 1955 and 1960 plays, incidentally, Anne's affair with Willie seems to be common knowledge to everybody but Jack and Adam. Even Tiny Duffy knows all about it and assumes, until Sadie Burke tells him otherwise, that Adam was given the hospital job to keep him quiet about Willie's shenanigans with his sister.

In the play the impeachment crisis is deemphasized. Although the hospital project and the original investigation of Judge Irwin are motivated by an impeachment crisis, the final squeeze on Judge Irwin (and, when that fails because of Irwin's suicide, the agreement to the Larsen deal) is motivated not by that crisis (which seems to lose steam midway through the play) but by Marvin Frey's blackmail attempt against Tom, which Willie thinks of as MacMurfee's last stratagem, the impeachment attempt having gone sour. Warren thus, at the price of somewhat more complicated plot, is able to place Willie's relationship with Tom in a stronger light than in the 1955 play.

As in *Willie Stark: His Rise and Fall*, Willie delays cutting a deal with Gummy Larsen even after Irwin's suicide (when it becomes clear to everyone else that he will eventually have to do so), deliberately breaking an appointment so that he can see Tom play football. It is only after Tom's injury (as in *Willie Stark: His Rise and Fall* but not as in the novel) that Willie finally caves in and offers Larsen the construction contract. The final scenes of the 1960 play also owe a great deal more to *Willie Stark: His Rise and Fall* than to the novel, down to Willie's confession at the anti-impeachment rally. But Willie's acts, even his final words ("It might have been different, Jack—even yet—even yet—you got to believe that, Jack"), are allowed to stand on their own in the 1955 version and are subject to caustic reinterpretation here.

This reinterpretation is the work of a character Warren created for this version, the snide and cynical Professor, a Gradgrindish brute with immense respect for "the facts" and immense contempt for moral reasoning, which he dismisses as "vaporings around the facts." Jack Burden is in a struggle with the Professor for interpretive control of the play from the opening scene. Jack interrupts the Professor's Historical Materialist speech at the dedication of the Tom Stark Hospital in the play's prologue and jousts with him on and off throughout the play. The Professor even dismisses Willie's final turn against corruption as a pathetic and sentimental failure of nerve. Most readers think of the Professor as rather a disaster, and some recent productions of the play cut all of his lines. Warren had introduced similar interlocutors in other works whose interpretations and misinterpretations enable the audience to think through similar issues. But the "historian" of *World Enough and Time* at least has an engaging melancholy rather than mere snideness. And even the character R.P.W. of *Brother to Dragons*, almost as nasty a figure as the Professor here, never has quite the ability to tyrannize over the work that the Professor has. The chief fact about the Professor is that he does not know the difference between a tough-guy rhetoric and actual realism about human beings and human motivations. It is a curious piety of our age that those who adopt the Professor's style, those who mechanically take the most cynical and reductionist view of human acts they can come up with, often enjoy the unearned prestige of having superior knowledge of the world.

Readers of *All the King's Men* will recognize the Professor's disease as the disease of Jack Burden before he undergoes the transformations worked upon him by the dark events of the novel's plot: the Professor, like the younger Jack, is a believer in the "Great Twitch" theory of human nature, the theory that human beings are but mechanisms seeking power and pleasure, all other claims about their motivations being evasions designed to serve the purposes of power and pleasure. The invention of the Professor for the 1960 play may well be a consequence of that text's renewed foregrounding of Jack Burden as the moral center of the play. Jack Burden as a character, as opposed to Jack Burden as a narrator, had views rather like the Professor's, and the conflict between Jack and the Professor in the play is a way of representing the conflict in the novel between Jack's views as a character and Jack's later views as narrator.

Collectively, the three dramatic versions of the Willie Stark story that Grimshaw and Perkins have presented here show how alive all of the motivating ideas behind the novel remained in Warren's mind, even years after he published the book. Warren continued to rework not only details of plot and take but also the order of events, the structure of motivations, even some of the major themes of the work. Even the things that remain constant undergo changes in disposition. In every version, for instance, Willie at some point throws his drink in Tiny's face. But his motivations for that act are not always the same: sometimes he is enraged by a lascivious mention of Anne Stanton, sometimes he is enraged by the Larsen deal, sometimes he is enraged that he has been put in so desperate a situation that he has to agree to the Larsen deal despite himself. Clearly it mattered more to Warren that Willie throw his drink in Tiny's face than precisely why he does so — after all, Tiny Duffy has a way of providing occasions for such treatment. At the same time, the strong continuities among the versions concerning Willie's final turn — which is always a product of Tom's death — suggest that Willie's relationship with Tom has more emotional weight in Warren's imagination of the book than the scanty development Tom's character is given in the novel might lead one to believe. Willie's failed relationship with Tom outweighs even Jack Burden's driving of his father to suicide, which Warren felt free to drop. Grimshaw and Perkins's work in editing these three very different dramatic versions of the Willie Stark story shows just how much continued to remain open to Warren about this book, how many possibilities continued to be in play in his mind even after the official version was already part of the public mind. Even in the public mind, *All the King's Men* continues to unfold, whether in the different dramatic versions developed recently by Adrian Hall, Robert Walsh, and Lucy Maycock and Barry Kyle, in the opera by Carlisle Floyd, in the implicit allusion to Warren's book in Woodward and Bernstein's account of the Watergate scandal, or in the casual appropriation of Warren's thought and themes in recent political fiction. Huey Long has been dead since September 1935, but Willie Stark seems to keep on living.

Preface

This edition is inspired by a belief that an understanding of Robert Penn Warren's novel *All the King's Men* is enhanced by knowledge of the development of the Willie Stark story, which began as a drama, *Proud Flesh*, in the summer of 1937. That development continued through the 1960 publication of *All the King's Men (A Play)* and included the metamorphosis from drama to novel and back again to drama. A problem previously confronting readers, however, was the unavailability of texts for *Proud Flesh* and for *Willie Stark: His Rise and Fall*. We are pleased to be permitted to make available editions of those two texts now, along with the previously published version of *All the King's Men (A Play)*.

We believe that these three texts will provide readers with new insights and a better understanding of Warren's classic story about Southern politics and the ethical and moral dilemmas faced by people in positions of power. Central to those dilemmas is the age-old question, Does the end justify the means? In addition to the three stage versions of the Willie Stark story, we offer an introductory essay that provides an overview of their relationship to one another and to the novel. Four decades ago in an essay entitled "The Dramatic Versions of the Willie Stark Story," William M. Schutte recognized the significance of these dramatic versions; we are indebted to his pioneering work, which serves as a backdrop to this edition. Also included is a selected bibliography of works related to the dramatic versions of the Willie Stark story.

Drama was important to Warren. His novels are filled with elements of drama, and his early interests focused to a large extent on Shakespeare's plays. Scholars such as Mark Royden Winchell, Lewis P. Simpson, James A. Grimshaw, and others have noted echoes of *The Tragedy of Coriolanus*, *The Tragedy of Hamlet, Prince of Denmark*, *The Tragedy of Julius Caesar*, and the Henriad, an influence to which Warren himself alludes in several interviews and in his various introductions to his novel *All the King's Men*. That fascination, coupled with Warren's return to work with the dramatic version of *All the King's Men*, the film adaptation by Robert Rossen, other stage renditions such as the adaptations by Adrian Hall, and an opera by Carlisle Floyd, lend credence to the significance of and continuing interest in this particular story.

In choosing the three versions included in this book, we have kept three things in mind: that we are presenting the first version of the play and the final versions of two (of the three, counting the novel) variations of that beginning; that the texts should provide the reader some sense of growth of narrative material as it relates to the novel *All the King's Men*; and that since Warren was self-critical and constantly revising his dramatic work, we were not looking for a final authorial text of the plays. However, one might argue that the text published by Random House in 1960 constitutes the final authorial text of the play *All the King's Men* and that the text we have created here out of notes on the method of collaboration between Warren and Aaron Frankel constitutes a final version of *Willie Stark: His Rise and Fall*. Since the Cleanth Brooks version of *Proud Flesh* is the beginning of Warren's struggle to tell the story of Willie Stark, this volume combined with a copy of the novel should provide the reader with the alpha and the omegas, with the beginning and the various endings of Warren's several attempts to tell this compelling story. For the sake of consistency and because we are not trying to produce a facsimile edition, we have adopted a general format similar to the one used in the Random House (1960) version of *All the King's Men (A Play)* for the other two texts. We have also attempted to correct accidentals silently, that is, misspellings that we believe would have been caught in reading proofs. Rather than fill the text with a cumbersome editorial apparatus, we have restored the standard spellings.

The text of *Proud Flesh* presented here is based on the Cleanth Brooks copy. By plotting a progression in the development of Warren's leading character, we might discover three distinct phases, more or less distinguished by the three names Warren gives him: Strong, Talos, and Stark. Strong and Talos appear in different versions of *Proud Flesh*. A preponderance of evidence suggests that the text with Willie Strong is, indeed, the earliest text. It is the text provided in this volume.

The text of *Willie Stark: His Rise and Fall* presented here is based on the director's copy prepared by Aaron Frankel for the 1958 production at the Margo Jones Theatre in Dallas, Texas (Finley, Draft G). The authority for this version is established in a series of letters from Frankel to Warren written when Frankel was working on a version of *Brother to Dragons*. On 17 October 1967, Frankel wrote: "maybe we can go back to our 'Willie Stark' method, when I was at least able to confer with you by letter or telephone, when necessary." Then on 14 January 1968, he wrote: "I've otherwise followed our old 'Willie Stark' method, meaning that I've avoided writing a single line of my own, and every word left is yours only. I've done this with transitions, sometimes (not often) with whole speeches, or parts of a speech, or lines or parts of lines, and trying always to keep what I can sense is your metrical desire as well as the best acting answer." The text of *Willie Stark: His Rise and Fall* marked "director's copy" reveals two kinds of changes made by Aaron Frankel. First, he made cuts — cuts of lines, cuts of whole speeches, occasionally cuts of entire scenes. Clearly, these cuts were made in consultation (probably by telephone or in person) with Warren. In several places in the manuscript "STET" is written in the margin beside passages that have been marked out. The net result of the cuts Frankel made is a more manageable play. The play is still too long, but Frankel was able to root out most of the redundancies. The other changes he made, changes in language, we ignored.

In his letter to Warren about *Brother to Dragons* quoted above, Frankel says that in this revision, as in the one he did for *Willie Stark: His Rise and Fall*, he toned down Warren's language: "I think I shall haul ass" became "I think I shall haul tail"; "son-of-a-bitch" became "son-of-a-gun" or "spit-licker"; "bastard" became "swine" or "blood sucking louse"; "for Christ's sake" became "for cripes sake." We believe Frankel made these changes and Warren agreed to them with the Dallas audience in mind, but the changes create a semicomical undertone that reduces the effect of Warren's portrait of down-and-dirty Southern politics. In a 26 May 1997 letter, Frankel told us: "A word about my having 'toned down' the language. Your guess about Dallas is dead right. I was totally unprepared for the Bible Belt when I hit it. . . . I'd have had to cancel 'Willie Stark' without acceding to those changes. You're welcome to include this information and certainly to restore the language, with my thanks." In every case, we restored Warren's original language. By accepting Frankel's cuts and restoring Warren's language, we have created a text that was not performed but that probably represents the most accurate text that can be reconstructed from the available materials.

The text of *All the King's Men* presented here is based on the printed text of the 1960 Random House edition. That edition, in turn, is based on the 1959 version directed by Mark Schoenberg at the East 74th Street Theatre, a text that Warren said was the result of "a happy collaboration." We would have preferred to check the printed text against the setting copy and the page proofs of that edition, but neither of those copies was available.

This presentation of the three stage versions of the Willie Stark story provides a book for aspiring playwrights, for students interested in textual studies, for literary critics, for teachers, and for directors of future productions of this play. For readers who are intellectually curious, various comparisons among the texts — characterization, setting, structure, and language, for example — will challenge and reward.

Several people have been most kind in assisting with this project through suggestions, moral support, and permission rights. We thank the following people specifically and the many others who patiently listened to us discuss our thoughts and theories: Professor Emeritus Joseph Blotner, University of Michigan, Warren's biographer; the late Cleanth Brooks, who generously lent his copy of *Proud Flesh* and provided wonderful conversation about his life-long friend; Professor John Burt, Brandeis University, Warren's literary executor; Dr. Bob Dowell, editor of *Texas College English*, in which a portion of the introduction appeared as "Strong to Stark: Deceiver, Demagogue, Dictator"; Mr. Charles East; Dr. Sue Laslie Kimball, Methodist College, Fayetteville, N.C.; Professor of English and American Studies Emeritus R. W. B. Lewis, Yale University; Graduate Dean Keith McFarland, through whom part of this project was funded with a Texas A&M University–Commerce Organized Research Grant; Dr. William J. McTaggart, chair of the Department of English, Dr. Richard L. Sprow, faculty development officer, and the Faculty Development Committee at Westminster College, through whom part of this project was funded with a Faculty Development Grant; Ms. Carol Morrow, who helped type part of this manuscript; Boyd Professor Emeritus Lewis P. Simpson, Louisiana State University, former coeditor of the *Southern Review* and adviser and mentor; Mr. Al Sternbergh, former director of planning and placement, Westminster College; Dr. Patricia C. Willis, curator, the Yale Collection of American Literature, Beinecke Rare Book and Manuscript Library, Yale University; the National Endowment for the Humanities Summer Seminar for College Faculty; Owen Laster and Jill Westmoreland of the William Morris Agency; Ms. Karen Orchard, director, and Ms. Kristine M. Blakeslee, editor, University of Georgia Press; and Ms. Mary M. Hill, copyeditor.

A very special thank you to the Estate of Robert Penn Warren and to Rosanna Warren, Gabriel Warren, and the late Eleanor Clark Warren for their kind permission, which allowed us to provide this volume.

ROBERT PENN WARREN'S

All the King's Men

THREE STAGE VERSIONS

Introduction

By examining a text of each of the three versions of Robert Penn Warren's drama — *Proud Flesh, Willie Stark: His Rise and Fall,* and *All the King's Men (A Play)* — from the thirty-three manuscripts in the Robert Penn Warren Papers, Yale Collection of American Literature at the Beinecke Rare Book and Manuscript Library, we corroborate William M. Schutte's passing observation in 1957 that "each of the versions of Stark's story is a discrete entity" (76). And we reveal the development of Willie Strong (deceiver) to Willie Talos (demagogue), both of whom are stereotypical politicos in *Proud Flesh,* and then to Willie Stark (dictator), a more complex character whose transformation, Warren tells us, resulted from "many things, some merely technical" (Beebe and Field 28).

To demonstrate Willie Stark's development, we have selected three texts to edit for this volume. The *Proud Flesh* text we believe to be the first complete version of the Willie Stark story; the *Willie Stark: His Rise and Fall* text, based on the director's copy for the 1958 production in Dallas, Texas, reflects Warren's continued interest in the story, an interest that goes beyond the 1960 published text; and the *All the King's Men (A Play)* text represents Warren's attempt to blend novel and drama. The changes in the various versions are the focus of the following discussion, in which we shall refer to other manuscript drafts generally as illustrations of the play's evolution.[1]

We can speculate with some degree of certainty that the *Proud Flesh* manuscript, which uses the name Willie Strong, is the earliest version of the play and, indeed, of the story.[2] Warren stated that he began the play in Louisiana in 1938 and finished it in Rome in 1940 ("Introduction," *Tutti gli uomini del re* 1).[3] In an 11 January 19[40] letter to Brooks, Warren wrote that he was sending the manuscript of *Proud Flesh,* "which has been ready for some days." Also, Brooks's version is paginated consecutively from 1 to 106. In later drafts Warren uses the more sophisticated act/scene/page method of identifying pages, for example, III-i-2. Warren exhibits a similar learning curve in his fiction. The first draft of

The Apple Tree (or *God's Own Time*) is paginated consecutively. In Warren's subsequent novels, pages are identified by a chapter/page method, for example, X.2. In the folder marked 97.1812 in the Robert Penn Warren Papers, a note in Warren's handwriting appears: "This was the first fragment written for <u>Proud Flesh</u>, what later became <u>All the King's Men</u>. This is the opening chorus of the chorus of Highway Patrolmen. RPW." That chorus of Highway Patrolmen has about it a military aura as it introduces the character of Willie Strong. In a criticism of this version, however, Francis Fergusson pointed out to Warren in a 9 May 1941 letter: "As for the chorus, I think its story needs to be simplified. It is all for Strong in the beginning, gradually comes to doubt him, and at last reads him out of the party. My criticism of it at present is that its irony (conscious and unconscious) tends to grow too elaborate so that we lose our sense of the chorus as a force, an entity, a dramatis persona." This earliest version is structured in five acts, ten scenes, with choruses representing different groups: the Highway Patrolmen in act I; act II, a football chorus; act III, a chorus of women; and toward the end of act V, a chorus of surgeons.[4] Later versions of *Proud Flesh* reduced the various choruses to a chorus of surgeons, and Warren shortened its role to that of commentator, that is, one who draws the audience's attention to the implications of the past or to impending action — at times philosophical, at other times factual.

Willie Strong dominates the play, and his character seems to be based on the notion Warren mentions in an interview with Frank Gado: "The notion — or *a* notion — behind the play was that a man gains power because he is drawn into a vacuum of power. In one sense, is a creation of history. There was the germ of this in the first version. . . . For each individual, the 'strong man' is a fulfill-ment" (74–75). Strong's character has no past good against which he can be measured, and his deceptions are recounted matter-of-factly by other charac-ters. For example, Keith Amos (Adam Stanton in the novel) says to his sister, Anne, who is trying to persuade him to accept Willie's offer to direct the hospital,

> I'll not be
> Glove to his hand, haft to his grip, or be
> Whatever slime it is he spins to cradle
> His vanity's softness, spins to swaddle and sheathe
> That vanity's sickness, worm-fatness, to cuddle its
> Dark dream in whatever bloated chrysalis
> It is. (CB, I.ii.30)[5]

Clara (Lucy), his wife, pleads with Willie not to ruin their son, Thomas, but Willie remains head*strong*, and she grieves over his own blindness to what he has become (CB, I.iii.43). In retort Willie uses an appropriate chameleon metaphor that ironically captures the essence of deception (CB, I.iii.44). The closest reference to his past comes in act IV.i when Willie tells Sue Parsons (Sadie Burke) that it is over between them. Sue reacts violently and rails at him and belittles him, to which Willie responds in a somewhat self-deprecating tone:

> What I was then I scarcely now know, or guess;
> Who have, in the cistern of time's stagnation, peered
> At the drowned, the glimmer-fractured face — and winked,
> Like the hotel-drunk at the wash-room mirror's stranger.
> I have stood in the rain and tortured history,
> Under the street lamps stood, asked eyes and the sudden faces;
> Asked: "Have you seen him?" Asked: "Is he well?" Asked:
> ["]Where is he now? Did he leave no message for me?"
> But bells labored in the dark condensation of air,
> And I lacked courage. (CB, IV.i.86–87)

Those lines, reminiscent of T. S. Eliot's "The Love Song of J. Alfred Prufrock," are the deepest spoken by Strong. Warren uses many of those phrases in the novel. Willie's mistress, Anne Amos (Anne Stanton), who thought it might be different, later attempts to explain, all too poetically, to her brother, Keith, her relationship with Willie (CB, IV.ii.95). Anne's speech pattern maintains a poetic quality in the novel.

In Greek chorus fashion, albeit within the five-act structure of a Renaissance drama, one of the surgeons says about Willie's chances for survival after Willie is gunned down by Dr. Amos: "The question of the patient's survival may, therefore, hinge upon such an imponderable as his 'will to live.' . . . The phrase the 'will to live' we may take simply as a metaphor, the will to live — or will in any connection — being, as it were, a function of certain subtle biologic processes which have, thus far, eluded precise definition" (CB, V.ii.104).

The tension in the play relies first on the hospital deal that Tiny Harper (Duffy) manipulates for his friend Bob Satterfield (Gummy Larson), second on the reversal caused by Tom Strong's football injury and subsequent death, and third on Sue Parson's revenge through Tiny. Jack, a newspaper reporter and friend of Dr. Amos, appears in the last act. In a 1957 interview Warren told Ralph Ellison: "He [Jack] was an unnamed newspaperman,[6] a childhood friend of the assassin, an excuse for the young doctor, the assassin of the politician, Willie Stark, to say something before he performed the deed" (Ellison and Walter 44). He has also asked Tiny to get him into the hospital waiting room; there, he speaks a scant four lines that enable Tiny to mouth the words: "I just don't know what us boys is gonna do, now the Big Boss is gone" (CB, V.ii.106).[7]

In a revised version of *Proud Flesh* (Draft D), Warren reduces the play to three acts but adds one scene. The Governor is Willie Talos (Stark) now, and a number of minor characters are introduced with small speaking parts.[8] The chorus is more interspersed in Draft D and ebbs and flows more with the action. The first act opens with a meeting between a group of doctors and Willie Talos, who is handing them plans for an eight-million-dollar hospital. Draft D has the same focus as the earlier version, but Clara's (Lucy's) concern over their son, Tom, becomes an issue between them in act I.iii. In a like manner, Anne's part in talking her brother, Keith, into taking the directorship of the hospital comes to light, and Willie explains to Anne: "there's always somebody down in the ditch. Even if your brother isn't. What do you make bricks of? Mud. To make bricks, somebody's got to get down and paddle in the mud" (Draft D, I.iii.10–11).

These two versions of *Proud Flesh* emphasize the triangle of familial emotions between Clara and Tom, between Willie and Tom, and between Willie and Clara. They highlight Willie's ambition, his willingness to do anything for the desired end, and of course his mistake in eventually letting his means destroy the people he comes to realize he loves the most. In act II.i.8, just after Tom's injury on the field, the chorus comments: "Like father, like son—that's a good definition of fate":

> So the sins of the father are visited on the child,
> Of the father's father are visited on the child,
> And visited on us, on him, on you,
> While under the ground, the mouths that you never knew,
> That never kissed you through their nicotined beards,
> Speak, and their utterance is louder than words.
> O, it's no zombie, it's not the bugaboo,
> It's just grandpa's glands crawling in bed with you! (Draft D, II.i.9)[9]

In the following scene, too, the Chorus observes in response to Willie and Clara's argument over Tom: "In action only is answer, and a way of knowing" (Draft D, II.ii.3). From these exchanges and choral interpretation, the theme of love surfaces. Willie's lack of understanding of love—he has, after all, professed romantic or erotic love to Clara, to Anne, and to Sue (Sadie) at various times— becomes the basis of his downfall. Those three principal female characters in Willie's life form one of the dialectics in the play: Anne as the romantic version of love who, as the Chorus Leader cautions, tries to "get more out of love than there is in it" (Draft D, II.iii.9); Sue, as the lustful version of love who when scorned reacts as violently as her concept of love shows her to be: "But he [Willie] knows where to come when it's not taffy he craves" (Draft D, II.iii.2); and Clara, whose love transcends even Willie's shortcomings, which she recognizes all too painfully: "O, be what you are, and I love you, but let our son now / Be what he is, and no preposterous mirror / To what you are, no peg to hang your old coat on" (Draft D, II.ii.3).

In *Proud Flesh* Willie Strong/Talos is archdeceiver and demagogue, but in the intervening years between the conception of his verse drama and the conversion to the novel, Willie Stark (all three names work as far as his character goes) gains some depth through the addition of a second major character, Jack Burden. About this addition Warren wrote:

> Picking it [*Proud Flesh*] up three years later I decided to start all over again with a novel. Decisions of this kind rarely come with perfect clarity, but I suppose that what I wanted was the "follower" to go with my "leader"—a follower whose modern frustrations and aimlessness would, in a complicated ambivalence, be set in relation to the will of the leader. So Jack Burden, who had been glimpsed before as only a nameless newspaper man in the last Act of *Proud Flesh*, entered as narrator and chorus. (Quoted in Kuehl 260)

In *All the King's Men (A Play)*, the Chorus is replaced by one character, the Professor of Science, an interlocutor who pricks Jack's conscience as Jack attempts to defend what Willie Stark has done. The manuscript version (Draft B) that seems very close to the 1960 published play has a prologue and twenty-five designated scenes in three acts.[10] The scene designations disappear in the published version, which calls for scene shifts through lighting effects in what Brooks Atkinson refers to as a "stream of consciousness style" (27). In outlining some of the changes in Stark's character from this version, we remember that the published version is not the latest one developed among the stage versions, as Schutte rightly points out (84).

Warren must now grapple with the changes he has made in the story as novel, and Jack Burden must be reckoned with. The manuscript version relies on flashbacks. The Professor, a pompous scientific pragmatist, and Jack argue about Willie's character in the prologue; Jack defends Willie's motives through the hospital Willie created:

JACK. He got the idea for the hospital, because he owed it to something he was.
PROF. Something he was—by ordinary standards he was a cheap demagogue, a ruffian, hag-ridden by vanity, a skirt-struck reprobate, a drunkard. (Draft B, prologue 2)

Other characters—Anne Stanton, Tiny Duffy, Sadie Kovak (Burke), and Adam Stanton—make their brief comments about Willie as well.[11] He is still the focus, but Jack now dominates thirteen of the twenty-five scenes. And with Jack comes the Judge Irwin episode and a very subtle father-son parallel to the Willie-Tom motif. Within the first act Willie makes his midnight visit to Judge Irwin and tells him about "dirt" (Draft B, I.iv.3), and two scenes later the audience sees Cousin Willie at Slade's, where he meets Tiny Duffy for the first time. This added background to Willie seems to be Warren's attempt to put the fictional character on stage and consequently provides a moral past against which

Stark's actions can be judged. It is, however, a thin attempt. The first act ends with the making of a demagogue; Willie cries to the crowd, "Gimme that meat-ax! BLOOD ON THE MOON!" (Draft B, I.viii.3).

After Willie throws over Sadie, he says introspectively: "The truth, plunged into the bath of Time, dissolves. What truth I had was dissolved in the cynical clarity of that liquid. But the atoms of that truth had kept their geometric secret, the ineluctable structure of the crystals that will form again. I saw them form at last, solid and clean. And saw what I had to do. I tried to do it. Was it too late? I have asked myself, and I do not know" (Draft B, III.iv.4). Later he utters the enigmatic words from the novel, "It might have been different, Jack—even yet—you got to believe that, Jack" (Draft B, III.vi.2), to which the Professor responds: "No, Mr. Burden, No! No! These words were only the final indication of Stark's failure of nerve. For in his last phase—after the death of his son—Stark became the sentimental, confused moralist, unable to deal with reality. . . . the morality of an act is not an absolute. It is the index of the society in which the act takes place" (Draft B, III.vi.2). But Jack, true to the end, concludes this version of the play with these words: "For action is our only truth. That is our fate" (Draft B, III.vi.6).

Wolcott Gibbs was less than kind in his criticism of the Erwin Piscator staging of this version of the play in 1947. Gibbs blames the play's failure on Warren's and Piscator's lack of selection of material, on the "bleak narrative sequences," on the separation of abstract argument from concrete happenings, and on the set itself (43). His comments possibly prompted the next version, which Warren entitled *Willie Stark: His Rise and Fall*. Divided into three acts and twelve scenes, the movement of this version is smoother and seems more suited to the story. Dr. Shipworth, director of the Tom Stark Memorial Hospital, returns from *Proud Flesh*, and Warren adds a football teammate of Tom named Talley. Otherwise, the cast is recognizable from the novel. More noticeably, the story returns to Willie; Jack's story is basically eliminated, and his role is subordinated. Like the *All the King's Men* version, it uses flashback. Stark is dead, and the hospital is being dedicated. Stark dominates acts I and III; Jack moves the action in act II.

Certain subtleties in Stark's development have been added. In his midnight visit to Judge Irwin, Stark is not quite as abrasive with the Judge, and Judge Irwin makes a telling observation: "Yes, Willie, we *did* get a lot of fine reforms. But Willie, I have begun to wonder. I wonder if sometimes—just sometimes, mind you—the price isn't too big that a man has to pay to get even the good thing he wants" (Draft G, I.i.8). In essence, does the end justify the means? We believe this question is one of the central issues in this version of the drama and also in the novel. Stark's subsequent reaction follows the novel's characterization. Stark tells Jack to find something on the Judge, citing his oft-referred-to biblical passage from Psalm 51:5: "Man is conceived in sin and born in corruption, and he passeth from the stink of the didie to the stench of the shroud. There is always something" (35th Anniversary Edition, 61; the line is not finished in Draft G, I.i.17). Willie begins to absorb more of what is said about him, a fact that may have caused his sudden lack of nerve, his hesitancy to act at the crucial moment. In an argument with Jack about the "purity" of the hospital, for example, Willie is confronted with Jack's observation: "Yeah, I understand. I understand that you have to talk this way to keep on operating" (Draft G, II.i.8). Out of Jack's mouth comes the rationale for Willie's kicking Tiny around, for "living," for just "being Willie Stark" (Draft G, II.i.9). Jack can realize ironically this trait in Willie because Anne points out to Jack that "a man's got to want to live in the world—to make his life mean something. Oh, Jack, you didn't want anything" (Draft G, II.i.16).

In the hospital waiting room in act III.iii, Willie shows more signs of stress and suppressed anger than Warren permits him to show in earlier versions. He quarrels with Lucy, suspects the nurse who comes in to change the flowers, and provokes Lucy to say, "You ruin everything you touch" (Draft G, III.iii.15). She follows up with the observation that Anne makes in *Proud Flesh* (CB) and that Willie modifies in *All the King's Men* (Draft B) version: "If you had loved me, you would have made things all different" (Draft G, III.iii.16). He protests, not understanding her meaning, and she continues: "Oh, if you had, all the world would be different. Different—yes, different—not everything ruined when you touch it" (Draft G, III.iii.16).

In the last scene, Stark confesses to the voice of the crowd, and they cry louder for him. The assassination follows. The epilogue allows for an exchange between Jack and Dr. Shipworth, similar to the one Jack has with the Professor in the *All the King's Men (A Play)* version. And Jack renders his concept of history and the spider web theory of relationships: that things might have been different matters, "it matters, it matters! I matter because everything is part of everything else. All the past—the past is part of—" (Draft G, epilogue 1).

What do we find, then, among the assorted stage versions of the Willie Stark story? We find the germ of the idea for Robert Penn Warren's best-known work in the guise of a stereotypical Southern politician, Willie Strong, who plays rough and dirty without much introspection and with somewhat singular ambition. We watch him blossom into a full-blown demagogue with political aspirations to become president of the United States. And finally we see the dictator emerge. As John Burt has observed, "The most engaging thing about Willie is the candor about the immorality of his means. The most difficult thing about him is the sincerity of his devotion to his ends" (142). The elements of character are furthered in the latest version through a better developed supporting cast and the addition of Willie's "other voice," Jack Burden. Thematically all three versions deal with the idea that absolute power corrupts absolutely; with the ethical dilemma whether the ends justify the means, which for Willie

Stark they do; and with the power of love, the emotion that might have made it all different for Willie.[12] And, with the introduction of Jack Burden as a significant character, Warren confronts the concept of the truth of the past and its relevance to the present.

That the drama appeals to directors and producers is evident by the continued performances; that it fascinated Warren is obvious from the variations that exist. As G. Thomas Tanselle reminds us, "Of all the historical activities of textual study, the effort to reconstruct the texts of works as intended by their creators takes us deepest into the thinking of interesting minds that preceded us" (92). Although this volume does not represent a textual study, what these three selected texts represent gives readers a glimpse of such a mind.

Yet, paradoxically, when critics extol the virtues of Robert Penn Warren, they usually do not emphasize his plays. After all, Warren won three Pulitzer Prizes, one for fiction and two for poetry, but his ventures in drama were not similarly recognized. Warren wrote six plays, including a version of the narrative poem *Brother to Dragons*.[13] Many of these plays, including the third version of the Willie Stark saga, *Willie Stark: His Rise and Fall*, were written between 1951 and 1956, when Warren was teaching play writing at the Yale University School of Drama.

At the time Warren joined the faculty of the School of Drama in 1950, the only plays he had written were *Proud Flesh* and an early version of *All the King's Men*, which Erwin Piscator directed for the Dramatic Workshop of the New School at the President Theatre in New York in 1948 (L.B. 19). Warren studied drama, especially English Renaissance drama, and he had the tutelage of several eminent critics, including Francis Fergusson, Eric Bentley, and his longtime friend Cleanth Brooks, as he found his way into the genre. But his appointment at Yale probably was the result of Yale's desire to have a Pulitzer Prize—winning author on the staff and the result of Brooks's and Warren's desire to reunite the team that had already produced *An Approach to Literature* (1936), *Understanding Poetry* (1938), *Understanding Fiction* (1943), and *Modern Rhetoric* (1949).[14]

Beginning in 1937, Warren wrote three dramatic versions of the narrative material contained in his 1946 prize-winning novel, *All the King's Men*. In an initialed holograph note on a typed fragment (mentioned in our preface), Warren identifies the first draft of *Proud Flesh*. From that start he went on to write sixteen drafts of a verse play bearing the same title before converting the dramatic material into a novel.[15]

Warren writes one of the best short accounts of the writing of the novel and its relationship to the three dramatic versions that ultimately emerged. The following introductory note for the publication of an Italian translation of the play *All the King's Men* appeared in the magazine *Sipario*.[16]

ALL THE KING'S MEN

In the 1930's I lived in Louisiana. Until September 1935, when he was assassinated by a young physician [Dr. Carl Weiss], Huey Long was the scarcely challenged master of the state. In that atmosphere, punctuated by gun fire in the Capitol, the story that was to become *All the King's Men* began to take shape.

The first form—like this, the last—was a play, a verse play called *Proud Flesh*. I began work on it in Louisiana, worked on it in Italy, in an olive grove overlooking Lake Garda, in the summer of 1938, and finished it in the winter of 1939–40, in Rome, to the music of military boot-heels on the cobbles. So the shadow of a European as well as home-grown American dictatorship lies over the composition. I say "shadow," for my Willie Stark is no more like Huey Long than he is like Mussolini. He is, I hope, himself, and more humanly acceptable, I hope, than either.

My play is, indeed, about power, its genesis and the temptations it carries for both leader and follower; but I wanted my story to be personal rather than political. I wanted the issues to come to crisis in personal terms. I wanted to indicate some interplay, as it were, between the public, political story and the private, ethical one: a mirror held up to a mirror.[17]

To return to the old play *Proud Flesh*. I finished a draft and laid it aside. *Picking it up three years later I decided to start all over again with a novel.* Decisions of this kind rarely come with perfect clarity, but I suppose that what I wanted was the "follower" to go with my "leader"—a follower whose modern frustration and aimlessness would, in a complicated am-bivalence, be set in relation to the will of the leader. So Jack Burden, who had been glimpsed before as only a nameless newspaper man in the last act of *Proud Flesh*, entered as narrator and chorus.[18]

After the publication of the novel *All the King's Men*, Eric Bentley read the old play, liked it, and arranged for a production at the theater of the University of Minnesota. Shortly afterwards, Irwin [*sic*] Piscator, then liv-ing in America, became interested and offered to produce and direct the play. By the time preliminary work had begun on this production I had discovered that *Proud Flesh* was a very different thing from *All the King's Men* and that I should like to keep Jack Burden in the important role he holds in the novel.

So this led to a new play. It was produced by Piscator at the President Theatre in New York, under the auspices of the New School. Subsequently it has had numerous productions in America, one at Cambridge University in England, and several in Germany, where it was published.[19]

A little after 1948, when Piscator first produced All the King's Men, *I be-*

gan to grow more and more dissatisfied with my own work. I felt, in fact, that it was too close to the novel, too much an adaptation. In 1956, with Aaron Frankel, I prepared another version which he, in 1958, directed at the Margot [*sic*] Jones Theatre in Dallas. *But I was still dissatisfied, and when, in 1959, Mark Schoenberg, then a young assistant producer at the Theatre Guild, came to me, I thought I had sorted out the reasons for my dissatisfaction.*

The play that was developed in a happy collaboration with Mr. Schoenberg's direction is offered here. Whatever it may be, it is the final form. It may not be the play I had once dreamed, but when, a year ago, I saw Clifton James as Willie Stark confront John Ragin as Jack Burden on the handsome stage of the Seventy-Fourth Street Theater, they endowed their roles with such reality that I felt I could put them away from me for good and all. [Emphasis added]

The passages above marked for emphasis tell the story of an accomplished and demanding writer working his way into a new genre and being frustrated and dissatisfied again and again with his progress—at least thirty-three times. We have charted the growth of that work below.

Proud Flesh   1937–1940
All the King's Men (novel)   1943–1946
All the King's Men (drama)   1947–1948
Willie Stark: His Rise and Fall   1956–1958
All the King's Men (rewrite of 1947–1948 version)   1959

Warren had good mentors in his attempt to learn the art of play writing. During the composition of *Proud Flesh*, Warren wrote from Rome to Cleanth Brooks:

I shall have your MS of *Proud Flesh* in the mails next Monday or Tuesday. It has been ready for some days, but I discovered that the copy I had for you all was the only copy left which had in it a number of revisions, and so I had to hang on to it, or try to go back and remake the revisions. So I hung on to it, and made another copy. When you have time, please write me in detail about it, all your suggestions and criticisms. For I don't regard this draft as final. In fact, I am almost certain that if the thing is produced— which, I am sure, is quite unlikely—I shall have to do some heavy cutting in the second and third scenes of the first act. And I imagine that there will be other important revisions to make. But for the time being I am going to lay it by, so that I can have the benefit of the comments of a few people and the benefit of a little perspective.[20]

On 8 June 1940 Warren wrote to Brooks: "For the present I'm here working with Francis Fergusson on a revision of my play. (If you have any suggestions I wish you'd spring them now, while I can bring them to bear on the present process of revision.) He is going to put on a couple of scenes experimentally this summer, and talks about doing the whole thing next year, if some of the revisions pan out."[21]

As early as April 1940, Francis Fergusson was involved with the revision of *Proud Flesh*. Fergusson believed from the beginning that the play was worth working on. In his first response he noted three major problems: "First of all, the story is not quite clear. . . . A more serious trouble is that you seem to have no very consistent convention for the use of verse. . . . The third general point I have in mind has to do with the texture of the dialogue or dramatic writing itself. This needs tightening and simplification."[22] As indicated in the letter to Brooks quoted above, Warren spent time in Vermont in the summer of 1940 working with Fergusson. Following that time together, Fergusson continued to work on *Proud Flesh*. In March 1941 he wrote to Warren: "It was good to hear from you, and learn that you are back on the play again. I have marked up the first two of the scenes you sent me. As they stand, what they chiefly need I think is cutting for shape and intelligibility. This I have done roughly, not to say brutally, just as I did last summer with some of the scenes we worked on together." On 9 May 1941 Fergusson sent Warren four scenes (eighteen pages) of *Proud Flesh* with a cover letter that opened as follows: "I'm returning at long last four scenes which I have worked over and annotated and generally cut up. They are I think all much improved, but I have shortened them still more, and marked some passages which I think should be rewritten for clarity." As late as March 1947 Fergusson was still involved with and supportive of *Proud Flesh*. He wrote to Warren, "I hear from Eric . . . that the U of M[innesota] theatre will do it this spring. That is very good news indeed. If even part of your intention could be got onto the stage, we should have *the* American play to date."[23]

The Eric to whom Fergusson refers in his letter is Eric Bentley, who arranged for the world premiere of *Proud Flesh* at the University of Minnesota under the direction of Frank Whiting from 28 April to 4 May 1947.[24] But Bentley made those arrangements only after continuing the mentoring that Brooks and Fergusson had begun. Bentley was particularly worried by the Chorus and wrote Warren from Alta, Utah, on 17 August [1946]: "The Chorus remains a problem. I think your script should indicate exactly how you want it handled. One has the impression that the author sometimes forgets the Chorus is onstage and leaves it just standing there dumb for long and embarrassing stretches."

Of course, by the time Bentley made this comment about the chorus in *Proud Flesh*, Warren was already at work on an adaptation of *All the King's Men* that would replace the Chorus with Jack Burden as both narrator and commentator and would be directed at the President Theatre in New York by Erwin Piscator, to whom Bentley had introduced Warren.[25] For Warren play writing was a collaborative process, a learning process. In drama he may not have found his voice yet, a speculation to which Bentley seems to allude in a response to a tape-recorded reading of Warren's "The Wedding Ring" (based on the Cass Mastern story in chapter 4 of the novel):

> David Clay gave me the tape recording, and I heard two of the three acts, but didn't bother about the last: the reading was quite bad, I finished the play reading to myself.
>
> I am still deeply interested in the work but would not wish to direct it as it stands or even with minor revisions. Therefore if you and the Stevens office wish to go ahead now, you should feel free to do so without me. Naturally, though I owe you an explanation. Here it comes.
>
> There *is* a play here, once the first act is rather severely cut down to size. And if you go ahead with it, I wish you all the luck in the world. I myself lack confidence in this play because —
>
> Well, first, the rhetoric. If you prune your dialogue, you will presumably feel that I have not understood the intention of your style, the nature of this sort of speech, the idea of poetic prose and poetic drama. I should retort that I don't think this rhetoric is succeeding. For example, Cass's dying speeches. To me, there is a lack of dramatic progression in the speeches. They hang in the air. I say this after certain experience with your work. You were right to de-theatricalize DRAGONS, because your mind tends to a philosophical poetry, a rhetoric which is non-theatrical. Some of the passages in PROUD FLESH were non-theatrical in the same way. They didn't have the drive and thrust *forwards into the action* which I require from theatre-poetry. Please make allowance in these statements of mine for the oversimplification and dogmatism that come from trying to set down opinions and impressions too briefly. I feel that the rhetoric of WEDDING RING c[oul]d be worked on until it *is* theatre, but I am not sure that *you* w[oul]d like the result, or that you really want to push it in that particular direction. In urging you, I may be urging you against the grain; so I don[']t urge, but, instead, write you this letter.[26]

Bentley's impression of the nature of Warren's mind seems fairly accurate; it is a mind interested in and in fear of abstractions, a mind that creates fascinating if somewhat difficult novels and great poetry, but a mind that creates problematic drama. Is *All the King's Men* a play that focuses on a general social problem, as Schutte suggests? Or is it focused on Willie Stark's character, which offers a more philosophical and psychological dilemma? Can it be both? This presentation of the three dramatic versions of *All the King's Men* allows readers to observe in a small way that mind at work and to ponder those questions.

In summary, then, Warren's fascination with the relationship between power and corruption and with the effects it has on the relationships of the characters involved lingered beyond two decades (1937–60). The central character, Willie Stark, develops from a rather flat, one-dimensional character in *Proud Flesh* to the round, three-dimensional character in *All the King's Men (A Play)*. His development is achieved, in part, with the addition of the other central character, Jack Burden, who in the novel moves from "brass-bound idealist" to a synthesis between the man of action (Willie) and the man of ideals (Adam). He learns to accept responsibility, and with that acceptance comes Jack's belief that "it might have been all different."

What might have been all different for Willie was his love for family and friends. Ironically, however, that difference might also have precluded his political success, which the Chorus in *Proud Flesh* notes (Schutte 80). For Willie, the difference would have been a 180-degree reversal; the ends would not justify the means. With the hospital Willie is caught in an ethical dilemma: a virtuous end but by unvirtuous means. These three stage versions of the Willie Stark story dramatize that dilemma and its consequences.

NOTES

1. Unless otherwise noted, folder and draft references are based on the William K. Finley catalog of the Robert Penn Warren Papers, MSS 51, Yale Collection of American Literature (YCAL), Beinecke Rare Book and Manuscript Library, Yale University, New Haven, Connecticut, August 1991. The letters used in this introduction, unless otherwise indicated, are also from the YCAL and are used with the kind permission of the Beinecke Rare Book and Manuscript Library and the William Morris Agency.

2. One reason we feel obliged to present evidence in support of this contention is the "Author's Introduction" to the 35th Anniversary Edition of *All the King's Men*: "By this time [1940] the name Talos had been discarded as being too fancy and had been replaced by Strong" (xix). In his 11 January [1940] letter to Cleanth Brooks, Warren refers to a copy of the manuscript that is undergoing revision; Brooks's copy, however, has the character named Willie Strong. Francis Fergusson's 9 May 1941 letter also refers to Strong. In his "Author's Introduction," Warren mentions completing the draft of his play in December 1939 and sending copies "to several friends, including Allen Tate, Kenneth Burke, . . . and Francis Fergusson." Another consideration, moreover, is the structure of these versions. The text that uses the name Talos is in three acts; the text that uses the name Strong is in five acts. Why would Warren have changed from three to five acts, especially when his friends who commented on the manuscript suggested simplification? But his beginning with a five-act structure seems plausible. It relates to his involvement with the Shakespeare classes that he was teaching at Louisiana State University in

the late 1930s. The structure of the traditional Renaissance play is in five acts, and the influence of Shakespeare might have led Warren to try a similar structure. The newspaper reporter *is* named in both versions. In the Strong text, Jack is referred to in the stage directions as "an old friend of Dr. Amos" (V.i.100). However, Jack is identified as Dr. Keith Amos's *boyhood* friend in the Talos text, a link that is a later development in the story's characterizations and more closely akin to the novel. Furthermore, in a 1945 letter to Warren about the novel, Lambert Davis asked Warren to change the name from Talos to "a name of less ambiguous pronunciation, and one that suggested more definitely an American origin." The name of the governor was changed in the setting copy (Finley 101.1869–76) of the novel from Talos to Stark.

3. Our dilemma is consistency versus accuracy. For example, evidence from the Warren-Brooks correspondence suggests that Warren started *Proud Flesh* in the summer of 1937, yet in print Warren refers to the summer of 1938. In Warren's biography Joseph Blotner refers to Warren's having done "a few fragments of a play" by the fall of 1937 (164). Notwithstanding possible confusion, we use the dates cited in the articles we quote.

4. The five-act structure is consistent with Warren's statements to William Kennedy: "Back then — and now — I was much more soaked in poetry and Elizabethan drama than I was fiction. . . . The literal plays behind the novel [*All the King's Men*] were two Shakespearean political plays, *Julius Caesar* and *Coriolanus*; they were there consciously. And then, less consciously, Webster's *White Devil*" (170). All of those plays are written in five acts. A case can be made for a five-act dramatic structure of the novel, *All the King's Men*, with each act containing two chapters. The first four chapters, then, are "exposition," the next four "complication," and the last two "resolution." For a thorough discussion of these three elements and the problems the dramatist shares with other writers and those he faces alone, see "Introduction to Drama," in Brooks, Purser, and Warren.

5. Arabic numerals refer to manuscript pages rather than to line numbers. The manuscripts cited are CB, a copy lent to Grimshaw by Cleanth Brooks on 4 November 1988; *Willie Stark: His Rise and Fall*, Finley Draft G; and the published version of *All the King's Men (A Play)*, which is dedicated to Francis Fergusson and to the memory of Marion Crowne Fergusson. Draft A (1955) contains changes to Draft G in lines and in pagination. Written on Draft G (first leaf): "CL-96234 This is director's copy for production at Margot [*sic*] Jones Theater [*sic*], Dallas — *November 1958* [William Morris Agency sticker] directed by *Aaron Frankel* AKM [circled] #3."

6. Actually, Dr. Amos greets him as "Jack" (CB, V.i.100), and the script identifies him as an old friend and newspaper reporter. For a perceptive discussion of Jack's development as a character, see Justus 194–203.

7. See also Casper's discussion of *Proud Flesh* (117–21) and *Willie Stark: His Rise and Fall* (134–36).

8. Warren comments on the "Talos": "For Talos was the first avatar of my Willie Stark, and the fact that I drew that name from the 'iron groom' who, in murderous blankness, serves Justice in Spenser's *Faerie Queen[e]* should indicate something of the line of thought and feeling that led up to that version and persisted, with modulations, into the novel" (Beebe and Field 27; reprinted from *"All the King's Men*: The Matrix of Experi-

ence," *Yale Review* 53 [December 1963]: 161–67, which appears as the introduction to the Time Reading Program edition [New York: Time, 1963]). We find that some critics have interpreted "first avatar" as first characterization and, therefore, place Draft D chronologically before the CB draft. Rarely would we not accept without question Warren's memory on such matters, but the other circumstances and evidence suggest that he perhaps reversed the names in his mind.

See Kuehl (261) for a listing of the effects of Jack Burden's newly defined role on plot and characters.

9. Readers will soon note the interrelatedness of Warren's writing. For example, compare Warren's poem "Original Sin: A Short Story." Randolph Paul Runyon has done a thorough job of analyzing this intertextuality in his two books, *The Taciturn Text: The Fiction of Robert Penn Warren* (1990) and *The Braided Dream: Robert Penn Warren's Late Poetry* (1990). *Proud Flesh* reverberates, as do the other two versions, with images that appear throughout Warren's poetry; that blending of genre may have been an obstacle to Warren's finding his dramatic voice. *Brother to Dragons*, a drama in verse, attests to Warren's struggle. Random House first published *Brother to Dragons* in 1953 and published "a new version" in 1979.

10. In the Warren Papers at YCAL, Draft B (box 103, files 1913–14), the characters are centered on the page. The last line is Jack's: "Yes, yes, The Truth action." Draft C (box 104, file 1919) was still in its black binder as of 19 July 1995, with Evelyn M. Keith's address label on the lower outside corner of the inside front cover. However, Sadie's name is Burke in this version, rather than Kovak. Therefore, Draft C does not appear to be the 1946–47 version that is quoted, but it may be a possible revision of Draft B. See note 13 for a discussion of the various manuscripts.

11. Warren continues to play with names. "Kovak," the Hungarian version of Smith (that is, worker with iron), suggests the hardness of Sadie's character. That Sadie's iron will is stronger than Willie's will of iron is not remarkable in retrospect. Sadie points out that Cousin Willie has been used by the MacMurfee faction, and Sadie's words to Tiny Duffy set in motion the assassination of Willie. She is, indeed, a woman with an iron will. For a more detailed perspective of women characters in Warren's works, see Ferriss.

12. Lord Acton wrote Bishop Creighton in 1887: "Power tends to corrupt and absolute power corrupts absolutely." In *The Oxford Dictionary of Quotations* (London: Oxford University Press, 1962), 1.

13. They include (a) "Proud Flesh," an unpublished play, 1939, first presented 28 April–4 May 1947, University Theatre, University of Minnesota, directed by Frank Whiting; (b) "The Wedding Ring," an unpublished play, copyrighted 24 July 1951, revised and copyrighted 27 December 1955, version D dated 1 June 1959 and titled "Listen to the Mockingbird: A Drama of the American Civil War"; (c) "Willie Stark: His Rise and Fall: A Play in Three Acts," an unpublished play, copyrighted 17 October 1955, premiered at the Margo Jones Theatre, Dallas, Texas, 25 November–14 December 1958; (d) "Brother to Dragons: A Play in Two Acts," *Georgia Review* 30 (spring 1976): 65–138; (e) *All the King's Men (A Play)* (New York: Random House, 1960), directed in an unpublished form by Erwin Piscator, 1947, produced off-Broadway, East 74th Street Theatre, 16 October 1959, directed by Mark Schoenberg; (f) "Ballad of a Sweet Dream of Peace: A Charade

for Easter," with music by Alexei Haieff, *Georgia Review* 29 (spring 1975): 5–36, presented at the Loeb Drama Center Experimental Theatre, 27–29 April 1961. Warren collaborated with David M. Clay in writing "The Conway Cabal" for an unproduced television series, "This Very Spot," and with Max Shulman in writing "Don't Bury Me at All: An Original Story for the Screen." Warren was also a technical adviser for the film and script of the Academy Award–winning production of *All the King's Men*. He worked with Julian Barry and Robert Redford on an unproduced film script for *A Place to Come To*. See Grimshaw, *Robert Penn Warren*, for additional information about performances.

14. For an amusing account of that reunion, see Wellek.

Interestingly, *Understanding Drama* (1945) was written by Cleanth Brooks and Robert Heilman. Why Brooks and Warren did not collaborate on that text as well we cannot be certain, but a reasonable speculation might include Warren's other writing commitments, traveling abroad, growing marital problems, and finishing his novel *All the King's Men*.

15. The number of drafts of the three texts discussed here or the order of their composition is difficult, perhaps not even possible, to determine. When Grimshaw looked at the material in 1988, he dealt with thirty-three folders on deposit at the Beinecke Library: twelve folders of *Proud Flesh*, ten folders of *Willie Stark: His Rise and Fall*, and eleven folders of *All the King's Men (A Play)*. He also had the copy Cleanth Brooks had lent him. In a subsequent article on the texts, he notes that "some of those folders contain worksheets and fragments, some are duplicate copies" (Grimshaw, "Strong to Stark" 17). In that same essay, Grimshaw includes a "Table of Manuscripts" that briefly notes physical details of the manuscripts (table 1). Many of those physical details described by Grimshaw were lost or obscured by the time William K. Finley cataloged the Warren Papers. Internal evidence in the early versions of *Proud Flesh* suggests that scholars must question the order of composition implied by Finley's listing. For example, ink corrections on page 10 of Finley Draft B are typed perfectly on page I-i-11 of Finley Draft A. Determining the order of composition of the various drafts of the plays will be a long, complex task.

16. Two copies of this manuscript are housed in the Beinecke Library. One is a three-page original typescript (OTS), the other a six-page holograph (OH). References in this paper are to the OTS rather than to the *Sipario* translation. The translation was done by Gerardo Guerrieri. A letter indicates that Guerrieri began the project in 1958, translating the version of *Willie Stark: His Rise and Fall* (the version that is printed in this volume) that Aaron Frankel produced at the Margo Jones Theatre in Dallas, but Warren's introduction indicates that the final translation, *Tutti gli uomini del re: Un porlogo e tre atti di Robert Penn Warren*, that appeared in *Sipario* is of the East 74th Street Theatre version of *All the King's Men* produced by Mark Schoenberg in 1959. This version was the text published by Random House in 1960 and is the text printed in this volume.

17. In *An Approach to Literature* (shorter ed.), the authors write: "If in tragedy we stand side by side with the protagonist, even a protagonist like Macbeth, in comedy we stand in our sympathies with society itself, the laws or customs which the primary figure in the comedy is breaking" (Brooks, Purser, and Warren 516). Warren apparently was aiming for tragedy, that is, for a play in which the audience sympathizes with the pro-

Table 1

Table of Manuscripts

PF		AKM		WS	
1.	OTS (A) w/RPW note manila folder	1a.	OTS (46/47) brown binder	1.	OTS (WS) worksheets manila folder
2.	OH, OTS, CTS worksheets (FMW) manila folder	1b.	CTS (old version) brown binder	2.	OTS (RPW/55) manila binder
3a.	OTS (B) manila folder	2a.	CTS (f5) prompt script manila folder	3.	OTS (MacBond) MacCabee Bond black binder
3b.	CTS (CB) Cleanth Brooks	2b1.	CTS (f6) black binder	4.	CTS (Lucy) light blue binder
4.	CTS (C) manila folder	2b2.	MTS (f6) prose version	5a.	(see #3) CTS (f3)
5.	CTS (D/frag) manila folder		manila binder		Fitzall, 6 June 1955
6a.	OTS (E/frag) manila folder	2c.	CTS (f7/old version) black binder	5b.	MTS (f3/old version) blue binder (see #3)
7.	OTS (F) manila folder (see #4)	3a.	OTS, CTS, MTS (EP$_1$) Erwin Piscator gray folder	5c.	MTS (f4/old version) blue binder (see #3)
8.	CTS (G) folder	3b.	MTS (EP$_2$) purplish-gray folder	6.	MTS (f5) [MJ58] Margot Jones blue binder [Draft C]
9a.	OTS (H) black binder	3c.	CTS/MTS (EP$_3$) gray binder	7a.	CTS (WM) Wm. Morris Agency gray binder
9b.	OTS (I) folder (see #9a)	4.	MTS (Frankel) mailing envelope 19 April 1954 [later rev. Draft A]	7b.	CTS (WM) gray binder
10.	CTS (MN prod. 46/47 [RPW]) grayish binder [Draft J]	5.	MTS (74th St./1959) black binder		

tagonist. Based on those distinctions, *Proud Flesh* seems to be more of a comedy, *All the King's Men (A Play)* a tragicomedy, and *Willie Stark: His Rise and Fall* the tragedy in which "the issues come to crisis in personal terms."

18. See note 2 regarding Warren's accuracy on some of the early details.

19. Warren, *Blut auf dem Mond*. Counting this published version of *All the King's Men*, four dramatic renderings of the narrative exist. Since Warren never published this version in English and since he reworked it with Mark Schoenberg to create the East 74th Street Theatre version, which was later published by Random House, we consider the two versions as one play with a somewhat convoluted history of composition.

20. Letter from Robert Penn Warren to Cleanth Brooks, dated Rome, 11 January 1939, in the Cleanth Brooks Papers, MSS 30, YCAL. The actual date of this letter should probably be 1940. Warren himself said that he completed the play during "the winter of 1939–

40, in Rome." Since he implies in this letter that he is sending a complete MS to Brooks and since the first paragraph of the letter refers to the contents of the *Southern Review* 5.3 (winter 1940), which would carry a publication date of January 1940, Warren must have done what we have all done during January—written the incorrect year. Thus, Brooks received the *uncorrected* version with the name Strong in it, the same version Fergusson would first see. Brooks's reply is not in either the Brooks or Warren Papers in the YCAL. For more information on their letters, see Grimshaw, *Cleanth Brooks*.

21. Letter from Robert Penn Warren to Cleanth Brooks, marked General Delivery, North Bennington, Vt., 8 June 1940, in the Cleanth Brooks Papers, YCAL.

22. Letter from Francis Fergusson to Robert Penn Warren, dated Bennington College, 1 April 1940, in the Robert Penn Warren Papers, YCAL.

23. The emphasis in the phrase "*the* American play to date" is Fergusson's. This praise is strong indeed from the man who was, at the time of the writing of this letter, two years away from writing *The Idea of the Theatre*, perhaps the most important single volume on drama written in the United States.

24. Warren was at the time on the faculty in the Department of English at the University of Minnesota. Joseph Warren Beach was chairman of the department then. The University of Minnesota production, however, was entitled *All the King's Men*; the playbill includes a special thank you to Eric Bentley.

25. Several other dramatic productions of *All the King's Men* have been staged, but without Warren's assistance with the script (for example, Adrian Hall's *Prologue to "All the King's Men*," an adaptation from chapter 4 in the novel, the Cass Mastern story, at the Dallas Theater Center basement theater, 2–21 January 1990). Hall also has a more recent adaptation of the entire story.

26. Letter from Eric Bentley to Robert Penn Warren, dated Riverside Drive, 28 March [1955].

Proud Flesh

A PLAY

IN VERSE AND PROSE

BY

ROBERT PENN WARREN

Cast of Characters

Warren had not included a cast of characters in the manuscript to Brooks.
This one is added by the editors.

Place: One of the Southern States of the United States.
Time: The present.

Any resemblance between the characters of this play and any real persons,
living or dead, is purely accidental.

Proud Flesh

I:i

(The curtain rises on a group of men who, dressed in blue uniforms and black leather boots, goggles, and caps, are standing in military formation, in postures of wooden rigidity. Behind them is another curtain.)

CHORUS. What hand flings the white road before us?
  What hand over hills and the damplands,
  Over the highlands and swamplands,
  Gully and bayou? And flings us
  Fast as the slug from the gun-mouth,
  Hard as the word from his own mouth —
  Us nameless, and yet he has named us,
  And aimless, and yet he has aimed us
  And flung us, and flings us, a handful
  Of knives hurled, edged errand — O errand
  Blind with the glittering blindness of light!

(At this point one of the members of the CHORUS detaches himself from the group, moves diagonally forward toward the edge of the stage, pushes up his goggles, and speaks in a ruminative, almost conversational tone. The other members of the CHORUS begin to relax into slouching, natural positions.)

PATROLMAN. Yeah, when I wasn't much more'n a kid, they begun putten that highway past pappy's place, and then hit wasn't no time to speak of till the Big Boss commenced to take holt of things, and they give hit a concrete top, first-rate. And I'd be worken in the field on pappy's place and I'd see them highway cops go by on their motorcycles, lickety-split, burnen the road. Saturday afternoons and Sundays and sich I hung round the fillen station and got so I could ride me one of them things. And I always was right handy with a gun, if I do say hit. And I got on the highway force. One day I was hangen round up at the Capitol, and the Big Boss was standen there, and he said, "Boy, what's yore name?" And I said, "Al Suggs." And he thumped me on the chist, and said: "Damned if you ain't a likely-looken specimen. I think I'll put you on my personal detail." And God damn — *(The patrolman strikes his right fist into his left palm with a boyish gesture of excitement.)* — God damn, if he didn't go and do hit!

(The patrolman steps smartly back into his place in the CHORUS, *adjusting his goggles, and the other members resume their former postures, and speak.)*

CHORUS. Let us praise now the wheel, for he gave it.
    Let us praise now the wheel, for it knows no
    End and no ending, and knows no
    Beginning, no crossed aims, distractions,
    Confusion or sick heart; knows only
    The suction of distance, the hunger
    Of time out of time whirled, the wind-roar;
    In swift ear the speech of the wind's roar:

(Spoken retardedly as in a ritual.)

    Road-roarer
    Way-wailer
    Light-dazzler
    Space-eater
    Time-cheater
    Distance-betrayer.

(They remove their revolvers from the holsters and gaze at them.)

    And name now this other, and praise it—
    This, this, he gave it, we praise it,
    The steel husk wherein sleeps amazement,
    Steel pod where the dark drowses darkly
    Like seed locked, like light locked in darkness,
    Like love locked, like flame locked in stone;
    Like death locked, which will blossom in bone.
    What wind will fumble the pod-latch?
    And catch it, and take it, and shake it,
    What wind rises to break it and shatter
    Pod-chamber?— O wind, which will scatter
    The cold seed to blossom in blindness of light;
    The cold seed whose name is the silence:

(Spoken retardedly, as before.)

    Far-speaker
    Fire-darter

Light-quencher
Slug-hurler
Flesh-plugger
Brain-darkener.

(They replace the revolvers.)

What wind? What pod-shaker?

(The patrolman whose name is AL SUGGS steps from his place, pushes up his goggles, and saunters toward the curtain behind the CHORUS. The other men move raggedly offstage, while the curtain rises. The curtain exposes a car, a roadster with the top down, parked at the edge of a highway, and a motorcycle. In the car, two men are seated. AL SUGGS lounges toward them, and when the last member of the CHORUS has disappeared, speaks.)

AL. Fer Christ sake!

(Almost at the car, he stops, places his hands on his hips, and appears to be scrutinizing the two men in the car. The man at the wheel is about thirty-five years old, rather handsome, with a dark, brooding, unsatisfied face. He is KEITH AMOS, a surgeon. The other man, also a doctor, has a full-fleshed, rather round face, with a blond mustache, and wears glasses. His name is BILL SHIPWORTH. When he speaks his voice and manner are bland and soothing, in contrast to the truculence of his companion. After insolently inspecting the two men in the car, AL SUGGS, with a scruffing sound, puts his feet on the running board, and speaks again, almost aggrievedly.)

AL. Fer Christ sake, what do you think this is? What do you think this is, any-how? Seventy-five miles an hour and on them—

AMOS. *(In a restrained voice, as though suppressing irritation.)* I wasn't aware that there is a speed limit in this state, on the highway.

AL. Reckless drive-en, there's reckless drive-en, all right, if there ain't no highway speed limit. Seventy-five miles an hour, and on them curves! Buddy, I'm doen you a favor, hit's a favor—

AMOS. All right, officer. Let me have the ticket, if that's what you're getting ready to do. I'm in a—

(BILL SHIPWORTH leans toward the PATROLMAN, putting his hand restrainingly on his friend's arm, and speaks with a controlled, purring voice.)

SHIPWORTH. Now, officer, you're perfectly right. We were going a little fast. But it was necessary. Now this— *(With his free hand he indicates DR. AMOS.)* —is Dr. Amos. Dr. Keith Amos.

AL. I didn't see no doctor's sign on this car.

SHIPWORTH. There isn't one. You see, this is my brother's car. We borrowed it. But this is Dr. Amos, all right.

AL. *(Leaning to inspect, suspiciously, the face of the driver.)* Are you a doc?

AMOS. I'm Dr. Amos. But I don't see what—

SHIPWORTH. Show him your driver's license, Keith.

AL. Well, for Christ sake, doc, watch hit on them curves, or you'll be docteren on yoreself. But I ain't gonna stand in the way if you're gitten to somebody what's sick. *(He takes his foot off the running board of the car.)*

AMOS. *(Slowly and distinctly.)* There's nobody sick. I wasn't going to anybody who's sick.

AL. *(He puts his foot back on the running board, and addresses DR. SHIPWORTH.)* So somebody was sick, huh? Oh, yeah? Sick, huh?

SHIPWORTH. I said nothing of the kind. What I said—

AMOS. Give me the ticket. I'm in a hurry.

SHIPWORTH. What I said was that he *is* a doctor. If you will reflect for a moment, officer— *(His voice is insulting in its suavity.)* —you will realize that I said nothing about anyone's being ill. If you will reflect.

AL. *(He lowers his head like an animal sinking into an anticipatory crouch, and spits out of the side of his mouth, then puts his foot over the spot on the pavement.)* I oughter give you a ticket, too. Durned if I oughtn't. *(He spits again, and fumbles for his pad and pencil.)*

SHIPWORTH. Officer, do you know why we're in such a hurry?

AL. I don't give a fart. *(His face is twisted with effort as he writes.)*

SHIPWORTH. Officer, I was preparing to say when you interrupted me, we happen to be hurrying to keep an appointment with Governor Strong. You know, you must have heard of him—even if you don't read the papers?

AL. Oh, yeah? An appointment with Governor Strong. In a pig's twat. But me— *(He leans toward them, almost confidentially, a boyish, stupid pleasure showing on his face.)* —I'm going to keep an appointment with him this mornen. He's come-en in from New York this mornen, and I'm keepen an appointment. *(He taps himself on the chest.)* —I'm on the Big Boss' personal detail. Hit's a fact.

SHIPWORTH. You won't, you know, be on it if you finish that ticket.

AMOS. Hurry up!

SHIPWORTH. You won't be on the Governor's personal detail. You won't even be on the patrol. You'll be busted.

AL. Oh, yeah? You and how many more's gonna bust me?

SHIPWORTH. I am Dr. Shipworth, and I am Professor of Clinical Pathology at the State University Medical School. You don't know what Clinical Pathology is, but take my word for the fact that Governor Strong will listen to me when I tell him why we are delayed. *(He presents his card to the* PATROLMAN.)

AL. Durn— *(He speaks peevishly, aggrievedly.)* — durn, why didn't you go and tell me you was worken fer the Big Boss, too? Why didn't you say you was on the pay-roll? I was just doen what come to me.

SHIPWORTH. And my friend here—

AL. Him, too. Durn, they wasn't no way fer me to know. They wasn't—

AMOS. Officer, you say I was driving seventy-five miles an hour?

AL. *(Slyly.)* Yeah, but that ain't nuthen, that ain't—

AMOS. And on those curves?

AL. Yeah, but—

AMOS. And I passed a car at that speed?

AL. Yeah, but I never seen hit. I ain't seen a thing, doc. *(He leers cunningly at the two men.)*

AMOS. *(Sharply.)* All right. Fill out that ticket. Now.

AL. *(Plaintively.)* For Christ sake!

SHIPWORTH. Hell, Keith, leave the kid alone. He didn't mean any harm.

AL. I shore didn't. I didn't know. I just done what come to me.

AMOS. Give me that ticket.

AL. I didn't know—

AMOS. Didn't know! You knew I was driving seventy-five miles an hour. On those curves. You knew I was breaking the law. That's all you're supposed to know. Now— *(His voice takes on a vindictive quality, rising.)* — give me that ticket!

SHIPWORTH. Hell, Keith, what's eating you? We can't stand here all day.

AMOS. Give me that ticket!

AL. I can't give you no ticket. Not and you and him on the pay-roll. You ain't gonna ketch me that a-way.

AMOS. Before God, if you don't, I'll report you for neglect of duty.

SHIPWORTH. Come on, Keith, leave him alone.

AL. *(His voice is that of a big, clumsy boy confused almost to tears.)* I can't give you no ticket, doc. I didn't mean no harm.

AMOS. Harm? You fool. I want you to do your sworn duty. For once. Give me that ticket.

AL. Doc, I can't. I do, and you just got me.

AMOS. All right.— *(He speaks quietly now, almost musingly.)* —What's your name?

AL. *(Sullenly.)* Al Suggs.

AMOS. All right, Suggs.

AL. Well, I can't help hit if you do go and do hit. But I ain't give-en you no ticket.— *(He retreats from the car a little.)* —I got to be gitten to town. Before the Big Boss' train gits in.— *(He looks down at the left front tire of the car, pauses, then points to it.)* —You all got a flat, or mighty nigh. Hit won't hold up much longer.

AMOS. *(He gets out of the car, slamming the door behind him, looks down at the tire, and then kicks it experimentally with the toe of his heavy brown shoe.)* The steering was dragging the last couple of miles.

SHIPWORTH. *(He gets out and comes around the car.)* What next?

AL. Listen, I'll change yore tire fer you. Right now, in no time. *(He is suddenly excited, anxious to please.)*

AMOS. You better go on. To your appointment with — *(He hesitates, pronouncing the word as though the feel of it on his tongue were disgusting.)* —with your Big Boss.

AL. *(Paying no attention to DR. AMOS, he has hurried to the back of the car, where he fumbles with the spare tire.)* I'll change hit. In no time. I'll be glad — *(He hesitates, fumbling with the tire.)* —Hell, this tire ain't got enough air, neither. *(He strikes it with his fist, twice.)*

SHIPWORTH. Damn it, that nigger of Jake's has gone and left a flat on here again. He ought to break the black bastard's neck. *(This is spoken calmly, in his usual voice.)*

AL. I'd fix hit for you, I shore God would. If I didn't have to git on to the Big Boss, like I said. But they's a fillen station a piece up the road, and I'll make 'em git here in no time. I'll —

SHIPWORTH. That's fine. If you'll hurry.

AL. I'll shore hurry. I'll put a fire under their tail, too. I'd a-fixed hit myself, if —

SHIPWORTH. You better get on.

AL. *(Looking at DR. AMOS, who is standing a little apart, and who seems to have withdrawn himself from the events around him.)* And that ticket, now. You ain't gonna —

AMOS. I'll promise nothing.

AL. *(Standing in the middle of the highway, looking from one man to the other.)* Fore God, now —

SHIPWORTH. You better get on.

(AL SUGGS hesitates a moment, looking despairingly and confusedly from one to the other, takes a slow step backward, then moves to his motorcycle. He looks back, once more, appealingly. Then he starts the motor, and is gone, the motor roaring into the distance. When the sound has faded out, DR. SHIPWORTH turns to his friend.)

SHIPWORTH. What's eating on you, Keith?

AMOS. Nothing.

SHIPWORTH. Scarcely nothing, I'd say.

AMOS. Nothing. Nothing, only a man gets tired, no matter what he touches, of having his fingers get a stink on them.

SHIPWORTH. A stink? Really, now, Keith.

AMOS. A stink, and on a man's fingers,
 Whatever he lays hand to, it's there,
 And the stink climbs the multitudinous sweetness of air,
 Lovingly lingers, a kiss upon the tongue,
 And fouls the nostril's secret stair —
 Smell it, it's there
 On your fingers, and mine —
 Whatever you touch,
 The cup lifted familiarly, morningly, to the lips,
 The friend's hand — that delicate
 Film of moisture slick upon the palm
 There, there it will live, proliferate,
 Swelling like algae spored upon a pond —
 The flower you pluck, and the door-knob
 Kind to your fingers, accustomed, the door
 Which opens to the innermost room where love lies.

SHIPWORTH. That blundering bumpkin, now, afraid for his job — he's just another —

AMOS. That bumpkin, as you call him. He's nothing. I shan't report him. He's nothing. He's just a rotten tooth, but he isn't what makes the breath stink. It comes stinking from the belly, the death stink, the inwardness rotten. I shan't report him. You don't pull a dying man's tooth.

SHIPWORTH. Hell, Keith, don't be a Boy Scout. Things aren't all that bad. I admit Strong's a tough baby. I don't approve of his methods, exactly, and his best friend wouldn't say he's a gentleman —

AMOS. A gentleman!

SHIPWORTH. But he gets something done. This meeting, now — I wouldn't be surprised if we don't get a bang-up medical center, a real one. If something like that isn't on his mind, why all this pow-wow?

AMOS. All right, we get the medical center. All right. We patch up a few more bodies. A healthier people. Better babies. Apple week. Jesus Christ.

SHIPWORTH. That's something. It's what we're supposed to think about. You and me.

AMOS. Think. Think nothing. Listen — (*He leans toward the other man and seizes him by the lapel, drawing him.*) — did you ever ask yourself when you put your hand on some poor bastard's belly and sewed him back together — did you ever ask yourself what was in him?

SHIPWORTH. (*Amiably.*) Aw, nuts.

AMOS. What was in him? I'll tell you.
 The stink.
 If the stink's all, why bother?

Think?
But we don't, you and I,
Blind fingers, rag-pickers,
Mumblers and patchers of remnants.
For what?
To get the wind out of a worn-out gut?
We don't know.
Know!
The caterpillar knows its leaf, the mole
Its hummock, the fox the fetid hole,
The cat the cushion, the hog the sty
And the swill-trough, who
Has known his heart?
Who? Not I,
And Bill, not you.

SHIPWORTH. I know that pain's evil.

AMOS. An evil, but not evil.

SHIPWORTH. No, evil, evil itself. And we're the answer. The only one.

AMOS. There was a time there was another answer.

SHIPWORTH. Well, we get the center, we should worry. That'd be a mark for the Big Boss, all right.

AMOS. Boss —

SHIPWORTH. Now Keith. Power is power, whatever you call it. Or whoever has it. Somebody held it before Strong's time. Somebody. It's just that he's tougher than a whole pack, and has licked 'em.

AMOS. No, not that only.

SHIPWORTH. Aw, just about that, I'd say.

AMOS. We touch only the surface, and our fingers
Stink. Whiff only the breath breathed out,

(He shifts his attention more and more from his friend, as the light begins to fade, except on him.)

And it stinks.
But he lies inside.
He is deep inside.
He is growing,
A cancerous growth which now grows proud in the dark,
Iridescent in darkness, the flesh's final pride
Thriving on flesh; and the sluggish blood now sways
And swags to his mass, like sway of the sea's tide.
He burns, is peacocked in flame, but utters no light.

(The light fades rapidly now.)

Eastern and mogul, his mass savagely drowses,
His coils stir. Our name in him is essential,
O nomenclature swollen now! O splendid
And inward that apple, that fat fruit which gleams

(By this time, the light is entirely gone, and there is only the voice in the darkness.)

On the bough of our darkness, till dark itself is rescinded,
Till the night is ended
Till the dark
He is in the dark.

End of I:i

I:ii

(The setting is a long room in an old-fashioned "institutional" style, with high windows backstage. Through these windows, as at no great distance, can be seen the shaft of a steel-and-stone building. Scaffolding is still about part of the building and the boom of a crane can be seen to one side.

In the middle of the room, running lengthwise on the stage, is a long table about which a dozen men are seated. At the end to stage-right, a man is lounging back in his chair, in profile to the audience, seeming to be almost asleep. The arm toward the audience lies on the arm of his chair, and a cigarette, apparently forgotten, smoulders in his fingers. The smoke rises steadily upward from it. The man's face is, in repose, rather coarse and dull. His hair is unkempt and his vest is unbuttoned. He is the Governor, WILLIE STRONG.

To stage-left of the GOVERNOR, is standing a very large man, tall and paunchy, with thinning hair combed glossily back over his round skull. He is dressed in a well cut and obviously expensive dark suit. A very large diamond is on the little finger of his left hand. He is facing down the length of the table in the act of speaking to the men seated along it. As he speaks, he gestures with his left hand, in which he holds an unlighted cigar. The diamond flashes with the gestures. He is JOE (TINY) HARPER, the State Highway Commissioner.)

TINY.—has asked you gentlemen, who are the acknowledged leaders of the noble profession of medicine in our progressive State, to come together this morning because he has a very important message for you. It is a very important message, indeed, gentlemen. (DR. AMOS *and* DR. SHIPWORTH *enter unobtrusively and find seats.*) It will increase the health and happiness of the people of our progressive State, and will make you all happy to know you can use your skill to the uttermost, which hasn't never been the case, heretofore, to bring that condition about. That is what we are all working for, the health and happiness of the people of our progressive State. Now ain't it, parties regardless? But now I'll let the Governor give you his message.

(*When* GOVERNOR STRONG *rises, he pushes his chair raspingly back with one foot, sticks his forefinger into his collar to loosen it, and then lets his hands drop to touch the table. Meanwhile,* TINY HARPER *has let his bulk sink by degrees into the scarcely adequate chair, and has looked about him as though for applause. He exhales heavily through his meaty lips, and then wipes his face on a large white silk handkerchief, which he rearranges in the breast pocket of his coat.*)

STRONG. Well, now Tiny's shot his wad for the day and got his weight off his arches, I'll give you boys what Tiny calls my message. Though God knows where he ever got the habit of using that word. It sounds like a Baptist prayer meeting, and Tiny's a Romish mick. — (*The* COMMISSIONER *smiles, but without complete conviction.*) —He thinks he can buy both salvation and grammar. Well, what I've got to hand you is short and sweet. At least, I hope it'll sound sweet to you. I'm gonna put up the best hospital and clinic in this town money can buy. That is, the best one about eight million of money can buy. Then—

(A *large, somewhat pompous man, who is sitting about the middle of the table, facing the audience, leans forward and clears his throat as though about to speak. He is* DR. FAIRBANKS.)

FAIRBANKS. Eight million! That's—
STRONG. Hell, doc, ain't that enough?
FAIRBANKS. What I was about to say—
TINY. If you'll excuse me, Governor, the figure you got in New York, to carry out your ideas was about—was about nine million.
STRONG. Sure, sure. But I'm expecting you, Tiny, to save the State about a million or so. You know— (*He turns to the men along the table.*) —Tiny's a stemwinder when it comes to saving the State money. It's remarkable, every time he gets outer the State he saves it some money. He can save this State more money just listening to music and drinking champagne in Palm Beach than any man who was ever Highway Commissioner could sitting right here in his office. What about it, Tiny?
TINY. Well, Boss— (*He smiles again, looking covertly at the men along the table.*) —well—

STRONG.*(Ignoring the* COMMISSIONER.*)* I'll build you all the hospital. Eight million. More if you say the word. Then we'll stick 'em round over this whole damned State. Half a dozen. Hell, a dozen. What I want —

FAIRBANKS. Governor —

STRONG. *(He looks at* FAIRBANKS, *but continues to speak.)* What I want you all to do is to look over these drawings and specifications and stuff, and get together and talk it over, and let me know how it looks to you. So we can get down to rendering lard pretty quick. — *(He shoves a big roll of blueprints a few inches along the table, and prods a bulging leather brief case, which is lying before him.)* — How about it?

FAIRBANKS. Speaking for myself — *(He stops, clears his throat, and looks about him, as though for support.)* — I shall be happy to offer the benefit of my experience and training. And I know that there is need for further hospitalization facilities in this city. Yes, a considerable need.

STRONG. You've got 'em three in a bed, sometimes.

FAIRBANKS. A considerable need, I say. But eight million, Governor? And you speak of a program elsewhere in the State, on a similar scale. Now, I am sure, Governor, we can manage on something a little less — shall I say? — spectacular. We could have a very nice little annex for charity cases for, perhaps, about seven hundred and fifty thousand. This is a poor State, Governor, you must remember. A very poor State.

STRONG. There's a passel of poor folks living in it, doc. And that's why your very nice little annex wouldn't be more'n ham hock on a holiday. Why, there's no telling how many micks and wops down there across the tracks, where Tiny, here, come from before he decided to dedicate his talents to the public weal, and where he can still rally 'em round on election day for four bits and old times' sake, and most of those micks are porer'n a sick flea on a blind nigger's hound-dog. And the red-necks up the country where I come from —

FAIRBANKS. It's a poor State, I repeat, Governor. Statistics show it. And without extravagant improvements of late years — which, of course, Governor, do make very good newspaper copy — *(He nods toward the building beyond the window.)* — with our extravagant improvements, our resources are somewhat — somewhat depleted.

STRONG. Nuts, doc — *(He glances at the building beyond the window, then returns to* DR. FAIRBANKS, *and repeats, amiably, the word.)* — Nuts.

FAIRBANKS. I beg your pardon!

STRONG. Nuts. This State's got plenty of resources. It's just a question of who's got his front feet in the trough when slopping time comes. Well, the micks and the red-necks haven't — that is, except me and Tiny. We have.

FAIRBANKS. It's all very well, Governor, to —

STRONG. You're durned tooting, doc, it's all very well. I can figure out ways to raise money would surprise you. And you oughter see what Tiny can do if you give him a pencil and a piece of paper and let him get off in a corner to do his home work. It's a caution. Why, doc, we might even raise the income tax in your bracket, again. And all that stock you've got in Acme Electric —

FAIRBANKS. I fail to see what my personal affairs have to do with this discussion.

STRONG. Nothing, doc. Just that that stock might start paying you something a lot down nearer six percent if the State started to get a little return on what you quaintly term its depleted resources. Yep, doc, there's ways to raise money, and what's more, I can make folks like it when election day comes. Except— (*He grins, nodding.*) —you.— (*He stops talking and seems to be waiting for someone to answer. He lights a cigarette, takes a deep inhalation, and lets the smoke seep slowly from his nostrils, while his eyes seem to be almost closed. Then he opens his eyes, forces out the last of the smoke from between his lips, almost with an action of disgust, and speaks.*) —Well— (*He thrusts the roll of blueprints along the table.*) —how about it?— (*He takes another inhalation of the cigarette, waiting.*) —If you boys don't want to play ball, there's other pitchers in the league.

(*DR. FAIRBANKS' hand moves slowly, almost surreptitiously, toward the roll of blueprints, the full length of his immaculately gleaming cuff showing beneath the sleeve with the effort of stretching his arm. The other men are watching DR. FAIRBANKS' hand as it closes on the roll, and draws it slowly toward him. GOVERNOR STRONG speaks suddenly, his tone patronizing and ironical.*)

STRONG. That's the boy, doc!

(*DR. FAIRBANKS looks up at him, guiltily, wets his lips as though about to speak, and finishes boldly the action of drawing the roll to him.*)

STRONG. Well, you all look things over, and let me know when you're ready. I'll—

(*The door at stage-right opens to admit a woman, who stops just inside. She is of medium height, probably about forty years old, but seeming older, at first glance. She is wearing a formless and cheaply-made tweed suit. Her features have no distinction, but her dark eyes are large and intense. When she moves it is scarcely obvious that she has a slight limp. She is SUE PARSONS, the Governor's confidential secretary.*)

SUE. Governor—

STRONG. Be with you pretty quick, Sue. I reckon we're winding up.— (*As the doctors begin to rise, the GOVERNOR turns back to them.*) —Just let me know when you're ready. Thanks for coming round.— (*He starts toward the door at stage-right, then stops and faces the group.)* — Oh, yes, if Dr. Amos, Dr. Keith Amos, can spare a minute, I'd like to speak to him.

AMOS. I'm Dr. Amos.

STRONG. *(Nodding.)* I picked you for him. — *(He moves toward DR. AMOS, who stands his ground, his hands hanging loose at his sides. The GOVERNOR extends his right hand as he walks forward, but DR. AMOS shows, for the moment, no sign of seeing it.)* —Yep, I picked you for him. — *(He approaches DR. AMOS, grinning, his hand extended. After a moment's hesitation, DR. AMOS shakes hands. The GOVERNOR releases the handclasp, and as he withdraws his hand, grins again.)* — See, boy, it wasn't nearly as bad as you figured on. — *(DR. AMOS steals a glance at the hand which has clasped the GOVERNOR's, and the GOVERNOR stands before him, looking amusedly at him.)* —If you stick around a minute or two, Dr. Amos, there's something I'd like to say to you. As soon as — *(He hesitates, grinning again and looking toward the group near the door at stage-left, singling out DR. FAIRBANKS.)* —as soon as we can get shed of this assortment of ornaments of the medical profession and stuffed shirts.

FAIRBANKS. *(Clearing his throat.)* I beg your pardon!

STRONG. It's all right with me, doc, you needn't beg my pardon. Besides, the Good Lord did it, and he won't apologize.

(FAIRBANKS stands with his briefcase and roll of blueprints, his face purpling, but he does not manage a reply. Meanwhile the GOVERNOR has turned to DR. AMOS. The other men, with the exception of COMMISSIONER HARPER, who is again seated, go off through the door at stage-left. The GOVERNOR seems to discover COMMISSIONER HARPER.)

STRONG. That means you, too, Tiny. You're not a distinguished ornament of the medical profession, but there's something of the stuffed shirt about you. You can find some pictures to look at in my office.

TINY. *(He gets slowly to his feet, the same unconvincing grin on his large, round face, as before.)* So long, Boss. — *(He wags his head at DR. AMOS.)* —I'll be seeing you. *(He goes out the door at stage-right.)*

AMOS. Well?

STRONG. Well, boy, what do you think of it?

AMOS. I think that the people of the State will get some good out of it. And you will get your publicity and your votes. It's money better spent than for that. — *(He gestures, almost violently, toward the building beyond the window.)* —Six million for a new Capitol. Vanity, Governor, or worse.

STRONG. *(He has turned at the other man's gesture to look toward the building.)* It'll be there a long time.

AMOS. And what does that mean? You won't.

STRONG. *(Ignoring* DR. AMOS' *remark, he studies his face. When he speaks, his voice is measured and serious.)* Dr. Amos, I want you to be director of the new medical center and hospital. — *(As* DR. AMOS *seems to be collecting himself for a reply, the* GOVERNOR *raises his right hand sharply and commandingly.)* — Listen here, you're going to say, no. Just think about it a minute.

AMOS. For one thing, I couldn't put up with your interference. Or the possibility of it.

STRONG. Interference? I might fire you, boy, but I wouldn't interfere with you. And when I fired you it would be for incompetence. — *(His voice sinks to a harsh whisper, and he thrusts his head forward, toward* DR. AMOS.*)* —You got that straight?

AMOS. That's not all. There's —

STRONG. Listen here, I know what your political opinions are, and I'm not trying to buy you off. Boy, if you think so, you flatter yourself. I can run this State my way, and ten more like it, with you howling on every street corner like a pup with a sore tail. What I'm saying is, you run the hospital and I'll run the State. I wouldn't give a toot about you shooting off your mouth if it gave you any satisfaction. So long as you did your job.

AMOS. That's not the point —

STRONG. Well, the kind I do give a toot about when they start shooting off their mouths and trying to turn on the heat — well, I know more'n one way to skin a cat. Take the late Governor of this State, where is he now? He's not Governor, he couldn't even be elected sergeant-at-arms in a sanatorium for the feeble-minded. And he's broke, too. He's peddling no-good life insurance on the street corners, or damned near it. — *(He hesitates, grinning, leaning forward a little.)* —He'll be peddling fish to niggers before I'm through. And Senator Crosby, where is he?

AMOS. He's dead. He shot himself. You know that.

STRONG. Sure, I know that. But he ought never taken that little cut on building those municipal docks, when he was a bright young man, just getting a start. And then to sign his name to things. — *(He shakes his head commiseratingly.)* — Twenty years ago, but you know — *(His voice assumes a slightly ironical unction.)* — the Good Book says a man's sins will find him out. If he signs his name to things. A man ought to live so that when his summons comes to join that innumerable caravan which throngs the silent halls — *(He stops, leering amiably, and slaps* DR. AMOS *on the shoulder. Then he becomes serious.)* — About that hospital, I want to know pretty quick. But don't give me an answer off-hand. Hang around a half hour or so, and think about it. You can admire the view while you wait. — *(He gestures toward the building beyond the window, then looks at his watch.)* —Damn it, I've got to get the lead out. Sue'll

be pawing the earth in there. She'll be giving the stenographers heart failure.
So long!

AMOS. *(Before the* GOVERNOR *is out the door at stage-right,* DR. AMOS *takes a step toward him one hand out as though to seize him and detain him.)* Wait!—I—

(But the GOVERNOR *gives a jaunty wave of the hand, as he pulls the door shut behind him.* DR. AMOS *stands for a moment with his arm emptily outstretched, then lets it subside slowly. His gaze shifts about the room as though in search of something, and comes to rest on the stone shaft of the building beyond the window. He moves toward the window, and leans against one of the frames, facing stage-right.)*

AMOS. Vanity—
What holds the stone? Not the
Mortar.
What ties the steel? Not the
Rivet.
What bears the mass? Not the
Bedrock.
Vanity.
Not mortar, rivet, rock, not architect's
Sleight, nor builder's cunning, buttress nor
Strut-strength, nor stance and promise of arches, but
Vanity,
Vanity sleepless, uncrystalled, in steel's cold
Intenseness, crouched in stone-dark, eye lidless,
Sleepless in crevice, cat-footed, perpetual,
Ambient, flowing, unwinking in atom and sure,
Corridor-lurker, at home in janitor's cupboard,
The filing-case — spider, spinner of stone.
No, no — but the jelly-blob blind in the shell,
The slime-blob uncoiling slime into stone,
It is he, he — he is wrapped, is sheathed in stone,
In hardness is swaddled, mollusc enormous, blind,
Fat, unfolding, affirming — the valves pulse:
But think, think how in the center dark how soft,
Sick-soft and slime-slack, eyeless, nameless, he
Would quiver, jerk from a finger — Ah, see him!
See how the slime jerks, poor blob unfended,
I see you — Hi-spy! — I spy you, Governor —

(He looks out the window again, toward the shaft of the unfinished building.)

I will not, whatever I am—
The slime affirms the stone, nameless.
I will not—
And the stone nameless.

(While the preceding several lines are being spoken, the door at stage-left is opened, and a young woman quietly enters, standing for a moment with her hand on the knob of the yet unclosed door, and with her gaze upon the figure at the window. As she stands hesitatingly, DR. AMOS *turns, and, almost as though incredulous, peers at her. She is wearing a severely cut dark suit which shows to advantage her excellent figure. She has regular features, strong but not masculine. Her eyes are brown and her hair is blond. She is* ANNE AMOS, *the sister of* KEITH AMOS. *Still looking at her brother, she pushes the door shut behind her. Then suddenly, as with mutual recognition, she and her brother move rapidly toward each other, their hands outstretched.)*

ANNE. Why, Keith!

AMOS. Good Lord, Anne!— *(He seizes her hands, and looks at her, the pleasure obvious on his face.)* —When did you get in?

ANNE. This morning, on the late train. Just for the day.

AMOS. How's mother?

ANNE. Oh, she's all right. Feeling fine. Spends all her time gardening.

AMOS. I meant to come up last weekend, but, you know— *(His voice trails off.)*

ANNE. You never come anymore.

AMOS. I'm so busy. There's so much to do. Always more. I just can't get away. And there's nothing I like better than being home. With you all, you and mother. You know that?

ANNE. Yes, yes. Sure I know that.— *(Her tone takes on a touch of casualness and gaiety.)* —But imagine bumping into you here, of all places.

AMOS. *(He responds to her lightness.)* Imagine!— *(Suddenly, as though he has recollected something, the expression of pleasure passes from his face, and he seems to be peering at her again. A tinge of asperity appears in his voice.)* — Why—what are you doing here?

ANNE. Why, I'm going to see the Governor. What else would I be doing here? *(She speaks with a sort of playful defiance.)*

AMOS. *(He drops her hands which he has been holding clasped between both of his.)* He is a swine. *(He pronounces the words measuredly.)*

ANNE. No. Not that, exactly.— *(Her voice becomes serious.)* —He may do terrible things, I don't know. But that's not the word for him.

AMOS. It is the word. It's the filth of him.

ANNE. No —

AMOS. What do you know? Do you know him?

ANNE. *(She laughs.)* Sure, I know him. I've known him for weeks.

AMOS. You know him? Why do you know him? — *(He stops, peering at her again, so that she laughs.)* —What are you doing here now?

ANNE. Orphans. I'm here about orphans.

AMOS. Oh, those homes.

ANNE. That's it. Money, State money. We got some, and I'm after more.

AMOS. Somebody else could do it. You don't have to. You don't have to fool around with that swine.

ANNE. Oh, Keith, don't be silly. I have to spend my time some way. I'm getting on, Keith, I'm almost thirty, and I don't do anything. I'm not worth anything. It's the only sort of thing I can do. I don't want to just play bridge —

AMOS. You could let somebody else come up here, anyway.

ANNE. Don't be silly. It doesn't kill you to shake hands with the man. — *(At this Dr. Amos looks involuntarily at his own right hand, the same expression on his face as when he looked at it after shaking hands with GOVERNOR STRONG.)* — Oh — *(She pauses, her voice becomes almost gay again.)* — and what are you doing up here in this pesthouse?

AMOS. I shouldn't be here.

ANNE. Well, you are. And you don't seem much the worse for it. Except for your disposition.

AMOS. *(He looks out the window, away from his sister; then turns to her abruptly, as though with a decision.)* The Governor is going to build a hospital and clinic here. Eight million or better. There was a medical committee here this morning. I —

ANNE. Why, Keith! That's wonderful. That's what you've wanted.

AMOS. Wanted.

ANNE. Yes, what you wanted. That's what you used to say.

AMOS. *(Slowly, meditatively.)* Yes, I did say that.

ANNE. Well? And now here it —

AMOS. It won't help us. Not me, not you. It won't help anybody.

ANNE. *(Scanning his face anxiously.)* I don't understand you. What do you mean?

AMOS. Nothing.

ANNE. *(Lightly, again.)* Well, talk sense, then.

AMOS. It won't cure us. It won't —

ANNE. *(She steps toward him, lifting her hand.)* Keith —

AMOS. *(He takes her by the wrist of the lifted arm.)*

It won't cure us.

It won't, no matter how crafty the needle, sly;

How sure the bone-saw, scalpel insidious;
How quiet toward morning, like eaves-drip in dream,
Like clock-tick, the rubber heel in the hall,
The gauze no matter how sterile, how pure the love,
How practiced like a whore's the nameless hand,
The murmured word; no matter the rubber glove,
That glare all night, how incandescent and
How blazing-blue — steady, the blade gleams —
It won't matter. Listen — *(He draws her a little toward him.)*
ANNE. What, what is it?
AMOS. I have held a heart, alive, in my own hand,

(He leans as though to confide a secret.)

Beating, a tremulous blood-blob — it did
Not speak, it did not say a word, it said
Nothing.
ANNE. I don't know what you say, Keith. I don't know what you think, anymore.
Not like I used to, when we were younger. When we were little. Then —
AMOS. Then it was different.
We ran among the pines. I can remember
Your voice calling, the echo in the high pine boughs.
There was —
ANNE. Yes, yes, there was a place in the woods
Where the thickets were, it was dark, and there were rocks,
Old, and moss crusty above, but ferns
Below, where the damp was, and moss like velvet;
And we waited, watched —
AMOS. We waited for the fox.
ANNE. He came, he moved like the shadow of a bird's wing,
With no sound, gliding and swift, and his tail low,
And my heart stopped, for I loved him, it seemed,
But like a blink he was gone, where the ferns were.
That was all.
AMOS. And on the beach, you remember?
ANNE. Yes?
AMOS. We lay on the sand —
ANNE. It was warm and comforting-coarse,
Like father's hand inside, I thought.
AMOS. We lay
On the sand, and the sea was blue, how steady sound

But not loud, steady the light that stood
Over all, and the fish-hawk rose, rose into light,
In light lost, the last gleaming wing-wink
Of whiteness lost. And our eyes burned after him.

ANNE. He was gone — through slitted lids, how reeling and vast
That blazing bright palpitation of sky!
Blinded we lay, the talons of light as we lay
Were on us, were in us, the wing-beat, the beak:
Blind, but the blood-throb in eyelid was light,
Light was in us, like breath, and we were light.

AMOS. Why, Anne, it was our medium, we lay
Lapped and sustained, or motionless, yet plunged
Down tattered time and lifting spume of light,
Backward and roving porpoise-stride, the swell
Dividing, we dividers — it seemed true.

ANNE. True? Then, Keith.

AMOS. True now! Why stranded, shored,
Bitched up and bogged, flapping some mudflat, foul
With the sewer-stink, slime-laved — O tidal light!
I will not.

ANNE. You will not?

AMOS. (*Leaning toward her.*) Listen!

ANNE. Yes?

AMOS. He wants me to be director.

ANNE. Keith! — (*She seizes him suddenly by the hands, jerks him almost roughly toward her, so that, caught off balance, he seems to stumble; then she kisses him two or three times on the face. Standing a little back from him, but still holding his hands in hers, she regards him.*) —And who said the Governor didn't have sense?

AMOS. (*For an interval he does not speak. He slowly detaches his hands from hers, and slowly, almost dazedly, lifts his left hand, which is toward the audience, to the spot on his cheek where his sister has kissed him. He fingers the spot abstractedly, while he speaks.*) Sense.

ANNE. Sense, he's got sense. You're the man for it, Keith! (*She takes his right hand again, and again, he slowly withdraws it.*)

AMOS. The man for it. — (*He echoes her words with a touch of bitterness, scrutinizing her face. Then, suddenly, as though answering a question, he speaks.*) — I will not.

ANNE. You will, Keith! Of course, you will. You'd be a fool not to —

AMOS. I'd be a fool to do it.

ANNE. You ought to, Keith. What you could do—you know what you could do
for people. *(She becomes more insistent, taking a step toward him.)* What you
have always wanted to do. And all. What needed to be done—

AMOS. That's the bribe—that's it.

ANNE. The bribe?

AMOS. To yourself, that's it.

> To keep you from knowing what you know, to keep
> Truth quiet, the pap for conscience, the sugar-tit
> For the untoothed gums to mumble on, to coo
> And slobber while the world wags—O no!
> That jaw is toothed now—

ANNE. But, Keith, it's true!

AMOS. *(Ignoring her.)* A bone to throw to conscience, a bone for that

> Slack-bellied bitch, dry tits—those slatted sides
> Have dodged the boot-toe—cringing, ready still
> To love-lick any hand—

ANNE. But it's still true,

> If it's good, it's good, good in itself, Keith,
> No matter what Strong is.

AMOS. That: confusion's head, the cap and charge—

> That, that true, all acts but dead leaves blown
> In the street, decisions, occupations, all
> Unstemmed, trodden, wind-worried, snuffling the stone at night—
> Saliva bright under the streetlamp, cigarette
> Butts, gum, the cat's fastidious stance—
> Piled into corners, dung-damp and sodden, caught
> In the gutter grating at last. O disarticulate,
> What bough, green, broke?

ANNE. *(Breaking in, ignoring his words, which toward the last do not seem to have
been addressed to her.)* No matter what Strong is, the good

> is fact, no matter what
> The world is, even if it's not the world
> We thought—no lying on beaches now, and the light,
> Wings lost in that light, I remember, I
> Remember, it was once—but still it's a world
> To do what you can in.

AMOS. That's what they tell me.

ANNE. Oh Keith, be sensible, you're not a child anymore.

AMOS. Or a dog he can whistle in, to sit, fawn,

> Whine, pant, drool, a hog to come to his holler.

ANNE. Oh, act grown-up.

AMOS. That's it, I'm a man, and a man—

ANNE. *(She impulsively seizes him by the left hand, jerking at him as though to force him to come to himself, huddling her words together.)* It's what you ought to do, and you know it, Keith. To take the appointment. You owe it to people, you owe it—

AMOS. I owe it to myself not to. A man owes himself
Something. Sometimes. Not much, but sometimes something.
This much, at least, now.

ANNE. What? You mean what?

AMOS. To be precise, if you can't understand,
This: I'll be no tool for his vanity.
If you can understand this much: I have
No handle or hand-hold he can take and sweat on,
Wear slick with his fingers. No. And am no rag
To scrub and sop that muck his feet track in—
For who would squeeze me, wring me, wash me clean?
I ask, who? You?

ANNE. If you'll only stop, just stop for a moment and listen quietly, just listen to me till I can say something, say what I have to say. If you'll be quiet, if only—

AMOS. I can be very quiet, I've learned to be very quiet,
For there's nothing to words but the wind's scrannel squeak,
In and out, like an old bellows—the incalculable
Adaptation, the white cords cunningly fluttering in darkness,
The resonant chamber, all—wind in the alley.
In the gut, in the creek-canes the wind's transit.
I'll be quiet. But this much. I'll not be
Glove to his hand, haft to his grip, or be
Whatever slime it is he spins to cradle
His vanity's softness, spins to swaddle and sheathe
That vanity's sickness, worm-fatness, to cuddle its
Dark dream in whatever bloated chrysalis
It is.

ANNE. *(She looks at him with an air of discovery, and speaks very deliberately.)*
Not his vanity. But yours. Yours now.

AMOS. Mine? Well. *(The last word is spoken almost defiantly.)*

ANNE. Yours, you'd make the world
One thing, and the one thing you. But think: contusions,
Bone cankers, tumors, infections—they don't
Have politics, or only the old politics
Of pain, pus-caucus, the secret ballet of cocci,
The spirochete-poll, and the vote, the vote is always

Sure, is always for one name, is for
Death. Keith, Keith, you see!

AMOS. Men have died.
But sometimes for reasons. Or so I've read.

ANNE. Death. On the one side there, and there — there are
Your hands.

AMOS. My hands, yes.

ANNE. Yes, and not yours.
They are not yours, I'll tell you what they belong to:
The swollen abdomen and the gray lips,
The mouth which shapes like an O but utters no breath
When the pain strikes, the running sore and the sore
With the tentacled fingers which beckon, and beckon you,
The eyes which turn slow in the head and find
Nothing, have demanded nothing.

AMOS. *(Slowly.)* Nothing.

ANNE. Nothing,
And in the eyes there's nothing, and the nothingness
Devours, devours you, gray gullet, enormous, void —
And effortless that ingurgitation, and you
Defenseless. The fact. The act. You've seen it.

AMOS. I have seen it.

ANNE. *(She touches him on the arm.)* You've seen it. Well?

AMOS. *(He shakes off her touch as though in anger.)*
But there you are, yourself.

ANNE. Vanity.

AMOS. Yourself,
What man can name it, what he is, can name
The flame which at center does not bend, the essence unending?
Who has named it?

ANNE. *(Almost scornfully.)* Only children try.

AMOS. O Anne,
There's a tooth which gnaws, and gnaws our definitions,
A current in things, we look and their shapes alter
And falter, we falter, doors bang, bang open
On dark and the wet: cold gust at the ankle, the flame
Jerks from the wick, the wick stinks in the darkness.

ANNE. *(She lays hold of his arm and draws him.)* Say you will, now!

AMOS. We have lived in the house, have heard the rustle at night. I'll say nothing.

ANNE. Say you will!

(The door at stage-right opens, and SUE PARSONS *enters and stands just inside, with her hand on the knob.)*

ANNE. Oh, howdy-do.

SUE. *(She continues to study* ANNE AMOS *distantly before she answers.)* The Governor can see you now, Miss Amos.

ANNE. Thank you.

SUE. You can come in this way, if you like.

ANNE. *(To her brother.)* I'll call your office. You'll do it?

AMOS. *(Bitterly.)* Go ahead in. You have an appointment.

*(*ANNE AMOS *goes out the door at stage-right, leaving* SUE PARSONS *standing there looking across at* DR. AMOS. *He turns slowly toward her.)*

AMOS. You are Miss Parsons, aren't you? I've heard of you.

SUE. Yes. And I've heard of you. *(She stands with her hand still on the knob, as though grudging him the delay.)*

AMOS. You can tell the Governor— *(He hesitates, gropingly, his attention seeming to leave her.)*

SUE. Yes?

AMOS. You can tell the Governor I said, all right.

SUE. *(Studying him across the distance.)* That's what you want me to tell him? All right?

AMOS. *(Sharply.)* Yes. That's what I said.

SUE. *(Beginning to smile tolerantly at him.)* Well, that costs me five bucks, doctor.

AMOS. Five dollars?

SUE. Yes, I bet the Big Boss five bucks he wouldn't hook you.

(She goes out quickly, closing the door with a little more noise than seems necessary. He makes as though to follow, then stands with one arm raised, as when the Governor left him alone.)

End of I:ii

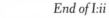

I:iii

(The scene is the bedroom of a hotel suite. It is rather plainly furnished. A bed is at stage-left, a bureau at the rear, and an easy chair toward the front to the right of the bed. The door is at stage-left, toward the rear, and on each side of it is a

straight chair. On a night table at the head of the bed, on the side toward the audience, are a telephone, a small radio, and three bottles of whiskey, one of scotch and two of bourbon. A bowl of ice, a large glass pitcher of water, and several siphons of soda are on the floor by the table. The floor, the foot of the bed, and the top of the bureau are littered with newspapers and stacks of books. Here and there a book lies face down on the floor.

GOVERNOR STRONG, in shirt sleeves, with vest unbuttoned but with shoes on, is propped on pillows against the head of the bed. One heel is dug into the pale blue bedspread; the other dangles loosely off the bed on the side toward the audience. The GOVERNOR holds a high-ball glass in his right hand. His hair is rumpled, but he does not seem to be affected by the liquor.

Eight other men are in the room. In each of the two chairs flanking the door is a uniformed highway PATROLMAN; the nearer man is AL SUGGS. They sit with their chairs propped back against the wall, their booted legs dangling, their hands lying idly on their laps, their faces impassive.

TINY HARPER is seated in the easy chair, stage-right, front. He does not lie back comfortably in the chair, but sits forward, now and then shifting his bulk uneasily, and moving his hands together on his lap. Occasionally, he inspects the diamond on the little finger of his left hand. He does not have a drink.

Two other politicians are in the group. One of them, BENET PILLSBURY, is seated in the straight chair between the bureau and the door. He is medium-sized, bald-headed, and has a pale, splotchy skin. He wears a high, stiff collar, a dark tie with a pearl stick-pin, and a black suit, meticulously pressed but rather loosely cut. The pince-nez, set low on his rather sharp nose, helps to give the impression of a small-town banker or a city preacher. He holds his glass primly, and takes precise, finicking sips; but he takes them often. The other politician is a gaunt, bony man, with a sun-burned, wind-roughened face, like a farmer. He wears shiny blue serge, like a farmer's Sunday clothes. With an air of abstraction, he slowly moves his jaws, working his quid of tobacco; now and then he decorously and modestly lets a blob of juice drop into the spittoon near the bureau, against which he leans. His name is TAILLIFERO MEEKS.

The other three men are NEWSPAPER REPORTERS, two of them young and cocky, as though aware of the theatricality of their profession. The other is a middle-aged man, shabby, colorless, and aggressive or slightly cringing by turns. The reporters lean over the foot of the bed, wander about the room, or perch on the arm of COMMISSIONER HARPER's chair or on the foot of the bed. They all have glasses in their hands.)

PILLSBURY.—and sister, he says, sister— (*He speaks with a confidential, smirking air, fingering his glass, and lifting it for a sip between phrases.*) —sister, did you ever see anybody try to play a trombone in a telephone booth?

(The reporters laugh in an arbitrary, practiced fashion, nodding at the narrator as though in approval. COMMISSIONER HARPER emits two or three nervous, unnatural wheezes, scarcely laughter, and steals a glance at the door. The farmer-like politician nods, while a slow, brotherly grin spreads over his face.)

MEEKS. Durn!—*(He obviously shifts his quid.)* —Durn, a trombone, one of them things.

(The OLDER REPORTER, still laughing, looks toward the GOVERNOR, who shows no sign of amusement.)

OLDER REPORTER. He's a card, ain't he, Boss?—*(The laughter passes from his face, as he sees no response from the GOVERNOR.)* —That's a good one, ain't it?

STRONG. Hell, no.—*(He says this amiably. Then he turns with an air of casual conversation to BENET PILLSBURY.)* —You know, Pill, you could be teaching the Lord's prayer to a small child and out of your mouth it'd sound like something written on a fence.

PILLSBURY. *(With the deprecatory air of a man trying to pass over a compliment.)* Now, Boss—

1ST YOUNG REPORTER. *(Picking up a book from the bed.)* What you been reading, Boss?

STRONG. A book.

1ST YOUNG REPORTER. *(Inspecting the cover.)* Vanity Fair. I been meaning to read that.

STRONG. You'd find it helpful. It's about a tart. A tart who knew what she wanted and knew how to get it. Only— *(He drinks.)* —she didn't.

2ND YOUNG REPORTER. It was in a movie. I saw it twice.

MEEKS. The Boss, he sets up nights reading them things. Not all the time about tarts, neither. *(The word tart comes from him with an inflection of self-conscious unfamiliarity.)*

OLDER REPORTER. Don't you ever sleep?

STRONG. Some. Too damned much. Somebody's got to keep an eye on these birds.— *(He nods toward the COMMISSIONER and then toward the other two politicians.)* —Turn your back on 'em and they'd pull down the new Capitol and sell it to some kike second-hand man for junk.— *(He pauses.)* —Don't print that, though.

OLDER REPORTER. Aw, Boss, you get your cut.

STRONG. Sure, but just try and pin it on me. Pin it on me, and that damned yellow sheet of yours would raise you ten bucks a week. They love my guts.

OLDER REPORTER. Hell, it's all in the game, Boss. A feller's got his job.

STRONG. Well, be sure you keep yours. Even if it isn't such a hell of a good one.

1ST YOUNG REPORTER. Come on, Boss, come on and spill something about this hospital business.

STRONG. Go on and ask Tiny over there. *(He takes a drink as though dismissing the subject.)*

1ST YOUNG REPORTER. Can the Commissioner make a statement?

STRONG. Sure, he can make a statement. Did you ever see him when he couldn't? But don't believe a God-damned word of it. He doesn't know a God-damned thing about it. — *(He heaves himself over on the bed, pours some bourbon into his glass, fishes over the side of the bed for ice, and adds a little water.)* —Not a God-damned thing.

(There is a knock at the door, and AL SUGGS, at a look from the GOVERNOR, reaches up and jerks on the knob, so that the door swings inward. A YOUNG MAN, timorous and apologetic, enters.)

YOUNG MAN. Excuse me, I just wanted to speak to the Commissioner, if you please. *(He looks at the GOVERNOR, in question.)*

STRONG. Come on in, boy. — *(As the YOUNG MAN still hesitates on the sill, the GOVERNOR turns toward the COMMISSIONER, who is leaning forward nervously in his chair.)* —Hey, Tiny, somebody wants to confide in you!

TINY. Yes. Yes. — *(He goes to the door, where the YOUNG MAN says something in a low tone, then retires, closing the door. The COMMISSIONER turns back into the room, and goes toward the little table where the bottles are.)* —I reckon I will take a drink, Boss. I reckon I will take a little scotch.

STRONG. Help yourself. — *(He watches while the COMMISSIONER picks up the bottle of scotch.)* —But I wouldn't take scotch if I were you.

TINY. Huh?

STRONG. It's foreign. What would the voters say if they could see you reaching for a bottle of foreign likker? If you ever want to be elected to anything, you better stick to the domestic product. — *(He inspects his own glass, turning it in his hand.)* —Like me. I attribute my success to the domestic product. I stick to old red-eye. — *(As the COMMISSIONER hesitates, and then, with almost an air of bravado, picks up the bottle of scotch, the GOVERNOR shakes his head.)* —That's just my advice, Tiny. You can take it or leave it. — *(As the COMMISSIONER squirts the soda into his glass, the GOVERNOR turns toward TAILLIFERO MEEKS.)* —How about you, Meeks, want a little foreign fire-water?

MEEKS. I had me some red-eye, Boss. I reckon I'll finish my chaw, then I'll take me another toot.

TINY. Boss —

STRONG. Yeah?

TINY. *(He takes two long gulps of his drink, as though to brace himself.)* Boss, there's a feller here wants to see you.

STRONG. Bring him in. Give him a drink.

TINY. *(He hesitates, and rolls his eyes significantly at the others present.)* Well, you see, Boss—you see—he's

STRONG. Why, hell, Tiny, it's all friends here. Bring him in and tell him to speak up like a man. No secrets here. Never had a secret in my life.

TINY. Well, Boss—maybe he'll just wait a little while—he's been waiting, and he's come quite a ways, but maybe he'll wait a little while—you see—

STRONG. Aw, buck up, Tiny, get the phlegm out of your throat. You're blubbering. Who the hell is this pal of yours, anyway?

TINY. It's—it's Satterfield.

STRONG. *(Almost gaily.)* Never heard of him.

TINY. Why, Boss— *(Reproachfully.)*

PILLSBURY. Satterfield, Satterfield! Old Bob Satterfield! *(He sits forward in his chair, a kind of excitement overcoming his primness.)*

1ST YOUNG REPORTER. Old Gummy Satterfield! Like a bluebottle round buttermilk. If he's hauled his up here, boys, it's churning-time!

TINY. *(Trying to manage a smile as though for a wayward child.)* Boss, you know Gummy. You've seen him a hundred times.

PILLSBURY. Slickest lawyer in the South.

OLDER REPORTER. Hell, he never made his in the courts. You know—

1ST YOUNG REPORTER. He made his keeping out of the courts.

2ND YOUNG REPORTER. Yeah, right now he owns more'n half interest in the Morton Bridge and Construction Company. For a fact, I know—

TINY. *(His confusion and fury being controlled with difficulty.)* I wouldn't be so sure. I wouldn't say off-hand, now—

2ND YOUNG REPORTER. Acme Electric, too.

STRONG. *(With excessive blandness.)* I never heard of the son-of-a-bitch.

TINY. You know him, Boss. Sure, you do—

STRONG. *(With a hint of mincing parody in his tone.)* I cannot say that I have ever had the pleasure. And— *(His tone changes suddenly.)* —God, I've had too damned much pleasure already tonight of that kind.

TINY. *(Pleading.)* He's come a long way, and—

STRONG. Tell him I said there's a cheap hotel round the corner if this one's too rich for his blood—

OLDER REPORTER. Jesus!

STRONG. —and if he's on his uppers, to try the Salvation Army flop-house.

TINY. Boss—he's setting out there, he's—

STRONG. The Son of Man had not a place to lay his head. Do you expect me to burst into tears because that blot on my divan out there, hasn't got himself a room yet?

TINY. Can he see you tomorrow?

STRONG. No.

TINY. Can I make an appointment?

STRONG. Sure. Four-thirty in the afternoon, sometime next year.

TINY. Boss —

STRONG. Go tell him what I said! Every damned word of it.

(*COMMISSIONER HARPER turns ponderously to the door, opens it, and goes out.*)

OLDER REPORTER. (*In a voice touched slightly by awe.*) Old Gummy Satterfield!

1ST YOUNG REPORTER. Boss, everybody knows something's up. Everybody knows about the hospital business. Come on, tell us what your hospital program really is.

STRONG. My boy, program is the mother of dissension.

2ND YOUNG REPORTER. Aw, spill it, Boss —

STRONG. Hell, if I told you all then you'd print it and everybody'd know as much as I do.

(*COMMISSIONER HARPER enters and stands beyond the bed.*)

OLDER REPORTER. Aw, Boss, come on, Boss — (*An insinuating, almost rhythmic quality comes into his voice.*)

STRONG. Don't bother to ask me. Go on and print what you want to. That's what you do anyway.

OLDER REPORTER. Aw, Boss, now, Boss —

STRONG. And God damn it, I'm not your boss. If I were, I'd fire you — (*The OLDER REPORTER grins, for the GOVERNOR is speaking in a half-bantering fashion, but the grin gradually fades from his face as the GOVERNOR, in the same tone, proceeds.*) —You know some of these days I'll buy your sheet. Cheap, too. And I'll fire you.

OLDER REPORTER. Hell, Boss, it's all in the game.

STRONG. You ever heard what the old nigger said a monk was?

PILLSBURY. (*Leaning forward.*) Naw, naw. What is it?

STRONG. The old nigger said, now a monk, he ain't nuthen but a buck-nun. And by God, do you know what a newspaper man is? — (*No one answers, as he swings his gaze from one to the other.*) —Well, a newspaper man is a buck-whore.

(*The men, with the exception of the COMMISSIONER, who only smiles, and as though by effort, laugh boisterously. Before they have ceased, there is a knock at the door. As before, AL SUGGS looks questioningly at the GOVERNOR, and then reaches up to open the door. The same timorous and apologetic YOUNG MAN enters, and stands with his hand on the knob of the door, which he has closed behind him.*)

YOUNG MAN. (*Speaking softly and seeming to address no one in particular.*) There's a lady out there wants to see the Governor.

PILLSBURY. She knows about the right time to come, huh, Boss?

STRONG. What's her name?

YOUNG MAN. I don't know. She didn't tell me. She just said she had to see you and you'd see her, Governor.

STRONG. Well, find out who it is.

(*The* YOUNG MAN *goes out, closing the door.*)

PILLSBURY. Yes, sir, the gals all like the Governor. She said she just had to see you. (*He renders the last with a mimicking falsetto.*)

TINY. I bet it's that Amos bag. That doctor's sister. She's hanging—

(*As the* COMMISSIONER *begins to speak,* GOVERNOR STRONG, *apparently paying no attention to him, is lifting his half-filled glass to his lips. Suddenly, but without turning his head, he dashes the contents into the* COMMISSIONER'S *face. Then, still not giving the* COMMISSIONER *any attention, he rolls his body toward the front of the bed, reaching for one of the bottles of bourbon. He begins to prepare another drink for himself. At the instant of the impact, the* COMMISSIONER *seems about to hurl himself upon the man on the bed, his arms lifting with fists clenched. But* AL SUGGS, *who had seemed so completely detached from the scene, is instantly on his feet, half crouching as though to spring.*)

TINY. (*Almost plaintively.*) Boss, now God damn it—

OLDER REPORTER. (*Slowly, almost reverently.*) Fer sweet Jesus's sake.

TINY.—Boss, what made you go and do that?

STRONG. (*Still preparing his drink, and not turning his head toward the* COMMISSIONER.) It just struck me as a good thing to do.—(*He takes a drink from the newly filled glass.*)—Something I'd sort of neglected in the past.

TINY. (*Mopping his face with his handkerchief, and then trying to grin as though the whole matter had been a joke.*) Well, Boss, you sure got me wet. For a fact—

(*The door opens and the* YOUNG MAN *enters, and stands respectfully, only stealing a hurried glance at the disheveled* COMMISSIONER.)

STRONG. Well, boy, who is she?

YOUNG MAN. It's your wife. It's Mrs. Strong. She says—

STRONG. (*He pushes himself up on the bed.*) Yes. Yes.

YOUNG MAN. She says it's important.

STRONG. Yes. Tell her to come in.—(*He sets his glass on the table by the bed, and swings his feet over the side of the bed toward the audience, getting ready to stand.*)—Go tell her.

(The YOUNG MAN *goes out. The other men move toward the door, and stand there looking at the* GOVERNOR *with a kind of covert curiosity.)*

STRONG. *(Giving an off-hand wave toward the group.)* Well, good night, boys.

(The men go out slowly, and the two PATROLMEN *rise and follow them,* AL SUGGS *last, closing the door behind him. Almost immediately, the* GOVERNOR'S *wife enters, shuts the door softly, and stands before it, waiting, looking for her husband. She is wearing a cloth coat, which, like her plain felt hat, is dripping wet from the rain. Her face is pale, and her eyes dark. She is scarcely a handsome woman, but her face indicates dignity, patience, and fortitude. Some of her dark hair has slipped down from beneath her hat, and glistens with moisture in the light.)*

STRONG. *(He rises slowly from the bed, and with a show of deliberation, sets down his glass on the table by the bed.)* Hello, Clara — *(When she makes no answer, he studies her for a moment.)* — Nice night for ducks.

CLARA. I want to talk to you, Willie.

STRONG. I didn't reckon we had much to say.

CLARA. I haven't had, for a long time. But I have now, Willie.

STRONG. *(Speaking detachedly.)* You better take that wet coat off before you catch cold.

CLARA. No. No thanks. — *(But she takes off her hat, shaking off the drops of water, and pushes her hair up.)* — I won't be long. I saw in the paper you came up from the capital this afternoon. And I wanted to talk to you.

STRONG. Well?

CLARA. I don't ask for anything for myself. Nothing
For myself. For I am nothing now, am only
Like wind not blowing, blown; the memory
Of mirrors in darkness. No, rather, am all,
Need nothing now, being all; all, because now
I approach, thankful, a knowledge of what I am.

STRONG. *(He looks at her meditatively.)* You haven't changed much, whatever you are.

CLARA. In knowledge the active fulfillment, not the whore's peace,
Panhandler's belly-peace, snow peace, the peace
Of the ether-mask, the capsule at twilight, easy.

STRONG. Christ sake, Clara, you talk like an old woman.

CLARA. Not old, but new, and will be no older, but you
Are older, more fallen-off, fragmentary —

STRONG. Me? — *(He pulls himself erect, wavering slightly, as though feeling the whiskey for the first time.)* — I reckon I can still dish it. — *(Then he looks at her in sudden irritation.)* — What do you want?

CLARA. I want nothing; not wanting, can give, now,
    What little I have to give, which is my love.
    I still love you, Willie.
STRONG. I thought we'd settled all that.
CLARA. Love you, but differently now, as the cold seed
    Un-numbing in darkness, unfolding, fumbles for light,
    As the word unfolds in act: differently now,
    And better, no longer in dark who lift lightward.
    You must do one thing for me.
STRONG. (*Grudgingly.*) What?
CLARA. It's Thomas. You must make him stop football.
STRONG. For God's sake! The best thing we've had in the backfield in six years.
    And you want him to stop. My God, and you want him to stop! He may not
    be big, but hell, Clara, he's plenty tough. He won't get hurt, he's too smart —
CLARA. It might be better if he did get hurt.
STRONG. What's eating you?
CLARA. It's ruining him. Not the playing, but thinking he's a hero, what people
    say. The people he goes with. The girls. There's one —
STRONG. Girls? What do you want him to be? A cushion-toter in a harem? Hell,
    he's a man, Clara.
CLARA. There's one —
STRONG. Look here, you mean there's one trying to put the bee on him, huh?
    By God, just let any little four-bits' worth just try to get rough with him —
    What's her name? What's her father's name? He must be making a living
    some way. Who's running this State anyway?
CLARA. Oh, Willie, Willie, it's not anything anybody can do to Thomas.
    It's what he is, what he thinks. Because he can run, can kick,
    Catch, throw a ball, better than most, a ball —
    Hollow, puffed up with wind, with words, and blown
    Like a bladder, a child's balloon, their spittle on him,
    And feeds on their words, their darling, their daisy, till — pop!
    Till he's done. — Ten years, and whose pass made the touchdown?
    The sport-page is yellow now, the shouting dream-dim. —
    Or, pop! — Till eye wavers, foot slows — till bang! the balloon.
    They grieve? The idiot leer, the lunatic laughter,
    The baby's coo for the bang; then cheer some other.
    And he is our son.
STRONG. Yep. He's a chip off the old block, all right. He's tough.
CLARA. You can save him, Willie.
STRONG. Save him! Hell, he knows football won't last, he knows —
CLARA. What he is becoming will last. That's the trouble.

STRONG. — he knows there's something after football. Something tougher to kick
    round. Hell, that boy'll be Governor, Clara.

CLARA. Yes, he may be Governor.

STRONG. Well, what's eating you?

CLARA. Blind, blind all these years, and the gray film
    Grows, unwinking in sun-blaze, is fat now, thick,
    Curdles on eye-ball, and the keen steel yearns.
    Blind, bat-blind, head downward in daylight, wait,
    Hanging fruit-heavy, wait twilight; or mole-blind, move —
    I see you, I an eye in the earth-dark —
    Move now, grind earth, heave sod, and the green roots scream.
    I see you, the tooth enormous on the green root.

(She holds up her hand before him as if to test his sight.)

    O can't you see! See what you are, see what
    You are who once were different, whom I loved;
    And love.

STRONG. What I am I am, and perhaps do not see it.
    But I see this, what men are, and what
    Is to be done, am not afraid of names
    Of things that must be done, necessity
    Flows downhill only; while the constant temptation
    To feed on words, as some chameleon puffs
    His ruby-bladdered throat upon the vine,
    Must be denied, to mumble air, to such
    What honeyed definitions would like dope
    Unstring the hand, blur vision; but the fact —

CLARA. You say you live by fact, know men, I know
    Them too, know all the grabbers, bluffers, sneaks,
    The snitchers, snivelers, snatchers, all the lot
    Who love you so, say yes, yes boss, who hate
    The very guts coiled in your belly, steal
    When your head's turned —

STRONG. They stole before, will steal,
    And I know only a fool would scrutinize
    Too close the stick he grabs in a fight.

CLARA. You think you use them, they use you, will use
    You till you're done, sucked dry, will outlast you,
    Being true sons of fact, the dollar's darlings,
    Loving, sure, whose fluctuations are

But the sea's faithful sway to that bright disk
Whose lunar excellence gauds any dung.
They will inherit. You, the sucker, stooge,
Fanatic bastard to a word, to wind,
Clenched fist of air, power—

STRONG. It's a big word.

CLARA. It is the last delusion, the gut-gnaw
Of those born empty, of the insatiate
Hollowness of heart, who have no inward answer,
Who would devour the world, drowse listening
In what aridity of the deep dark
To their own gut's rumble, rapt and lulled, alone
In darkness, the shudder in solitude.

STRONG. Listen:
It was a house set on the bare ground,
House bare, bony, set on the chunks of stone.
Shutterless, night's blind eye pressed to the pane.
The boy lay, tick-straw harsh to the bare side, heard
The oaks utter under the wind's long drag.
Under the unremitting percussion the timber,
Cold-taut, groaned, and I saw how across the Dakotas,
The icy and pearl-blind plain, the Ozarks, the wind
Came, and did not stop, and I did not know
The name of what was big in me, but knew
It. And once, sun hot on neck, I lay
On the brown grass, and felt beneath my palm
The enormous curvature of earth; and wept.
It has no name but the act, no being in the bland
Intermission of blood, between the stroke and stroke,
But its heat fuses all the mind to clarity,
As the whistling-white blast of the furnace, sand to glass,
For the world fulfills itself, for the perched stone
Throbs for the depth, and the dynamite atoms strain,
In their structures creak like a ship's metals in travail,
Groan; and I knew it. Who knows it and would deny it
Turns the knife on himself, the cut boar grunting for slop,
Fat dog in the sun. Which you, no doubt, admire
As exemplifying some superior principle
Lacking to me, and to, thank God, my son.

CLARA. You cause, they say, a general weakness, a failing,

A falling-off, and the slackness of principle,
Fear among friends and distrust on the street corner—
But I do not know—

STRONG. Well, I'll tell you this: folks get more for their money with me than they ever did. With only a small percentage for— (*He pauses, pours himself a rather stiff drink, neglecting to add either ice or water, leers at her, and gulps it down.*) —for lubrication.

CLARA. And those who speak against you are silenced,
Who move are undone, they say, and you do not forget—
But I do not know—

STRONG. What do they expect me to do? Pension 'em? Put rats in the pork barrel?

CLARA. But I do not know, nor now care, it is not
What happens to others, the outward corruption of power,
The sick-sweet encroachment, the blind rust creeping
With the inimical sentience of a groping hand,
Of ice that all night seeks the stone's fissure,
Sugar that dotes on the tooth's rotten spot—

STRONG. Hell, the *peepul* is like a girl in her first hot, she may squeal but she loves it.

CLARA. What happens to them, that glacial and lulling persistence,
Is outward, not essence, only the accidental
Corruption of power; not accident, essence in you.
For slavery corrupts the slave, but the master more,
And Dives shall lick Lazarus' sores, with relish,
And what in society is relative defect,
In you absolute, and darkness swims, and choice
Drools like an idiot—but O, my Love, a garden
Where bees weave the glinting sun, the summer.

STRONG. For Christ sake. (*He sits down abruptly on the bed, a little drunkenly.*)

CLARA. (*Slowly, as though collecting herself.*) As for our son—

STRONG. Our son— (*He begins to laugh, leaning back on the bed, only pausing to take a drink.*) —My son.

CLARA. (*She moves away from the bed, her gaze fixed on him.*) Good-bye, Willie.

(*He continues to laugh, paying no attention to her. She goes to the door, and goes out, closing it softly behind her. After a moment, while he continues to laugh, the radio on the table by the bed gives a few sounds, resembling static; then, as the sounds proceed, they gradually become comprehensible.*)

RADIO. —no doubt one of the most interesting political phenomena in the country today. His spectacular rise to power within the last five years has been based on two things: he delivers enough of his campaign promises to keep the voters happy in a State where campaign promises have rarely been delivered, and with political enemies and recalcitrant supporters he is ruthless with an unprecedented ferocity. His sense of political strategy has been, to date, impeccable. And he has an insatiable appetite for power. Where will this lust for power lead him? That question now concerns all political commentators. It is said that no price is too heavy for him to pay for power, that he —

(*GOVERNOR STARK leaps from the bed, tears the radio loose from its wires, and throws it to the floor. Then he drops across the bed, face down. After a moment, the radio, which is lying on the floor with its wires disconnected, resumes.*)

RADIO. But voices are gathered, and gather, and congregations of whisperers
 Nod like sedge with a dry sound,
 And the July-fly, the cricket, have made his heart stop, and in the summer
 Noonday, blood stammer;
 But not in fear, who fears nothing as men fear,
 Fears nothing, not himself but fears that emptiness of self the cricket names
  and calls to,
 Fears nothing but self, but self nothing, fears nothing therefore,
 But yet fears the more,
 Though the fact of the voices, the whispers, proclaims his essential success,
  which follows,
 Success as the sea's hissing wake creams after the rudder;
 Proclaims, he shall prevail.
 Whence the inimical sibilance therefore, the chuckle of rushes, windless, the
  cricket's dry glee?
 Or do those things demand, what do your works of hand commemorate,
 What fact the fitted stone? Commemorate only
 A bubble of pride in the belly, like wind, the itch in the brain-pan,

(*The light begins to fade, and leaves the stage in darkness before the last words are spoken.*)

 The lonely
 Name of a transient incertitude
 Who had a name?
 Who walked upright and had a name
 A name.

End of I:iii

II:i

(The curtain rises to disclose a CHORUS *composed of some twenty men dressed in football uniforms, with helmets on. They stand in a double row, very rigidly and woodenly. Behind them is another curtain.)*

CHORUS. What is enough? The thew, the swiftness, the cunning?
　To live by? The piston-like impact, the act, the sly running?
　To love by? The thud, and the punt climbs the tall gold light,
　The ends follow like hounds; or the snap and the plunge and the tight
　Heart tighter, and blood in the mouth; and the stands quiet?
　To live by, to love by? In its secret the flesh's fiat?
OFFSTAGE CHEERING. Rah, rah, rah! Rah for State!
　Our Alma Mater, she is great!
　We will fight and die for State!
　Rah, rah, rah! Die for State!
CHORUS. *(Joining in.)* Rah, rah, rah! Rah for State!

(Here, one of the members of the CHORUS *steps out of formation, and pushing off his helmet, lounges forward confidentially toward the audience, grinning ingratiatingly and embarrassedly. He is a powerful, stupid-looking fellow, a* LINEMAN *apparently. As he moves forward, the other members of the* CHORUS *relax into natural postures.)*

LINEMAN. Now, I'll tell you, it ain't exactly fair the way some folks talks about us football players. Now, don't get me wrong, I don't mean our fellow students, for our student body, except for a few little stuck-up horses' butts, is behind the team, yes sir. I mean to say they got spirit, the old school spirit, and they support their team. And some of the perfessors is OK, too. They will understand how it is and will co-operate. And they know where their bread is buttered, too, they know a winning team ain't going to hurt none when that good old pay-day comes round. Naw sir, not on your life. But some folks, now, they run off at the mouth, saying us players are just hired hands, and don't think of nothing but what we get out of it. But I'm here to state we don't git as much as you think. It's a fact, I don't get as much right now as when I was running me an ice-route. We want a ejucation, just like everybody else, and we play football to get it, and folks talk about us like we didn't have no feelings or nothing. We love our school, I'm here to state to you. We fight for our school, because ain't she our Alma Mater? Just to show we got feelings, that time we was trailing two touchdowns at the half, against Stafford, it just looked like wouldn't nothing work that day, and us outweighting them bastards twelve pounds on the average, and the Big Boss, the Governor—I mean to say he gives us players some appreciation—he come down to the lockers and what he called us, God-a-mighty, names I wouldn't call a nigger, names I never even heard before, and then he said, "That ain't nothing to what you boys'll be calling yourselves if you let Stafford run over you. Stafford, and them pretty little pukes' papas paying big tuition so their little boys can play football, and I go out and bring you boys in and give you a ejucation and fix you up, and you let them pretty pukes cut you down. By God, I'll put you back to chopping cotton, you let the old school down. You let me down. Think of the old school, boys, they're out there pulling for you—" By God, the boys just sat there and cried. I'll be free to admit it, listening to him, I just sat there and bellered like a snot. And folks say we ain't got feelings.

(He steps back into his place in the CHORUS; *the other men assume again their rigid postures, and begin to speak.)*

CHORUS. Not the appetite blind, no, not even—nor faceless
　　The glory, nor faithless blood-clamor, heart-clanger,
　　Nor fruitless, for the ever-returning, fulfilling intention
　　Fulfills us, fulfilling the ant's sacred endeavor,
　　The pitted cock's rattle, the blood-cough; and voices
　　Are more than, at twilight, bat's whimper, owl's hoot,
　　For the tongue's chisel-cunning has cut, out of air, names,
　　Though the names have stuck in our throats, are not spoken,
　　For we only perform them, like dancers, the names which
　　We cannot name, which wink us like wing-beats,
　　Like wings over hills, the light high; definition
　　Is ours now, who after may lose it, be lost, who trod
　　Under the autumn's long light the ritual sod.

(Off stage, as at a considerable distance, there is a long cheer, which continues as the curtain behind the CHORUS *slowly rises to reveal at stage-right, as in a cross-section the Governor's box in a stadium, and before it, almost at right angles to the audience, and toward the center of the stage, the players' bench. In the box is* GOVERNOR STRONG, *standing and waving his hat, and beyond him,* COMMISSIONER HARPER. *As the curtain rises to its full height, the* CHORUS *begins to break up, prancing as players do suddenly, as at a signal, eleven of them run back past the bench and out on the field, disappearing in the wings, while the cheer becomes more emphatic. The other members of the* CHORUS *take their seats on the bench.)*

OFFSTAGE CHEERING. Rah, rah, rah! Rah for State!
　　Our Alma Mater, she is great!
　　We will fight and die for State!
　　Rah, rah, rah! Rah for State!

STRONG. By God, they sure look good this year! We won't lose a game, not a game.

TINY. *(Unctuously.)* Not if all of 'em put out like your boy. That Tom Strong, now, he's hell on wheels, he's—

STRONG. *(He turns to HARPER as to a friend, the warmth and pleasure obvious in his manner.)* He's that, for a fact. Slick and tough. He can take it and dish it!

TINY. *(Even more unctuously.)* What I was saying the other day now, to some of the fellers, I said, yes sir, I'll give them bastards twenty points next Saturday. With that Tom Strong to carry the mail. He's my boy, now. That's what I said. You ask any of the fellers down at the Highway office, you just ask 'em.

STRONG. *(Abstractedly, watching the field.)* Sure, sure. *(He sits down.)*

TINY. Yeah, what I like about Tom Strong is he ain't like some of them boys, he ain't just beef and beller. He's slick, he tricks 'em. What I always say, I like 'em smart. And Tom Strong, he's smart. He's like his old man, huh?— *(He slaps the GOVERNOR on the back, watching the GOVERNOR's face narrowly from behind his mask of joviality. The GOVERNOR is watching the field intently, and seems to pay no attention to HARPER.)* —Yeah, that's what I—

STRONG. *(Leaping to his feet.)* Look! By God, it's Tom. He's getting away. No, no— *(He sinks back into his seat.)* —But it's thirteen yards.

OFFSTAGE CHEERING. Rah, rah, rah!

Strong, Strong, Strong!

STRONG. He almost got away that time, now.

TINY. He can sure pick a hole. I mean he picked one that time. He can pick a hole, like I always say. Like his old man.

STRONG. I mean he picked one that time now!

TINY. You can pick 'em, too, Boss. Like that time you caught old Judge Wilson short on that stock-law question and ruined him for Congress. And he hadn't been licked in twelve years. You picked a hole—

STRONG. Tiny, you talk too God-damned much.— *(Amiably.)* —Why don't you watch the game?

TINY. Aw, Boss— *(He waits for a little, then resumes.)* —You know, we're gonna lose the Fourth and Fifth Districts for Congress. You know we ain't never carried 'em. Well—

STRONG. Hell, Tiny, watch the game.

TINY. *(After a moment.)* But I don't get to talk to you none, anymore. You don't spend no time with the boys anymore. You're always off with that—

STRONG. *(Wheeling suddenly on HARPER.)* Don't you say it. You remember that time I threw that drink in your face? Well, it won't be a drink next time. It'll be— *(He lifts his left fist and pats it with his right hand just under HARPER's nose.)* —this! And I mean it's not liquid.— *(He grins suddenly, slaps HARPER on the back.)* —Aw, hell, Tiny, let's watch the game.

OFFSTAGE ANNOUNCER. It is third down and five yards to go. The ball was carried by Coy.

TINY. Sure, Boss, sure — (*He hesitates again, then leans toward the* GOVERNOR, *tapping him on the shoulder.*) —Listen, there's a way to get those districts. Now. This fall. There's a hole, Boss. If you pick it.

STRONG. What is it?

TINY. It'll be a deal, Boss.

ANNOUNCER. It is six yards and a first down. The ball was carried by Strong.

(*The* GOVERNOR *steals a glance toward the field, the expression on his face changing to pleasure. While his attention is diverted,* HARPER *signals to someone in the stands behind the box, that is, off-stage. The* GOVERNOR *returns his attention to* HARPER.)

STRONG. Well, what is it?

TINY. Well, somebody's got next to some of the big boys over in them districts. There might be a split vote over there, and we'd get ours. For a change, now. If you pick the hole.

STRONG. Who is it got next to 'em?

(*Before* HARPER *can answer a man enters the box from stage-right. He is a very small man, swathed in a heavy overcoat buttoned up to the chin, although neither of the other men has a coat. He carries his hat in his gloved hand. His head is bald and his features nondescript. His manner is excessively deferential and oily. He seems always about to bow. He is* GUMMY SATTERFIELD.)

TINY. Why, it's Mr. Satterfield! Howdy-do, Mr. Satterfield. (*But he steals an apprehensive look at the Governor's face.*)

GUMMY. (*He bows, and then hunches his head and shoulders forward several times in quick succession, as in abortive efforts to bow again.*) How-do, howdy-do.

TINY. (*Looking appealingly at* GOVERNOR STRONG.) Why, Boss, you remember Mr. Satterfield.

STRONG. Who could ever forget him! How's tricks, Gummy? — (HARPER *seems appalled at the use of the name, and* SATTERFIELD *winces.*) —You still cold, huh?

GUMMY. I do find a little chill in the air today. My constitution, you know. — (*He bows, and coughs once or twice, guardedly.*) —My constitution.

STRONG. Hell, Gummy, you ought to get an amendment to your God-damned constitution.

GUMMY. (*Hunching as though to bow.*) I beg pardon. An amendment?

STRONG. Sure, a big hot-shot politico like you ought to be able to get an amendment to any constitution. Even your own.

GUMMY. *(Coughing apologetically.)* I'm just a plain businessman, Governor. And a lawyer. A plain lawyer.

STRONG. Fancy, Gummy, fancy. They tell me you're getting ready to be the financial Madame Pompadour of this sovereign State. At least, over in the Fourth and Fifth Congressional Districts, huh?

TINY. Well, now, Mr. Satterfield—the Boss and me—we was just discussing—sort of in general—I mean not mentioning names—just before you dropped down—

STRONG. Hell, Tiny, do you think I'm blind? You did everything but whistle to the guy. And you'd done that if he hadn't been squatting on his mark like a dash-man. Weren't you, Gummy?

GUMMY. Well, Governor, now to tell the truth—

ANNOUNCER. State's ball on the eleven-yard line.

STRONG. Come on, Gummy, talk turkey. I want to watch this game.

GUMMY. It just so happens, Governor—you see, it's this way—

STRONG. You've got the Fourth and Fifth Districts sewed up. Or you think you have. You've got next to some of those bastards, and Gummy, it must have cost you something pretty. And now you want to horse-trade with me, huh?—*(SATTERFIELD hesitates.)*—Spill it, Gummy, spill it!

GUMMY. I just thought, with all this new building program, this hospital and all, a little more equitable distribution of contracts in the State—and there's a concern hasn't had its share, you might say, a very worthy concern, and I happen to have a friend connected with it—

STRONG. The best friend you ever had. Yourself, Gummy. You're the Morton Bridge and Construction Company.

GUMMY. Well, now—

STRONG. I can bust those babies over in the Fourth and Fifth next election. It'll just take that time to bust 'em. Bust 'em later, or buy 'em now. Time is money. Well, Gummy, I'll buy. If your figure's right.

GUMMY. The hospital contract—

STRONG. You better make a pretty low bid. And the penalties right.

GUMMY. As far as I can make out, Governor, and I have, I may state, looked into the matter, the cost will be a little more than you have probably anticipated. Probably eight million, seven hundred thousand, instead of eight million. For the type of construction which, of course, you want.

STRONG. You break eight million, two hundred fifty thousand, and the deal's down the drain. And we might start to investigate utilities in this State. You know, the Acme Electric. You've got a good friend in that, too, I reckon?

GUMMY. But—I'll have to think—

STRONG. Well, do your thinking somewhere else. And think about this: no contracts signed until after election—till you deliver. You get that?

ANNOUNCER. It is a touchdown for State. The ball was carried by Tom Strong. Six points for State.

STRONG. *(He leaps to his feet.)* God damn it, and I didn't see it. Why don't you all watch the game and not talk so damned much?

ANNOUNCER. Tom Strong was injured on the play, but it does not appear to be serious.

STRONG. Hell, he just got the breath knocked out.— *(He turns suddenly to* HARPER, *his face shining, and slaps him on the back.)* —Now, didn't that boy carry the mail, huh?

ANNOUNCER. Tom Strong was, apparently, struck on the head. He has not re-gained consciousness. He is being carried off the field.

OFFSTAGE CHEERING. Rah, rah, rah!

Strong, Strong, Strong!

STRONG. He just got the breath knocked out.— *(He turns to* SATTERFIELD.*)* — And by the way, Gummy, if you build that hospital and every window-latch isn't exactly like those specifications read, your address is gonna be the State pen. That is, the address of what's left of you after I take you apart with my bare hands. You get that?

(A MAN *runs across the field and approaches the Governor's box. The* GOVERNOR *rises and leans over to wait for him.)*

THE MAN. The doctor says it doesn't look serious, as far as he can tell. They're taking him to the field house. The doctor said to tell you so you could come if you wanted to.

STRONG. Hell, he just got the breath knocked out of him. He's tough— *(He nods to* THE MAN.*)* —Thanks all the same.— *(As* THE MAN *withdraws, the* GOVER-NOR *sits down, then turns to* HARPER, *almost appealingly, as though for cor-roboration.)* —It's not a thing. Not a thing. He's tough, huh?

TINY. Sure, Boss, tough as they come. *(He slaps the* GOVERNOR *on the back.)*

STRONG. Sure, sure.— *(He moves restlessly in his chair.)* —If I went over there Tom would be sore as hell at me. For a fact.

TINY. Sure, Boss.

STRONG. Nothing but the breath knocked out. *(He rises suddenly, hesitates a second, then, as though oblivious of the other two men, vaults the railing be-tween the box and the field, and moves hurriedly, almost at a run, offstage, crossing diagonally stage-left, front.)*

TINY. *(Looking after the* GOVERNOR's *retreating figure.)* Tough, huh?

GUMMY. *(He coughs slightly.)* A difficult man. A very difficult man to do business with.

TINY. Sometimes I just figure I can't get his number. He don't make a thing outer his opportunities, sometimes.

GUMMY. A very difficult man. — *(He coughs, hunching his shoulders.)* — But you and I, Mr. Harper — you and I — I believe we understand each other?

TINY. I am proud to say it, Mr. Satterfield, proud to say it. *(He gathers courage, apparently, to slap SATTERFIELD on the shoulder.)*

GUMMY. If you should ever decide to retire from politics, Mr. Harper, there would be, I think I can speak with assurance, a place for you with the Morton Bridge and Construction — an executive position — *(Coughing.)* — for a man of your wide experience.

TINY. Thanks, Mr. Satterfield, thank you, sir. It's an honor —

GUMMY. Or perhaps you might prefer to remain in politics — with a — with a broader field of usefulness than has — *(He coughs.)* — been yours in the past. This Strong, now — conservative opinion, sound business opinion will not accept his eccentricities for an indefinite period. The people will come to their senses. Then, Mr. Harper — *(He coughs again, and his voice trails off.)*

ANNOUNCER. The kick is good. The score is seven to nothing. Tom Strong, who carried the ball to the one and only touchdown, has not, we regret to report, regained consciousness.

(A CHEERLEADER, wearing white flannel trousers and a green-and-gold sweater, and carrying a megaphone, appears from the wings beyond the box, at stage-right. He is cavorting as though leading a cheer from an invisible cheering section.)

OFFSTAGE CHEERING. Rah, rah, rah!
Strong, Strong, Strong!

(The CHEERLEADER moves downstage, toward the center, but still faces stage-right. He begins to speak in the manner of college student orators, too emphatically, waving his megaphone. All the while, and until the end of the scene, HARPER and SATTERFIELD whisper earnestly together.)

CHEERLEADER. Now you never saw a finer thing than what Tom Strong did today. He gave his all for State. He certainly did put out, now I'll say. He fought and fell for State, just like the song says we all ought to do, but he'll be all right soon, and we're all gonna pull for him. But meanwhile — *(His manner changes to one of dignified earnestness.)* — meanwhile, let us analyze more closely the nature of his act and our response to it. His deed — why does it affect us so deeply? It is —
An instant window which, though blurred
And cracked and bleared, from the shuttered room
Of the heart's indignity and doom,
Gives on a scene none had inferred
In our confusion — wide waters, stern
And measured to the sun's wide eye:

White wings under that uncontrollable sky,
Astonishing, in distance yearn.

For all felicity is fed
From that dark stream whose secret is
On the darkling tentacles the kiss;
Root, shoot, so ignorantly bred.
And under our diurnal ice
In the blind channel's probe and coil,
Yet deftly, darkly, waters toil
That, ignorant, the bough rejoice.

O, let our ignorance be lit
By that bold moment's rift and gleam
That accident and fragment seem
Fulfilled and for the pattern fit,
That we mark out the measure full,
That all our days, like straw, burn
In instant flare before they learn
The mule's shuffle, the hog's drool.

(The CHEERLEADER begins to wave his arms. At the first words of the following song, the curtain begins to descend.)

CHEERLEADER. Now we're all gonna sing. Sing so good old Tom can hear it.
  That'll let him know we're all pulling for him. Come on!
OFFSTAGE VOICES. For good old State we'll give our all!
  For good old State we'll fight and fall!
  Give our all,
  Fight and fall!
  For good old State!

End of II:i

III:i

The curtain rises to reveal a CHORUS of women, all of whom, with the exception of CLARA STRONG, are in evening dress and are masked. In the front row, with CLARA STRONG, are ANNE AMOS and SUE PARSONS.)

CHORUS. See, see, the painful and tentative
    Return, who went forth, as at a gong's danger,
    Confirmed not by dry palm, the tinker's heart, to live,
    Not by the fashionable compromise, the insidious languor,
    To live, who loved life as a school
    Where only the finger-sucking fool
    Could fail to learn
    Joy's mathematic, the blessedness, that in
    All beauty excellent and unabused,
    Is squared all grace, all casual softness, with a stern
    Unfathomable function fused.
    Failing, fading, return:
    Unwitting, unwilling explorers of what Antarctic,
    Of the warm world no news, in the phones the ironical cackle of static,
    The black wind's voice,
    Information of ice.
    Fading, failing, return:
    Inhabit the heart's cellarage, dry scamper on stair.
    Fading, return:
    Now quick, quick, throw the precautionary switch in the head,
    To huddle, lightless, under the spawning air,
    Expecting the raid.
    We said: we shall not be as they are,
    For it is better, far
    Better, to praise, devoured, the devourer
    Than be the house-huddler, the corner-cowerer,
    For man in his prayer in part is creator, not creature:
    Therefore, affirm the mask, conceal
    The sad individuality of feature,
    Affirm the magnificent abstraction, repeal,
    Deny the neck's sly hinge,
    And past the personal itch, vain verity,
    Past the stitching tooth of distraction, plunge
    With wisdom of plummet, plunge
    Past definition into definition's intensity.

(CLARA STRONG steps forward from her place, and speaks musingly.)

CLARA. I, too, said that once; but have eaten
    My words, which clove, dry, to the palate, clung
    Pulp-like to tooth, exacerbated the tongue;

Know now the moment-kissing deceit in
Whose multiple bland dexterity
Eyes blink. — Then let no more
Occasion breed necessity,
For the vision lives not in surrender but labor,
Nor yet in the instancy of passionate conquest, fury's affirmer,
But in purgatorial knowledge: I would touch
With flicker of friendliness their fingers
Who peer from the interstices of the personal shadow;
Would do this, though it is not much.
In these words there are only the late, and few, singers.

(CLARA STRONG returns to the CHORUS, and the women resume their formal rigidity of posture. Then, ANNE AMOS moves forward, and lowers her mask.)

ANNE. Life pays a price for life, and I know it.
For vitality, violence, for good, evil — our doom,
And only the butter-hearted deny it,
Whose praise would retch at the dunged rose's bloom.

(She returns to the CHORUS, and again puts on her mask, as SUE PARSONS, unmasking, advances.)

SUE. Well, I knocked the nonsense out of that boy a long time back, a long time back. When I took him in hand a red-cap at the Union Station could have sold him a gold brick, that bat-sense wife of his had him so hopped to the eyebrow, he believed what the fat boys say on the Fourth of July. But it didn't take him long to get her number. Well, I put him in the big-time, and he knows it. He can have all the little fly-by-nights, and all the little Oh-it-must-be-grand-to-be-so-big girls, and help-the-people-too. He's had 'em. But he knows where to come when it's not taffy he craves. He always comes back.

(As the curtain behind the CHORUS rises, there is the sound of dance music. Men in evening dress appear from the wings, and the dance begins. ANNE AMOS dances with her brother. GOVERNOR STRONG, wearing a shabby and ill-fitting tuxedo and a rumpled shirt, appears from stage-right. He approaches DR. AMOS, and touches him on the arm.)

STRONG. Good evening, doc. You mind if I try to dance with your girl? If she can put up with it?
AMOS. Good evening. *(He releases his sister and turns abruptly away.)*
STRONG. The doc acts like he had something on his mind. — *(He leads her a few steps in the dance, while the other couples gradually withdraw to the rear of*

the stage, where they are in shadow.) —Hell, let's don't dance. I don't want to punish you. I just wanted to say something.— *(He leads her toward stage-right.)* —That's why I came.

ANNE. All right.

STRONG. Yeah, the doc acts like he had something on his mind.

ANNE. You must have something on your mind. It must have been awful when your son was hurt this afternoon and didn't revive right away. I'm glad to hear he's so much better tonight.

STRONG. He's all right. I was over at the hospital a half hour ago, and he was laughing and talking with some of the boys. He was sore because I came over to the field house. Like I thought he would be. He's tough.

ANNE. I'm so glad he's all right.

STRONG. Well, your brother's not. What's eating on him?

ANNE. Oh, nothing.— *(She hesitates.)* —Unless it's overwork. He's just that way sometimes. Crabby.

STRONG. *(Laughing.)* Well, I just asked him to run my medical outfit. I didn't ask him to love me.

ANNE. I love you.— *(She touches him on the lapel.)* —A lot. Isn't that enough from the family?

STRONG. That depends on how much you love me.

ANNE. A lot. I said a lot, didn't I?

STRONG. *(Seriously.)* A lot?

ANNE. Yes, a lot. Enough to risk what passes for my reputation, by messing round with a married man—to use the phrase the old women will use if they ever find out. And maybe they will, with me meeting you the way I do, and all. Going to—to our place.

STRONG. Do you think I like that?

ANNE. Well— *(She laughs.)* —I can recall some moments when, to all appearances, you did. But, of course, I may flatter myself.

STRONG. *(He does not respond to her levity.)* You know what I mean. This hole-in-a-corner stuff.

ANNE. *(She wags her finger at him.)* Tut, tut, Governor, what an unpleasant name for what I regard as my high romance.

STRONG. Don't be funny. It's not funny. I don't know whether I can put up with it much longer.

ANNE. *(Still banteringly.)* From what my operatives report, you have put up with a good deal of this hole-in-a-corner stuff for a good many years. With, of course, other ladies. *(She becomes prim.)*

STRONG. Yes.— *(He stops.)* —There was a difference. There—

ANNE. And did these other good ladies know there was a difference?

STRONG. I don't give a God-damn what they knew. What—

ANNE. Don't be ruthless. Though— (She shakes her head sadly.) —that's what I read about you in the paper. Ruthless. Plain ruthless.

STRONG. But why I came here is to tell you something. What it is—well, before I say it— (He stops, as though collecting himself.) —I want to tell you this. I made a deal today.

ANNE. A deal?

STRONG. One I never thought I'd make. No, no— (He holds up his hand.) —don't get me wrong. I don't mean to imply I never made one before. I've made God's plenty. I know what the rules of this game are, and I've even made up a few new rules of my own. It's just I never thought I'd deal with this particular outfit. A man with hay fever and upwind could scent those bastards a mile. The gang over in the Fourth and Fifth Districts.

ANNE. Tim Cass and those people?

STRONG. Yes, but I can't say that I have, thus far, soiled my lily fingers by direct contact. Satterfield—you know, Gummy Satterfield—that pretty plug of ear wax, fair and without blemish—well, he bought 'em. And he's selling 'em to me.

ANNE. (A little puzzled.) And you've done it?

STRONG. Listen, why does a man buy him a shoat? Not for a pet. He buys it to fatten till hog-killing time. Well, the next time there's an election over there—I don't mean this fall, but the next one—by God, there's gonna be hog-killing weather. I mean a real meat-frost.

ANNE. What do you have to give those people, Willie?

STRONG. Nothing. It's what I give Satterfield.

ANNE. What?

STRONG. (Almost hesitantly.) The medical center contract. To the Morton Bridge and Construction.

ANNE. You gave him that contract?

STRONG. Not yet. After he delivers.

ANNE. It's the same.

STRONG. Hell, you don't know the worst. It'll cost the State about two hundred thousand for sweetening.

ANNE. Oh, Willie, Willie!

STRONG. Don't worry, it'll all look all right. — (He grins.) — On the books. And— (He is suddenly serious.) —it's worth every penny to the State to clear out that gang. They cost the State more than that every year. It's a bargain for the taxpayers.

ANNE. I know, I know—but isn't there some other way? Does it have to be like this? And the medical center contract.

STRONG. Buck up! It's no news. You know how things are.

ANNE. No. No news.— *(She faces him directly.)* —I know how things are. I'm not a child. What has to be done, has to be done. Oh, Willie— *(She hesitates, then reaches out to touch him on the lapel.)* —I love you.

STRONG. *(Apparently paying no attention to her declaration.)* I wanted you to know. Before I told you what I have to tell you. I want you to marry me.

ANNE. Willie, I—

STRONG. *(He lifts his hand as though to stop a protest.)* My wife will give me a divorce. She said she would if I ever wanted it.

ANNE. It would ruin you politically.

STRONG. We're separated now. People know that.

ANNE. It would be different. It would ruin you.

STRONG. I'd risk it.

ANNE. I have never thought of it, have never asked
    It, and will not ask it, for I am no haggler—
    At least—no moment-botcher, hour-mender,
    Keep no scrap-bag, and am not biddy-hearted to brood
    And fluff on opportunities like eggs.
    You'll admit that?

STRONG. Yes, not one of the squint-eyed girls who squinch
    At cracks, love apertures, and count on their fingers.
    That's true; and I love you.

ANNE. Love, and I love you, but it is not
    A bright contrivance, cock's hackle, cock's tail, or peacock,
    Quail-grizzle or dun, air-brightness of blue-bird, on steel,
    The wax-dab on barb, or sly silk-knot; is not
    Sun-glitter on ripple at morning, the riffle, the strike;
    Nor love's pleasure, the spinner, spoon glimmer, fly-quiver on barb.
    Whatever may be said, not that. I ask
    Nothing, have contrived nothing, and my hope contrives
    Nothing but not to live in a junk-shop,
    For I would have the blaze so bright, however
    Infirm in time not in intensity,
    That when I turn my face, dark stun like a fist,
    Better the bruise-throb of blackness on eye-ball for all
    The world, than crepuscular clutter of compromise,
    Nothing quite used, old vanities marked-down, the grease-spot.

STRONG. You have never asked anything, but I ask something,
    Need something now that has not been surmised
    In daylight, nor heard like a word sudden in the half-light

Of dawn, nor defined in the sleepless and grit-lidded hour
Before dawn; now need—
ANNE. Need, need what? who are so complete, whose acts
　　Thrust, unfold, as from the trunk, the branch;
　　So self-fulfilling, execution buds—
STRONG. One moment: my wife once looked at me, and said
　　I was more fallen-off, unstrung, more fragmentary,
　　And I, I said, "Hell, I can still dish it."
　　Dish it!—slop the hog, kick the dog, put out paste for the rats.
　　Oh, that tune is easy enough, and the fingering
　　On greed, fear, hope, hate, and all the heart's
　　Vindictive and sluttish register, no better than
　　The blind nigger's wheeze or squeak on the street-corner.
　　Shuffle the same old greasy pack, and deal!
　　Yeah?
ANNE. If you are fragmentary, what of the others?
　　Of me, whose need by your needlessness only
　　Is answered? What sick and dry-lipped conjecture
　　Would green, like mould, the magnificent immediacy—
STRONG. Sick? Perhaps. But I only know now
　　The young necessity, whose poor tongue twists
　　A little, and blurs; but know some necessity
　　To live in the house, to hold with myself the familiar
　　Conversation, to knit the eye to the responsible instant,
　　Not blinkered move like the old mule at the cane-mill.
　　I would like to be still for a little while; be still.
　　I would like to be still beside you for the devoted day.
ANNE. What do you expect of me? Be honest
　　Who have been honest with honesty of water or wind
　　Moving, guilelessness of glacier. Do you think love
　　Is a fix-it, a household cement, to patch pieces,
　　The putter and piddle of cupboards, will polarize
　　At a word the fragments, the fractures, the filings of all
　　The invidious iron disorder of the enormous world?
STRONG. Well, no.
ANNE. Well, then?
STRONG. Well, I scarcely believe what I read in the papers,
　　And pictures before taking and after: "Dear sirs, I have taken
　　Three bottles of your special emulsion of love, and find
　　I am much improved, can do my housework,

No longer experience that old pain in the chest,
Especially when fall came on, or before rain,
And I want to thank you, sincerely yours (Signed),
The Lonely Heart"—which is shaped like an apple, and has
A small worm at the core, and the worm has
A small tooth, familiar and hideously soft.
—Scarcely that.

ANNE. Well, what do you expect?

STRONG. Not too much, and nothing which you cannot give,
Give and not know you give, so natural
That efflorescence, expense unspending, unspent,
The uncrumbling of radium, in dark its unwinking
Absolute; or nearly that—

ANNE. I cannot.

STRONG. Cannot?

ANNE. Cannot. Later, perhaps. But I cannot
Now. Cannot, being what I am and knowing
What I know. For in my conduct has been
No accident, no casual remission of will,
But for once—and after I had seen time
Untwist, gather like lint under a bureau—
At last, for once, the unblinking discipline
Which repudiates that desperation drily bred
By the day-after-tomorrow; and I cannot
Permit that the motive, absolute, instant,
Be impugned, cannot cut across the grain, guess at
A smuggled secondary hope, and pick
The hangnail of speculation, at any late hour.
And whose fault? for before the lidless horror, before
The centrifugal dismay, what health, what purity
Of heart, but in the inflamed metonymy?
Whose fault, I ask you, for—

(*COMMISSIONER HARPER, during the utterance of her last words, has been approaching. He discovers them suddenly, and advances, almost breathlessly, with his hand outstretched.*)

TINY. Hey, Boss, Boss!

STRONG. (*He turns with an expression of scarcely suppressed fury on his face.*)
What do you want?

TINY. Boss—Boss, I been hunting you all over. There's a call—

STRONG. Yes, yes?

TINY. From the hospital. They say for you to come. The boy's taken a turn.

STRONG. (*He turns quickly to* ANNE AMOS, *obviously suppressing an impulse to reach out toward her.*) Good-bye, Good-bye. I'll see you later.

ANNE. Oh, I'm so sorry! I do hope —

(GOVERNOR STRONG *has hurried away toward stage-left, rear, and without looking back has disappeared into the shadow.* HARPER *peers after him for a moment, and then turns to* ANNE AMOS.)

TINY. Gee, it's tough. But — (*Brightly, with an air of discovery.*) — there ain't a thing we can do about it. Is there?

ANNE. (*Abstractedly.*) No. No.

TINY. Let's dance. Let's trip one of the light fantastic.

ANNE. (*She mechanically lifts her arms toward him for the dance as he steps toward her.*) Yes. — (*They take a few steps, as the music grows louder. Suddenly, she stops, and almost violently draws herself from him.*) — I can't right now. I'm sorry, but I can't.

TINY. Aw, come on — (*He tries to slip his arm around her again.*) — You were getting ready to dance with the Boss. Aw, come on.

ANNE. (*She pulls away from him again.*) I'm sorry. I can't. Now —

(DR. AMOS *appears from the shadow at the rear of the stage, and hurries toward them.*)

AMOS. (*He surveys them detachedly.*) Well? — (*He waits as they look at him with a certain surprise.*) — Will you dance with me, Anne? (*He speaks with exaggerated formality.*)

ANNE. No, Keith. Thanks. Just now — you see — I was just saying to Mr. Harper here, I didn't feel like dancing —

AMOS. That was what I had assumed.

ANNE. (*Shocked.*) Oh, Keith!

TINY. (*Mincingly.*) Oh, don't mind me. I'm just waiting for a streetcar.

ANNE. Mr. Harper — I —

TINY. (*He bows with ponderous irony.*) I'll be seeing you. (*He walks away toward stage-left, rear.*)

ANNE. Why did you have to insult him?

AMOS. Why do you have to be seen with him, put up with him. Strong is bad enough, but at least you don't have to drink the scum off the pot.

ANNE. In any case, I can manage my own affairs. You don't have to bother about me.

AMOS. I'm not. I'm bothering about myself.

ANNE. Well, you didn't have to be rude to him.

AMOS. I didn't have to. It was a luxury. A small luxury which I allowed myself, but which you seem to find too expensive for yourself.

ANNE. Oh, Keith, Keith, let's don't quarrel. Let's don't. Not with everything the way it is, at least we don't have to quarrel.

AMOS. I was scarcely quarreling—

ANNE. Oh, Keith, let's be like we were, like we used to be. And love each other—

(A PAGE-BOY enters from stage-right, rear, and approaches DR. AMOS.)

PAGE-BOY. Dr. Amos, there's a call from the hospital for you. Urgent, they say. About the Governor's boy.

AMOS. Thanks, thanks.— *(To ANNE AMOS.)* —It's probably a consultation. Come on. I'll send you home in a taxi. Come on.

(He takes her almost roughly by the arm, and hurries away, as the music grows louder, and the shadowy forms at the rear of the stage become more distinct as dancing couples. The orchestra, which is in the shadows at stage-left, is playing "I can't give you anything but love." One of the members of the orchestra steps out to the stage, at the left. He is, apparently, the leader, for he holds a wand in one hand, and in the other a microphone, on an upright. He sets it down and begins to croon into the microphone, while he conducts, mechanically, with the other hand.)

CROONER. I can't give you anything but love, Baby.
    That's the only thing I've plenty of, Baby.
    Dream awhile,
    Scheme awhile,
    And you will find
    Happiness
    And I guess
    All those things you've always wanted,
    Diamond bracelets Woolworth's didn't sell, Baby,

(The music becomes very subdued.)

    More than that, a peace no tongue can tell, Baby!
    Choose but love,
    Lose not love,
    And your lost heart
    Will achieve,
    Though it grieve,
    Meaning past remorse of pleasure.
    What if worlds and cultures fall today, Baby?

(The music has almost faded out; the rendering of the words is almost a recitation.)

If democracy is in decay, Baby,
Crumbling now,
Tumbling now?
Yet though you find
Values shot,

(At this line the music bursts into hysterical violence, and the CROONER madly waves his wand.)

You have got
Love, love, love, love, love, love, loving!
Though the maggots now are in the cheese, Baby,
And constellations drift like falling leaves,
Glimmering, and by short-wave, when the weather's good,

(The music fades out, and the following lines are rendered as a recitation with heavily marked accents; and the last line is rendered in prose — the speaker seems to become abstracted, as though he has lost interest in what he was saying, and is concerned with the new and more fascinating idea of his radio's capacity.)

We hear the inspired idiot's harangue, the shout,
The frantic burst of applause like hail on a tin roof.
But sometimes we can only get the local stations.

End of III:i

III:ii

(The scene is a rather plainly furnished living room, the living room in the house of CLARA STRONG. A fire is smoldering in the grate at the center of the stage, rear. At stage-left, in an easy chair which is set at right angles to the audience, GOVERNOR STRONG is slumped down, with his head thrown back so that his eyes are directed at the ceiling almost above him. A cigarette is burning between the fingers of his left hand, but he makes no motion to bring it to his lips. He is wearing a black suit and a black tie, and an overcoat and hat lie on his knees. Toward stage-right, and toward the front, CLARA STRONG stands. She is in the act of taking off a black cloth coat. Beside her stands another woman, a little older, who solicitously takes the coat from her. This is a friend, DORIS.)

THE FRIEND. Now, Clara, you're sure you don't want me to stay? I'd want to stay, you know. And aren't you going to let me fix you a bite to eat?

CLARA. No, Doris, thank you. If I need anything, really need something, the maid sleeps here now.

THE FRIEND. I'd love to stay, Clara.

CLARA. I ought— *(She hesitates, then begins slowly to remove her hat.)* —I think I ought to be by myself. *(She holds the hat in her hand abstractedly for a moment.)* I ought— *(Suddenly, she drops the hat, and makes a blind, groping motion toward her friend.)* —by myself. He's gone, Doris, he's gone!

THE FRIEND. *(She puts an arm about CLARA STRONG's shoulder, supporting her. Meanwhile GOVERNOR STRONG has not moved; he has not even removed his gaze from the ceiling.)* Oh, darling, you've been so brave. You mustn't, now— now that it's over.

CLARA. *(Almost in a matter-of-fact tone.)* He's gone.

THE FRIEND. You mustn't think of it that way. Think of what the preacher said. That Tom was an ideal for boys all over the State, a fine, clean ideal, and how now he'll be an ideal for years to come. That he—gave his life—

CLARA. *(Almost to herself, soberly.)* The fool.

THE FRIEND. I'm sure he meant to say something that would be—would be—a comfort. And it's true. About Tom being a kind of ideal, and all—

CLARA. He was my boy, and he was playing a game and got hit on the head, and he's gone.

THE FRIEND. *(Apparently at a loss for a reply.)* Darling— *(She strokes CLARA STRONG's shoulder. Then, almost with the tone of one briskly changing a subject, she straightens up and speaks.)* You're sure you don't want me to stay?

CLARA. No, Doris. I'm perfectly all right.

THE FRIEND. I'll be going, then. I'll come by in the morning. *(She looks toward the chair where the GOVERNOR sits, motionless.)* Willie, I'll drive you to the hotel, if you want.

STRONG. *(Detachedly.)* Thank you, Doris. I'm going to walk.

THE FRIEND. It's coming up rain.

STRONG. I think I'll walk, anyway.

THE FRIEND. *(Standing at the door, before going out, she looks at the two intently, curiously.)* Good-bye. *(She goes out.)*

CLARA. *(She looks about the room, then moves to lower the shades of the windows on each side of the fireplace, for it is almost dark outside.)* Willie, the girl can get you something to eat if you want.

STRONG. I don't want anything, Clara. *(He does not look at her, even when he speaks.)*

CLARA. I'm going up and try to sleep, now. I haven't slept for a long time.

STRONG. Neither have I. For a long time.

CLARA. Good-bye, Willie.

STRONG. (*He watches, without changing his posture in the chair, while she moves toward a door at stage-right, rear. Just as her hand reaches for the knob, he speaks, but without moving.*) Clara!

CLARA. (*She turns, startled.*) Yes?

STRONG. I don't know what happened, or when, but it
    Happened, and happened long ago, and in darkness,
    The termite's powerful tooth set to the sill
    We walked on, but can walk on no longer.
    But now I know one thing — Come closer, Clara.

CLARA. (*She takes a few steps toward him, then stops, just to stage-right of the fireplace.*) Yes?

STRONG. You said you love me still, and I do not
    Demand, or cuddle the puling hope, that any
    Word can revoke the seminal assurance of time —

CLARA. I do love you, still.

STRONG. — do not, from that compunctionless sorite,
    Expect concession, who have seen the leaf whirled,
    Heard knee creak on stair, but ask, and humbly
    Some charity of your excess, the slosh
    Of what fullness you are, and my lips dry.

(*CLARA STRONG takes a couple of steps toward him, lifting her right hand, the hand toward the audience; then stops herself abruptly.*)

    I wiped my hand across my lips, like sand,
    Heard in the gutter rain murmur, remembered
    Snug weevil, and under the dead leaf the beardless
    Worm, where no face comes, saw it which suffers
    Only the consultation of grasses; and thought, Oh to be
    Now small, clean-furred, the small feet folded together,
    Asleep in rock-cranny, no thread there, the season
    Winter; or some small thing; my lips dry.

(*He rises suddenly from his chair, spilling the overcoat and hat to the floor. With a violent gesture he flings the cigarette butt into the fire, and takes one step toward his wife.*)

    I want to come back to you.

CLARA. I do love you, but what was once possible
    Is not now possible, at least not now,
    For darkness ticks like a watch, for I remember
    You said he was *your* son, not mine, and laughed.
    And now you have your son, the son you asked for.

STRONG. Clara!

CLARA. Not with the twisted tongue, for there is not
The wrung juice of rancor — my heart, like a raisin, dry —
I say it, say it because — and only because —
No, but in bitterness, which blind access
Warps will; and would unsay it now, my weakness.

(She moves toward him another step, again lifting her hand, as for a caress.)

STRONG. *(With a hint of artificial excitement, as when an adult makes a promise to a child.)* I tell you — I tell you, Clara, what I'm going to do. That new hospital, it's going to be The Tom Strong Medical Center! That's what it'll be.
CLARA. *(Her hand, which has been lifted toward him while he speaks, falls abruptly. She recoils a little.)*
And sports-page and pulpit have uttered their greasy gibberish,
Like a tube of patented salve, when you squeeze it,
Unction upon your official wound, and the manly
Tear, misting the lens, will aggravate catarrh,
And you have your son —
STRONG. *(He tries to interrupt her.)* Clara, listen —
CLARA. *(Ignoring him.)*
And you will have your son, a name chopped
Into stone, cast into bronze at a distant foundry,
And weather upon the tongue-tied syllables.

(He approaches, but she withdraws, holding up her hands, palms outward, as though to repel him.)

Oh, you will have him, but you cannot have mine,
Who does not belong to the public lie or the leering
Monument of easy emotion, who has withdrawn,
Brings all to silence and is innocent;
Participates now in the innocent ambition of the nameless.
And you will have your son, but than have such
I'd rather forget like the restless bitch with dugs swollen,
In that blunt-eyed degradation forgo the predictable
Pang when the pear branch unfolds the cold petal,
And the difficult crocus, and recollection lays
Its edge to the root of faculty. And you!
You have your son, and rain is on the ground.
Where is my son?
STRONG. Why, Clara! — *(He takes her by the wrist, shaking her arm.)* — Clara, stop it. Why, you talk like I had done it. Had done something. Like I had killed him!
CLARA. No, I did not say that, and have not thought that

You willed it, but know that your will is of death,
And frosty; responsibility has slept
Under carpets, has hovered like vapor in drains, left
No foot-print on dew, no cigarette-butt, and is
Delicately tentacled —

STRONG. Listen to me, Clara. — *(He tries to draw her to him, but she pulls away.)* —I want to come back to you. If you will hear me say it, I love you.

CLARA. But love would will a world that love can live in,
Stutters no starved economy, nor gnaws,
In the frothed incoherence of spirit, like the trapped fox,
The foot in the steel, and even desire needs belief,
And the arrogance gutters and bends, and the bestial
Enthusiasm will lift its weak hands;
As we once —and once —

STRONG. Give me your hand, Clara.

CLARA. As we once, but then it was another
Time, and another place, and we were then
Otherwise —

STRONG. Give me your hand.

CLARA. If it were not dark, or if it were dark and the dark
Were not vexed by ambiguities and if
I could know the nature of dark, not feel its uneven
Breath —

STRONG. Give me your hand, Clara.

(She extends her hand to him tentatively, and as he takes it, she suddenly sinks into the chair beside her.)

I have come a long way and —
Oh, Clara! And no ductile intuition had fingered

(He drops to the floor before her.)

The face which winks at me now. I've heard in my head
Blunt horrors lurch and grind like streetcars.
I hear doors creak on their hinges, shoes creak, approaching.

(He lets his face sink into her lap.)

CLARA. *(After a moment.)* He was a good baby, even when he was little.
He never cried.

End of III:ii

IV:i

(The scene is the Governor's office in the new Capitol. It is a high room furnished in a modern style, full of the glitter of chromium and glass. The GOVERNOR, when the curtain rises, is seated at his desk, but after speaking a few lines, rises and moves toward the windows at back-stage, which seem to look over a city.)

STRONG. The deed, plunged into the bath of time, dissolves;
    In that cynic transparency loses the intrinsic structure,
    Is of time, of the time; and the indifferent light revolves
    Its smile through that perjured innocence of tincture.
    O agitation! and no thumb resolves
    The uncarded snarl of nature, and the lunatic-tock
    Clock wigwags and the code-book lost and a small rock
    In the shoe and forest fires in Montana,
    And the Blackfoot spits and takes out his ten-cent bandanna;
    So history spat, shifts its slow quid.
    The deed, in time, out of time, the crystalline form at last.
    For, broth and brew, the coiling atoms nursed,
    Impassioned and solitary, that geometric secret:
    Which the lip on the day's dug can forget, regret.

(SUE PARSONS enters from stage-left, and closes the door behind her, but the GOVERNOR, for a moment, does not seem to be aware of her presence. She studies him intently, with an air of calculating patience.)

STRONG. Hello, Sue.

SUE. Hello, Boss. *(She continues to study him.)* How do you feel now?

STRONG. *(Abruptly.)* I'm all right.

SUE. *(After a wait in which the GOVERNOR seems to become oblivious to her presence.)* Didn't you want something? You rang my bell, didn't you?

STRONG. Yes. Yes. *(He moves toward her deliberately, and speaks almost formally.)* I want you to get together all the stuff we've got on the Morton Bridge and Construction, what they've paid taxes on, and on the Acme Electric. And start the digging for anything else. And get anything you can on Gummy Satterfield. I'm calling Tiny in here now— *(He presses a bell button on his desk.)* —and— *(He becomes almost gay.)* —when he comes out you'll see he's sweat off some weight.

SUE. I thought you were buddies with Gummy these days.

STRONG. Buddies. Listen, I love him like a brother, but the question is, is he gonna love me when I get through with him.

SUE. Sure, you love him. I had just forgotten your sunny nature.

STRONG. And get me two good accountants up here as soon as you can get them.

Miss Hawes will take charge of them. And boys who haven't got any friends. Get Jones. His own mother won't sit by him in church.

(*The door at stage-left opens to admit* COMMISSIONER HARPER, *who waves to both, and puffs once or twice before he can speak. He is carrying a derby hat and a cane in one hand.*)

TINY. Hello, Boss. Hello, Sue. (*He puffs again, and flicks out his handkerchief to wipe his forehead.*) God, them stairs is a pain. I was getting ready to go out and I'd been standing for the elevator ten minutes, it's a fact, when they come out to tell me you'd given me a ring. You stand ten minutes waiting for an elevator. Boss, we oughter fire them boys.

STRONG. (*Soothingly.*) Sure, I'll do it right away.

(SUE PARSONS *moves toward the door at stage-left, and at a nod from* GOVERNOR STRONG, *goes out quietly.*)

TINY. How you feeling, Boss?

STRONG. All right.

TINY. That's fine, Boss, that's fine! I knew you'd take it on the chin. And not give a blink. That's what I was saying to the boys yesterday, the Boss, he'll just take it on the chin, he'll be right back in harness. Yeah, and what the preacher said, it was a beautiful sentiment if I ever heard one. And the flowers. Now you take them from the Fifth Ward, that's what I call a real floral tribute! And I was saying—

STRONG. Tiny.

TINY. Yeah, Boss?

STRONG. Satterfield is your special pal, isn't he?

TINY. Well, now, I wouldn't say that exactly. I just thought—

STRONG. It's beautiful. That mutual confidence and perfect understanding.

TINY. I just thought—

STRONG. It is only proper that the nearest and dearest—that's you, Tiny—should break the sad news to him. You can put your hand on his shoulder.

TINY. What's that, Boss? (*A note of apprehension is in his tone.*)

STRONG. (*Again almost gaily.*) The deal's off, Tiny. That's what.

TINY. Boss!

STRONG. Yep!

TINY. (*Taking a step toward the* GOVERNOR.) Boss, you can't do that.

STRONG. I've done things I didn't think I could do myself. And that takes some doing.

TINY. You can't, and the election right here and all. And he's gone and fixed everything up already.

STRONG. Maybe he won't want to unfix it either.

TINY. Now, Boss— *(His tone becomes wheedling, sweetly reasonable.)* —Gummy's all right. You just don't know him, he's—

STRONG. I don't know his softer side, huh? The side the flies get stuck on?

TINY. He's all right. He's got plenty of jack, too, and he's got a slice of this State sewed up. Boss, you just don't make the most outer things sometimes. No offense, Boss, no offense, Boss, but you just don't—

STRONG. You do, Tiny.

TINY. Gummy's got plenty of what it takes, and we oughter co-operate. There's plenty in it for everybody. Sometimes, Boss, you just forget what makes the wheels go round.

(He puts his derby on his head, giving it a little thump, and takes a stance resembling that of a vaudeville comedian. After the first line of the following song which is rendered almost like a speech, the music begins, softly at first. HARPER punctuates the refrain with a flick of his cane and a thump on his hat.)

TINY. What puts the hop in the big grasshopper?
What makes the sweetie-pie say *Poppa*?
It's not what you think, it's the dollar.

What puts the doodle in the bug
And puts the spark in the old spark-plug?
What puts the grunt in the honey's hug?
It's not what you think, it's the dollar.

What puts the *Welcome* on the doormat
And makes the Madam take your hat
And puts the purr inside the cat?
It's not what you think, it's the dollar.

What takes the mouse away from the cheese
And whistles the birdies out of the trees
And gets the golfer away from his tees
And makes the *debitant* say *Please,*
And jerks the preacher off his knees?
It's not what you think, it's the dollar.

STRONG. And in what medium and murk the slow
Bulk cleaves, and scaleless, like the cat-fish couched
In cousinly thickets, cold, where the sun never
Comes, inhales the mire-sweet essences
And lolls and toadies to the channel's flux:
So, so!—and swollen on the black sewerage of circumstance—

Listen: I've seen the round eye's lightless stare.
Listen: and am untentacled, and no
Contagion laced to yesterday's indifferent honey,
Like the stuck fly, would bumble definition;
Which is clear. And may not be dispersed;
Nor I.

TINY. Boss, you just can't, you can't now —

STRONG. Can't what?

TINY. You can't do it. It ain't — it just ain't right.

STRONG. When you say that, Tiny, Jesus bleeds.

TINY. You can't do it, Boss.

STRONG. Who's going to stop me? Huh? (*He pushes a button on his desk.*)

TINY. Now, look here, Boss, the boys ain't gonna like it. Some of 'em.

STRONG. When, in God's name, did I ever ask them whether they liked it? Or you? Furthermore, you can tell your friend Gummy, after you've brought him round with the smelling salts, that maybe he won't want to alter his arrangements about the election, either. Right now Sue is getting stuff together on the Morton Bridge and Construction, and as far as the Acme Electric is concerned, the time begins to look ripe for an investigation of utilities in this State. And —

(*The door opens and* SUE PARSONS *enters. She steals a quick glance, full of curiosity, at the* COMMISSIONER.)

SUE. Yes?

STRONG. Tiny and I have just decided that there should be an investigation of utilities in this State. And soon. So we're having a special session of the Legislature. Say, in four days. So start the hog-calling.

TINY. (*Almost desperately.*) Boss, it ain't gonna do. I'm telling you. A lot of the boys won't like it, and there ain't any telling what'll happen, you get the Legislature on a thing like that. And —

STRONG. Gummy may think, or you may think, that he's bought up some of the boys; but it won't stick. He may give 'em twenty bucks, but I'll give 'em galloping paralysis. They get gay and there'll be a bear market on farmhands and barbers come the next election, for if there's anything cheap around here it's sweet potatoes and statesmen. They both grow on pore ground. And as for you — (*He suddenly whips out his finger at the* COMMISSIONER'S *breast.*) —

TINY. Boss, I —

STRONG. —you may be wearing a hundred-and-forty-dollar suit and a diamond ring, but on the hoof you're crow-bait, and boy! I can strip you to the blast.

TINY. Boss —

STRONG. Now get out.

(The COMMISSIONER *goes out quickly and quietly, with an agility notable in one of his bulk.)*

SUE. *(Shaking her head sadly.)* It just looks like he can't learn.

STRONG. The dog returneth to his vomit. — *(These words are scarcely addressed to her. He turns away abruptly, and steps to the windows and looks out over the city. Meanwhile she stands with the air of one adept at patience and calculation. He turns slowly back to face her.)* — Sue!

SUE. Yes?

STRONG. I'm going away. I'm going to my place up in the country. Until the special session. Send the stuff up to me when you get it.

SUE. How about me coming? I can bring it up. I'm getting fed up with city life, and I haven't been up since —

STRONG. No, Sue. Not now. Nor — *(He pauses, and seems to stiffen himself.)* — later.

SUE. For Christ's sake!

STRONG. No, Sue. It's over.

SUE. That Amos hag! I'll fix her, you'll be sic —

STRONG. No, she has nothing to do with it.

SUE. Gee, you're running through 'em fast in your old age! But you can't throw me. Listen here, I made you —

STRONG. Sue, I'm going back to my wife.

SUE. To that screwball! Hah! Don't make me laugh.

STRONG. If she'll have me.

SUE. Have you! I wish to Christ I'd never had you. And where would you be? Janitor in the City Hall by this time. Listen here, I made you, and you know it. And what do I get? A couple of hand-me-down kisses and a pinch on the ear and "That's-a-good-girl, Sue!" On a wet night or when you're too tired to go on the prowl. And what you were when I took you —

STRONG. What I was then I scarcely now know, or guess;
Who have, in the cistern of time's stagnation, peered
At the drowned, the glimmer-fractured face — and winked,
Like the hotel-drunk at the wash-room mirror's stranger.
I have stood in the rain and tortured history,
Under street lamps stood, asked eyes and the sudden faces;
Asked: "Have you seen him?" Asked: "Is he well?" Asked:
"Where is he now? Did he leave no message for me?"
But bells labored in the dark condensation of air,
And I lacked courage.

SUE. You'll lack something else, Buddy, if you try to dump me. You owe me something —

STRONG. (*He holds up his hand to stop her violence, and she pauses.*)
    I want to tell you, therefore, if it is possible
    To tell you what is to tell — Oh, who has not
    Lipped the common cup, swapped spit, who has not stood
    In the noisy congregation, or sly, beside the corrupter,
    Disturber, the unpartaker whose defiled
    Refusal spawns of strength inconsequence
    And ravels the fabric of the general human compact?
    I have, and see it, say it, now; have come
    By sleights and slanted alleys where the foot
    Slews in the scum of accident; but go
    In some hope now, but a hope that with the trail
    Of its poor history may slime, I know, the green
    Leaf, and snail-like now its prong's soft blundering
    Shivers in contact with the incorrigible future;
    Go in some hope, and hope to have whatever
    Friendship may be from what we were, are.

(*He advances toward her, extending his hand. She regards him, not moving a muscle until he is directly in front of her. Then, with a quick, flickering motion, she slaps him across the face. Very slowly, he lets his hand sink. Sue steps back from him, almost as though expecting a blow. He turns, picks up a leather brief-case from the desk, as though she were not there, and goes to the door at stage-left. After he has opened it, he turns again to her, his hand on the knob, and speaks somewhat formally.*)

STRONG. You will please send those materials up to me as soon as possible.

(*He goes out the door, closing it softly behind him.*)

SUE. (*Looking at the closed door for a moment before speaking.*) The lousy second-hand Christer! — (*While she yet stands stock-still, looking at the door, there is a knock at the other door, at stage-right. She turns quickly.*) — Come in!

(*The door opens to admit COMMISSIONER HARPER, who looks about the room inquiringly before speaking.*)

TINY. Has he up and gone?
SUE. Yes. He's gone.
TINY. When? When did he leave? Maybe I can catch him. (*He makes as though to go.*)
SUE. (*Deliberately.*) He's been gone a long time. You couldn't catch him.
TINY. I've got to see him. Maybe I can get him to see things. What he's doing —
SUE. He won't see anything.

TINY. By God! By God, he's gonna ruin us, he's done gone crazy, he's—

SUE. *(She moves quickly toward him scanning his face, and stops directly in front of him.)* Listen! Listen to me. Yes, he'll ruin us. But listen. He's throwing that Amos girl over.

TINY. Huh?

SUE. Yes. She may not know the bad news yet, but it's true.

TINY. *(Leering ponderously at her.)* Allow me to be the first—

SUE. Shut up! He's going back to his wife.

TINY. Sweet Jesus!

SUE. Listen!— *(She seizes COMMISSIONER HARPER's lapel.)* —Do you think that Doctor Amos knows he rolled Little Sister in the hay?

TINY. Well?

SUE. Hell, no, he doesn't know it. Or know that people— *(She becomes sly, insinuating.)* —are putting two-and-two together about how he got to be head of the hospital and all, when everybody knew he was against the Boss in politics. Or know why Little Sister is going to get her spare chemise cleaned out of the Boss' bureau drawer—

TINY. Huh?

SUE. Because that Amos killed his boy. Operated on him and killed him. And that's why he's gonna fire Amos out of the hospital. As soon as the special session gets started.

TINY. Is that a fact? A fact?

SUE. A fact? Does that matter a God-damn? Amos will think it's a fact. Every word. When— *(She comes closer to him, tugging at his lapel.)*

TINY. Huh?

SUE. When you tell him.

TINY. Jesus— *(His face lights up for a moment, then suddenly darkens.)* Sure, I'll get one of the boys—

SUE. Sure— *(Bitterly.)* —put it in the paper. You fool.

TINY. Well, now—

SUE. Sure, you're afraid of him when you tell him. And I don't blame you, not if he's what I figure—and pray to Christ—he is. But maybe you'll escape with your life. And then— *(She hesitates.)*

TINY. Huh?

SUE. And then!— *(She jerks his lapel, then releases him suddenly, and turns away, indifferently.)* —Take it or leave it. It's all your funeral, anyway.

TINY. *(Almost whispering, wetting his lips between words.)* All right. All right.

SUE. *(Distantly and indifferently, almost wearily.)* All right.

TINY. *(Enthusiastically, waving his arm.)* All right. Gee, you've got something on the ball! Satterfield, he'll fix you up!

SUE. I don't want anything he's got. If I'd wanted to, I could have been rich a long time back, panning in this muck.

TINY. *(He goes to her, and pats her on the shoulder, then rubs the palm of his hand between her shoulder blades.)* All the same-ee, Baby, a friend don't hurt. And Baby, I ain't gonna forget you. We might—

SUE. *(Not moving, she stands rigid under the motion of his hand, and speaks as through stiff lips.)* Take your God-damned greasy hands off me.

End of IV:i

IV:ii

(The scene is the consultation room of DR. KEITH AMOS. There are cabinets of instruments and large bookcases with glass fronts against the walls. To the rear are two large windows. A table is in the center of the room, and a large desk is at stage-left. DR. AMOS is standing in the middle of the room, as though just completing instructions to a woman assistant, dressed in the customary white, who is standing before him with a pad and pencil in her hand.)

AMOS. That's all, Lucille. But please ask him to have the report on those tests ready for me in the morning.

ASSISTANT. All right, Doctor.

AMOS. Thanks.

(As the assistant goes out the door at stage-left, there is a knock on the door at stage-right.)

AMOS. Come in.

(A woman SECRETARY enters, and closes the door behind her.)

SECRETARY. Doctor, there's a man to see you.

AMOS. Who is it?

SECRETARY. Well— *(She hesitates.)* —He didn't give his name. He just said—he said he was a friend. That it was something important.

AMOS. Well— *(He glances quickly at a pad on his desk.)* —Send him in. Now. But my sister is coming almost any moment now.

SECRETARY. Oh, I'm sorry! I almost forgot. She just called, and said she would be a little late. A few minutes.

(The SECRETARY goes out, leaving the door ajar. After a moment, COMMISSIONER HARPER enters, and the SECRETARY, who has ushered him in, softly shuts the door behind her as she retires. COMMISSIONER HARPER, despite an air of bravado, seems strained and nervous.)

TINY. Howdy-do, Doctor.

AMOS. *(Making no movement toward his visitor.)* Good afternoon.

TINY. *(Approaching slowly and almost warily DR. AMOS, who stands motionless.)* I just had something to tell you, Doctor. I hope I ain't intruding, but it's sorta important, it's— *(He lets his voice trail off, and suddenly stops his slow approach toward DR. AMOS; when DR. AMOS shows no sign of having heard, he resumes.)* You know—you know, the Boss—

AMOS. Boss?

TINY.—the Governor—well, you know he's back in town. He'll be up at the Capitol this evening, running the special session. That utility rate investigation—

AMOS. I should imagine it was time somebody put a shovel in that heap. But— *(He again seems to withdraw.)* —nothing will come of it.

TINY. Well, he'll be up there. And when— *(He hesitates, wetting his lips.)* — when it's over, you know what he's going to do?

AMOS. I am scarcely in the confidence of the—the Gang.

TINY. *(Leaning toward DR. AMOS, he lets his voice sink almost to a whisper.)* He's going to fire you! Out of the hospital job.

AMOS. It is of no interest to me. My resignation is prepared. It was prepared within twenty-four hours after I had accepted that appointment, and was dated and notarized that day. It is a very full statement. My attorney had held it since that time, with complete instructions as to its release. It is prepared in duplicate. One copy for the—Boss. And one for the press.

TINY. Huh?

AMOS. You can tell your friend that the resignation can be had at any time.

TINY. Listen, you got me wrong.— *(He speaks hurriedly.)* —You got me wrong. I just thought you'd want to know. And all. I just didn't like to stand by and see nothing rough—you know, nothing unethical, you might say—

AMOS. Christ!

TINY. Yeah, yeah, and you know why he's gonna do it?— *(He leans closer.)* — Because, he says, you killed his boy.

AMOS. Yes, that is one way to say it. I operated, and the boy did not survive the operation. Perhaps some other surgeon might have saved him. I cannot say. I operated at the insistence of the boy's father and of the attending physician. I did what I was capable of doing. And— *(He suddenly flares up.)* —I do not care to discuss the matter with you.

TINY. *(Recoiling a little.)* That's what he says, that you killed him. That's why he's firing you.

AMOS. My professional reputation, I believe, can survive aspersion.

TINY. And that's why he's throwing *her* over, too. And her a sweet kid, too. You know — *(He leans forward again, wetting his lips.)* — the confiding kind. — *(He scans the other man's face, which is expressionless. Then he resumes.)* — Yeah, the kind that gives her all. — *(He watches narrowly, but the face of* DR. AMOS *does not change; there is only a stiffening of his posture.)* —Yeah, yeah. — *(He pauses, after speaking the two words, softly, insinuatingly.)* —And you know why you got that job, they say. What they're saying. On account of — of —

AMOS. *(His voice is distant and grating.)* Of what?

TINY. Your si —

(Before the word can come from his lips, DR. AMOS *has leaped toward him, seizing him by the throat and the tie, driving him back against the table in the center of the room.)*

AMOS. Say it, and I'll strangle you with my hands.

TINY. *(He puts his hands ineffectually against the other man's shoulders as though to push him off, and speaks gurglingly.)* I didn't say nothing. — Not a thing. — It ain't me, it's them saying it. — I ain't done a thing. — It ain't my fault —

AMOS. *(He slowly releases the man's throat, with a thrusting motion as though to free his hands from a sticky substance. He holds his hands before him, at the level of his waist, looking at them.)*
Fault? Fault — and the swollen fly foots and sips
Garbage and blunders to bread — and the infection spangles
The palate, spores in the intricate blood — and it
Is guiltless. — *(Very softly, in contrast with the vehemence of the preceding words, almost parenthetically, he addresses* HARPER, *but does not turn toward him, his eyes still upon his own hands.)* — Go away — *(Then he resumes, while* HARPER, *with his hand touching his own throat, stares at him as if hypnotized.)* —For it lacks judgment, Lacking knowledge, lacking — Go, go away now — quickly —

(HARPER retreats slowly toward the door, still with his eyes fixed upon DR. AMOS; *then he goes quickly and softly out the door.)*

For O! what choice lives, judgment lights, in the tendon's
Twitch, in the precise secretion, the bubble of mire,
And what green definition we bragged on, and the delighted
Eye saw, ear heard, hope held, before the abrupt
Clutch, and absolute, stripped to the brute stalk

That bright and sun-pursuing exfoliation?
We should have walked softly, we should have walked
Softly on the pointed inquisitive toe, have fumbled
In darkness the wall's protuberances, the latch, have listened
For the sound of breathing in darkness; but no one had told us,
Said, "Listen!" But I—

(There is a slight knock at the door, toward which he has already turned, and taken one step. Almost immediately, while he stops and looks at it, the door swings inward, and ANNE AMOS *enters. She is white in the face, and strained. The two regard each other for a moment, before she speaks.)*

ANNE. *(She speaks tiredly, and as with an effort.)* I'm sorry I'm late. Something happened.

AMOS. *(Looking searchingly at her.)* Yes.

ANNE. You aren't angry, Keith?

AMOS. No. I am not angry.

ANNE. I'm sorry. Something happened. Something I could not prevent.

AMOS. Something happened.— *(He takes a step toward her.)* —Something has happened. And— *(He takes another step toward her.)* —and now I know.

ANNE. Know? *(She moves toward the table, drops her coat across it, and then puts her hand to the table, as though to support herself.)*

AMOS. I know. That man Harper—he has been here. And now I know. I know you. About you. And Strong.

ANNE. *(Not defiantly, but wearily.)* There is nothing to know.

AMOS. Nothing! You say it, who've fondled the foul hump
—And not for luck; flattered the essential deformity
Wherein all rectitude of nature is
Reviled—or nature's hope—and like the blunt
Child, have paddled the ditch's muck to make
What image, and given it what name—

ANNE. What I attempted I shall not name now,
For we have no language, at last; for we have no
Utterance for the great distance now, and ice on the wires—

(She sinks into the chair by the table.)

I had thought that it would be different—had thought to be stronger
At the time for strength, and on that frail predication
Had crutched—

AMOS. Strength? Christ!

ANNE. —but the hugged self-conception had not
Confronted the mirror of action, and in that warped

Gaze gone ghast; but knowledge is secret, he knows a
Small gate, is gum-shoe in alleys, and all our betrayals
Are but our own — and the liquor spilled, and the staves
Surprised, and the irreplaceable preciousness unbunged.
AMOS. What you are, or have been, is nothing to me, nor the febrile
Fingering of the scarce-scabbed fact, nor the crookt chirography
The unlegged consequences would crawl; but this —
ANNE. How can you say it, Keith! and we what we were?

(She stands up from the table, then sinks back.)

AMOS. But this: I practice no alacrity
To be, to pace and prink, the happy pimp
For the squint world's gape.
ANNE. *(She springs up from her chair, and seizes him, putting her arms about his
neck.)* No! No, Keith!

*(For a moment, he seems almost to succumb to her, putting one arm about her
shoulders. Then, but gently, he disengages himself, but still holds her by the upper
arm, with his own arm outstretched. He begins to speak in a low tone, which
gradually alters.)*

AMOS. For I had understood there was something to live by,
Not that sad sack we live by, glut and purge,
Or the other, secret-slung, sly purse of pleasure,
For the mechanic twitch of which throats have been slit,
And the wallowing whale coagulates ambergris
For sniff and spur, for which big enterprises,
Respectable, are flung to the preposterous ruin
That the newsboy crack his throat in the railway station.
And I've stood in districts of degradation where
Vile boys have stoned the windows of warehouses
And the sore's guilt gauds the corner of the mouth,
Have stood, and said, "There is an answer, there is
A word, a way." And I stood there. But there is
Not — *(At the word* not *he thrusts her from him sharply, so that she reels back
a little against the table.)*
ANNE. O Keith! Not after all —
AMOS. What's it to you? — And when did virtue lurk
In the rubber glove, or beatitude inhabit
The carbolic bottle? Or the enemy restrict
His householding to some small knot in the side?
ANNE. I have no enemy, and if I had

I should love him, for he would not leave me alone,
But would pursue, and like the unstumbling wind
Companion me in night's enormity.
He would name my name. I would hover under that wing.
AMOS. But I have one. And know his tread in the street,
Is monstrous, he wears many faces, he smiles, and I
Know him, and in that blessed knowledge shall know
Myself, for I know him now, and know that
His merds are found in the green wood-path, that he loves
To lean over bridge-rails and spit in the clear water.
ANNE. (*At her brother's last words, she has stepped toward him, raising her hand in protest.*)
Oh, Keith, it is not true!

(*She again tries to put her arms about him.*)

AMOS. And why should the whole unsmeared and wide world be
A back-fence for him to scrawl on? Tell me that!
But affirmation has a fist. And I— (*He flings her off.*)
And I—

(*He goes quickly from the room, jerking the door open and leaving it open behind him. There is the sound of a door being slammed in a farther room. ANNE AMOS sinks into the chair by the table, and lets her head sink down to its surface. After a moment, the SECRETARY steps into the room through the open door, hesitates, and then withdraws, closing the door softly behind her.*)

End of IV:ii

V:i

(*The scene is a corridor of the new Capitol, as in length-wise section. Along the wall at stage rear, that is, along a wall of the corridor, are recessed columns which reach up beyond the range of vision to support a high ceiling. The walls and columns are of marble, with a great bronze shield, the shield of the State, set in the wall. Toward each side, and to the front, is a column which corresponds to the columns in the rear. Against the column at stage-left, DR. AMOS is leaning. He is hatless, and has no overcoat or raincoat. His clothes are dripping wet, and he is splashed with mud almost to the knees.*)

AMOS. The pear is sun-fat, and the pear branch will sag;
  Absolute in light is the high hawk over the iron Wyoming,
  And he will stoop; the crag-familiar knows the crag,
  And the precinct of his pollution, the reverting dog.
  The mother turns to her child.
  Drop, stoop, return, turn: they are fulfilled.
  And all the driveled and disoriented at the unraveled hour of homing.
  And I: O motherly to the darling disaster!
  I bore it under my heart.
  It was of me the sacred part,
  But I slept, was sluggard in sun, and waster.
  I have felt the irreconcilable sweetness of its fingers clutch at my hem;
  I shall lean, and in my own hand take them.

(Along the corridor beyond DR. AMOS, groups of figures are passing and repassing. They are the types which one finds in the barber shops and hotel lobbies of a state capital. They gesticulate soundlessly together. One MAN, however, pauses and speaks to DR. AMOS. He obviously examines the wet and disordered clothing.)

MAN. Hello, Doc!
AMOS. Hello.
MAN. Gee, what you been doing? Swimming?
AMOS. No. No.
MAN. By God, you oughter go on in and hear the Boss tonight. You sure been
  missing something. He's on a tear, I'm here to tell you. He's like a one-legged
  man tromping out a prairie fire.
AMOS. Yes.
MAN. You can hear the squawking a mile. It's like a hoot-owl got in the hen-
  house.
AMOS. Yes.
MAN. I'm telling you, the air is full of feathers.
AMOS. Yes.
MAN. Well, I'll be seeing you.
AMOS. Yes.

(The MAN, apparently puzzled, turns and walks away down the corridor. He begins to whistle, like one who dismisses something from his mind. The other figures
pass and repass, gesticulating soundlessly together.)

AMOS. You labor for innocence but to learn
  That innocence is easy. Slip hawser and out,
  And without lights, on the late tide's turn;

And your friend Grover Whalen will not be about
To see you off at that hour,
Who was glad to know you and will do anything for you in his power.
Our fathers flinched, perhaps, and we revere them,
Who do not inherit the black mustache and the daguerreotype virtue;
But their lips clash only like grass-stalks, and we cannot hear them.
Is easy. And the environment breathless
In the powerful unfecundity of all farewell; but you farewell-less.
Is easy. Papers in order. No trouble at any frontier.
Farewell-less. And there is not even to remember
The hand which glimmers from any white verandah,
Between the jonquils, under the reasonable maples.
The tooth is now set through the thick rind.
Torsion and torment breathe, but like spaniels.
With what severe benignity returns the averted face.
I will not make a dry sound in a dry place.

(A *man about the age of* DR. AMOS *approaches from the opposite end of the corridor. He is somewhat shabbily and loosely dressed, with a sheaf of papers stuck into the side pocket of his coat, and his hat jammed jauntily on the back of his head. He has a raincoat slung over one arm. He does not see* DR. AMOS *until he is almost upon him. He is a reporter, an old friend of* DR. AMOS.)

FRIEND. Well, I'll be damned, if it ain't Keith! Damned if I've seen you in a generation. How are you, Keith?

AMOS. *(His face lights up for an instant.)* Fine, Jack. How are you making it? *(He puts out his hand to his friend, who takes it, and at the same time grasps him by the shoulder and shakes him playfully.)*

FRIEND. Oh, I'm getting along. Dishing out the dirt for the gentle reader. I've been up here covering the special session, but a fellow just relieved me. But you — I always knew you'd be a big shot someday!

AMOS. Well, not exactly.

FRIEND. Come on, come on! I read about you in the papers.

AMOS. Well —

FRIEND. Sure, I read the papers. When I ain't working for 'em. Yeah, old big-shot director of the Medical Center. Yeah, folks say you put that bug in the Big Boss's ear. He got an idea that time, all right. Yeah, I used to say all he needed was somebody to tell him how to heave his strength.

AMOS. I didn't —

FRIEND. But boy! he's sure heaving it tonight. He's God's gift to us reporters, for a fact. Well — *(He glances at his wristwatch.)* — I got to be shoving. I got to be back up here in half an hour. But say — why don't you come out with me some-

time? Come out and r'ar round with the boys, huh? We used to have some
pretty good times, you and me, a thousand years ago when we were kids.

AMOS. I'd like to. But I'm —

FRIEND. Busy. Sure, you're busy. I know. But you ought to knock off some night.
Give me a ring. You used to be human, before you were twelve years old.
Well — (*He seizes* DR. AMOS *by the hand again, and shakes it abruptly.*) —I'll
be seeing you. So long.

AMOS. (*He grasps his friend's arm and detains him.*)
Try to remember, try, if there is time
To remember, all our uninvolved delight,
All arbored afternoons and the slow sun's slant,
And how thin was the shout across the long water —
Before the great gear's toothed voracity
Had meshed, before — and let the late kildees cry,
And shake their hour, past all repudiation,
For the answer is not in a walnut-shell, and therefore,
Try to remember, and I, too, shall try.

FRIEND. (*Puzzled and embarrassed.*) Sure. Sure.

AMOS. You will try?

FRIEND. Sure. But — (*He looks at his watch, and* DR. AMOS *releases him.*) —I got
to be shoving. Good luck.

AMOS. Good luck, Jack.

(*The reporter passes down the corridor. He has scarcely disappeared when, from
the other side, the side opposite the spot where* DR. AMOS *is standing,* GOVERNOR
STRONG *enters. He is flanked on each side by a highway patrolman. The* PATROL-
MEN, *one of whom is* AL SUGGS, *carry submachine guns.* DR. AMOS, *at first, does
not seem to be aware of their presence, nor the* GOVERNOR, *who walks with head
bowed in preoccupation, of his. Then, seeing the group,* DR. AMOS *stiffens, stands
still for a moment.* GOVERNOR STRONG *sees him and lifts one hand in a salute.*)

STRONG. Hello, Doc.

AMOS. Hello.

(*The* GOVERNOR *extends his hand, and* DR. AMOS, *deliberately, takes one step
forward. Then, jerking a pistol from the side pocket of his coat, he leaps toward
the* GOVERNOR, *and fires twice. Almost simultaneously with the last report, there
is the burst from the machine guns.* DR. AMOS, *with arms outstretched, spins round
several times, as though suspended on a cord, and then collapses heavily, as
though the cord had been snipped. Meanwhile,* GOVERNOR STRONG *has stood
motionless, with his hands laid across his upper abdomen and chest, an expression of puzzled introspection upon his face. Then he staggers slightly. The body*

of DR. AMOS *has scarcely struck the floor, when* AL SUGGS *swings toward the* GOVERNOR, *dropping his weapon, which clatters upon the marble.*)

AL. Boss! Boss! He's done shot you!

STRONG. *(He speaks very soberly and detachedly.)* He has shot—me, Al. *(His knees sag, suddenly, and* AL SUGGS *seizes him and prevents him from falling.)*

AL. Boss, Boss! Does it hurt much, Boss?

(GOVERNOR STRONG's *head has fallen forward on his chest. People are running toward the scene from both ends of the corridor. The other patrolman is standing over the body of* DR. AMOS, *with his machine gun trained upon it, as though waiting for any sign of vitality.*)

AL. Boss, Boss! Does it hurt much?

End of V:i

V:ii

(*A* CHORUS OF SURGEONS *is revealed, standing in the same rigid and inhuman postures the previous Choruses have assumed. The members of the* CHORUS *are dressed as for an operation, the white robes, gauze masks, rubber gloves, caps. The light upon them is concentrated, almost as by a spot, and is blue, like the blue light of an operating room.*)

CHORUS. We do not envy them.
   Not the colonel, mahogany-phiz, unswaying in saddle and grim,
   Though his mount foot the roses, while the crowd's roar applauds him:
   He will make work for us.
   Not the capitalist, who shivers and smiles while they gawk through the glass,
   And box-cars and freighters and empires rattle like beads of a rebus:
   His money goes to a Foundation.
   Not the statesman, who stirs so profoundly the moral sense of the nation,
   And lingers under the bunting to define the historic mission:
   He, too, is our lackey.
   Colonel, capitalist, statesman, and all the nameless who glide
   Under the flung flags and confetti and are richly eyed:
   They move, iridescent like some on the disorder of the tide.
   They are tangential.
   We have moved among hands and the lips that move,

Have puttered among blossoms more precious than dahlias.
We are familiar to the room which is small and white;
Where all come at the twilit hour of worship.
They worship the twilit and featureless god of No-pain.
We have hung him up, in his muscular and metabolic perfection.
They long to see his face, which is featureless, white, and shaven like an egg.

(One of the surgeons steps forward from the CHORUS, *removing his mask, and begins to address the audience, with a tone of professional detachment. Meanwhile, the other members of the* CHORUS *relax into natural positions.)*

SURGEON. I shall not conceal from you that the condition is critical. Two bullets are lodged in his body. The patient is, of course, a man of very great vitality, and has, perhaps, a considerable reserve of strength. But, on the other hand, according to the subtle laws of compensation which we sometimes observe in such cases, that very vitality may, in the final analysis, prove to be a liability. It may, you might—ahem—say, prove to be a boomerang. For it has led the patient in the past into a very taxing and violent mode of life. The question of the patient's survival may, therefore, hinge upon such an imponderable as his "will to live." Yes, even as men of science, we are forced, at times, to admit this element into our calculations. But let us make no hasty generalization, certainly not one of a metaphysical nature, from this. The phrase the "will to live," we may take simply as a metaphor, the will to live—or will in any connection—being, as it were, a function of certain subtle biologic processes which have, thus far, eluded precise definition. But— *(He hesitates a moment.)* —I cannot help but take this occasion to make a comment of a more personal nature. Whatever we may have thought, as citizens, of the policies and methods of the patient during his incumbency as Governor of this State, we are bound in candor to confess that he did advance the cause of medicine and has provided more adequate facilities for the exercise of humanitarian zeal.

(The SPEAKER *steps back into the* CHORUS *and adjusts his mask. The* CHORUS *again speaks.)*

CHORUS. There is no dismay. No voice. Dubiety,
    Gust-screamer, rides like a gull the drowsy swell,
    Latched beak on bosom, tidy. And there is
    No knuckle at white lips, and no mouth mews
    Like a kitten at night, cold in the terrible grass.
    But hands will be devout in those high purlieus.
    And you—
    You should try to attend to the wintry palm at the window:

Its old blades rattle thinly and only as,
Nocturnal and despised, some recollection.
Tomorrow its blades will gleam in the sun, like tin.
Tomorrow is always a new day, and the different, undiffident faces.
It is difficult to name the year of the dispensation.

(From stage-right appears a wheeled stretcher, on which a figure lies, draped with a sheet. Only the face is visible. It is the face of GOVERNOR STRONG. He seems to be asleep, or drugged. The stretcher is pushed by a NEGRO who wears the white costume of a hospital orderly. His rubber-soled shoes make no sound. The wheels of the stretcher squeak very slightly. It moves at a slow, ceremonial pace. When it has passed the CHORUS, the surgeons, very slowly, follow it offstage, like a procession. When the forestage is empty, the curtain rises on the waiting room outside an operating room. There are benches along the rear wall, and a door in the middle of that wall. Toward the right, there is a table on which are piled magazines. Two chairs flank the table. A calendar is on the wall above the bench at stage-right, a calendar with a gaudy advertising picture. Above the bench at stage-left is a printed sign: No Loud Conversation. Please. *There is another door at stage-right, on the side wall.* CLARA STRONG, *very rigid, is seated on the bench at stage-left, under the sign. After a moment the door at stage-right opens, and ANNE AMOS enters. She seats herself on the other bench, under the calendar. After a little, by the same door, SUE PARSONS comes in. She glances quickly about her, then moves to the extreme end of the bench on which ANNE AMOS is seated. Then COMMISSIONER HARPER comes in, followed by JACK, the reporter. They take the chairs by the table. JACK leans toward the COMMISSIONER, and speaks in a loud whisper.)*

JACK. Thanks for getting me up here.

TINY. *(Whispering.)* Sure, I'm always glad to do anything for any of you boys. But— *(A little apprehension shows in his tone.)* —you ain't gonna tell the rest of 'em I got you up here, and them waiting down in the lobby?

JACK. Bite the hand that feeds me? Hell, no.

(JACK picks up a magazine from the table and thumbs idly through it. ANNE AMOS, after a moment of obvious hesitation, moves across the room, and sits on the bench beside CLARA STRONG, but at a little distance from her. But it is not long, before, with a quick, decisive movement, she has reached over to lay her hand on the hands of the other woman, which are folded together on her lap. The door in the middle of the rear wall opens, and a NURSE appears.)

NURSE. *(Very softly.)* Mrs. Strong! Please.

CLARA. Yes?

(The NURSE beckons to her. She rises, and goes to the door. The NURSE steps forward and to one side, as a SURGEON appears at the door. His robe is disordered and stained. He speaks to MRS. STRONG, but the words are not audible. The NURSE steps to MRS. STRONG's side as though to support her; but this does not seem to be necessary. MRS. STRONG, with the NURSE beside her, goes to the door at stage-right, and disappears. ANNE AMOS follows her, almost overtaking her at the door. SUE PARSONS, too, moves toward the door. After she passed the table, COMMISSIONER HARPER gestures toward her and calls in an excited whisper.)

TINY. Sue! Hey, Sue!

(Almost at the door, SUE PARSONS turns toward him with a white and convulsed face, and apparently tries to speak. But no word comes. She, too, goes out the door. Meanwhile, JACK has extracted from the side pocket of his coat a pad of papers and a pencil. He turns to COMMISSIONER HARPER.)

JACK. Well, Commissioner, I'd appreciate it if you can make a statement. You know, something—some expression.

TINY. *(For a moment he stares out over the heads of the audience, as into space, before he speaks.)* You know—you know, there ain't much for a man to say. Just this. I just don't know what us boys is gonna do, now the Big Boss is gone.

JACK. Thanks, Commissioner.

The End

Willie Stark

HIS RISE AND FALL

(Tentative Title)

BY

ROBERT PENN WARREN

Cast of Characters

THE TIME is present. THE PLACE is the southern United States.

A Note on the Production of "Willie Stark: His Rise and Fall"

Despite the several scenes of the play, no actual set changes are contemplated. Rather, the story is devised to move from scene to scene, and from place to place, by simple and fluent shifting of playing areas and lighting effects on a basic and permanent set.

This set is seen not as realistic but as a projection of free architectural forms organized on a stage to serve as easily imagined separate locales but making a whole design. It may or may not be based upon certain architectural styles common to state government buildings. Sections of it may be taken to represent an office or a living room or a corridor, etc., as needed. Within this scheme, two or three chairs, a desk, a lamp, a telephone, etc., moved from place to place, would be all the furniture required. The design would include several levels and platforms, the higher ones upstage, possibly surmounted by a domed platform alternately visible and invisible (lit and unlit).

This basic set occupies the upper two-thirds or more of the stage. Downstage, in front of the basic set, there should also be a forestage, or apron, completely bare. The action of the play will make apparent how the forestage is used. It will help to keep in mind mainly that the actors will pass back and forth from forestage to inner stage as the action demands.

As stated, the scene shifts will be accomplished by changing the playing areas and lighting effects, in a manner as simple, direct, and fluid as possible. These changes will not be indicated in the pages that follow in any precise detail but will only be outlined.

Prologue

(Stage Left, a raised rostrum with American flags, bunting, etc. and a speaker's lectern, with mike. The speaker's voice comes to the audience over a public address system. High, at extreme Stage Left is the impression of the facade of a modern steel and glass hospital. On the rostrum, to Stage Left beyond the lectern, are seated three men, TINY DUFFY, Governor of the State, HAROLD MACMURFEE, United States Senator, and WILLIAM LARSEN, a construction tycoon. DUFFY is an enormous, oleaginous man, expensively and flashily dressed, with diamond stick pin and diamond ring. He is accustomed to breathe on and then polish the stone of the ring, and he smokes with a long cigarette holder. MACMURFEE is a nondescript character, middle-aged. LARSEN — GUMMY LARSEN — is about sixty, thin, sharp-nosed, wearing pince-nez. DR. SHIPWORTH, at the lectern, is a self-important, unctuous person, given to wide gestures of excessive grace.)

SHIPWORTH. — come together today to dedicate this great hospital. As director of this great hospital and health center — one of the finest in the world I may say — it is my privilege to welcome you all and welcome our distinguished guests and speakers.

(As he names each he will now bow to the appropriate person.)

Aloysius Duffy, Governor of this State,

(Applause.)

Harold MacMurfee, United States Senator,

(Applause.)

William Larsen, builder, financier, philanthropist,

(Applause.)

All these men who have helped give a great dream the beautiful embodiment you now see before you.

(Gesturing toward the height of the facade.)

The Tom Stark Memorial Hospital — we see it before us at last. It bears the name of one of the greatest athletes this State has ever produced — young Tom Stark, who a few years ago received a fatal injury in that great stadium yonder.

(As SHIPWORTH gestures toward a hypothetical stadium at Stage Right, JACK BURDEN has quietly appeared on the Forestage. He is about forty, tallish, dark-haired,

somewhat careless in dress and manner. He stands inspecting the persons on the rostrum.)

SHIPWORTH. Tom Stark was the son of Willie Stark, who was once Governor of this State. Willie Stark, we all know, conceived the idea of this hospital. I am not going to say what Willie Stark was.

(High at Stage Center, in a growing light which reveals only the upper torso and head, WILLIE STARK appears. He is a rather burly man, of medium height, with deep-set eyes in a heavy face which can flash into anger or a grin with equal suddenness. Now his face is grave and composed, looking over the heads of the audience, as though into distance. On the Forestage, LUCY STARK appears, a woman about forty, plainly dressed, with a kind of domestic sweetness. She is looking up at WILLIE as the light grows on him. She lifts her arms toward him. SHIPWORTH is still speaking in pantomime.)

LUCY. Oh, Willie—Willie—I knew what you were in your deepest heart!

(SADIE appears beyond LUCY, on the Forestage. She is youngish, with burning dark eyes and hacked-off black hair, and is handsome despite her pocked face. She speaks toward STARK, with wrenched anguish.)

SADIE. Oh, what did you have to be that way for? Oh, Willie, you made me do it!

(ADAM STANTON appears beyond SADIE. He is in the middle thirties, a handsome man with dark hair, and a brooding face, somewhat too intense. There is a hint of the fastidious, the antiseptic, in his appearance. He lifts his right arm toward STARK in a denunciatory gesture.)

ADAM. Foulness—nothing but foulness!

(ANNE STANTON rushes from the darkness of extreme Stage Left toward ADAM, and seizes his arm in protest. She is in her thirties, has high-bred good looks, with something of the intensity of her brother.)

ANNE. Oh, Adam—Adam—can't you understand—even now?
ADAM. *(Lowers arm.)* And you were my sister and he—he was—

(ADAM lifts his arm again, as JUDGE IRWIN, a distinguished-looking gentleman of the late sixties, comes forward to comfort ANNE, even as he looks up at STARK, shaking his head as though, even now, unable to resolve a question. SHIPWORTH's voice, continuing his speech, is again audible.)

SHIPWORTH. No, I shall not try to say what Willie Stark—Governor Stark—was.

STARK. *(Looking over the heads of the audience, toward distance.)* I was a man, and I lived in the world of men.

(As STARK begins to speak, ANNE lifts her head from JUDGE IRWIN's shoulder, stares at STARK, moves from IRWIN's comforting, fatherly embrace, and raptly lifts her hands toward STARK. As she, and all the others on the Forestage, look up toward STARK, SUGAR-BOY appears at extreme Stage Left—an under-sized man of forty.)

SUGAR-BOY. *(Stuttering.)* The B-B-Big Boss—he k-k-kin talk so g-g-g-good!

SHIPWORTH. *(Continuing.)* No, what is important is this hospital. It does not matter how it came to exist.

JACK. *(Stepping forward, in excited protest, face toward SHIPWORTH.)* Oh, but it does matter—it must!

(ADAM surges forward toward JACK, ready to burst into denunciation, but ANNE restrains him.)

ADAM. It matters that foulness—

SHIPWORTH. *(Continuing, unaware of JACK.)* This hospital, with its modern facilities for the scientific practice of medicine, will make a healthier people. Therefore, it does not matter how it came to be.

(All the characters on the Forestage swing toward SHIPWORTH with simultaneous gestures and voices of protest. At JACK's voice they turn toward him, then move toward him, as the light fades.)

JACK. *(Interrupting SHIPWORTH.)* Oh, didn't it matter! *(Swinging toward audience.)* Didn't it matter? For if it didn't, then what—then what?

(Light has gone down on the entire stage except where JACK stands.)

It was night—late—and Sadie—Sadie Burke—the Boss's secretary—that girl from across the tracks, with the pocked face and all the answers—

(Out of the darkness toward Stage Left there is the voice of SADIE, as though on a telephone.)

VOICE OF SADIE. Yeah, Jack—get on down here, Jack—it has broke loose—what do you think I mean has broke loose?—hell has broke loose—Judge Irwin will pick you up—yeah, Irwin—

(The lights on the set go up.)

Act I

Scene 1

(JACK is moving into the set. It is a hotel room, at night. GOVERNOR STARK is leaning back in a chair, his feet, with only socks on, propped on the edge of a desk, a bottle of whisky on the floor beside him, a glass in his hand, half full. Before him stands TINY DUFFY, now Lieutenant Governor. His face is sweating with apprehension, and he stares down at WILLIE STARK, the Boss. Behind the Boss, to one side, propped back in a chair, is SUGAR-BOY. Stage Right, toward rear, SADIE BURKE sits at a little table, using a telephone. While she is on the telephone, JACK BURDEN, followed by JUDGE IRWIN, the Attorney General, enters softly, and stands surveying the scene.)

SADIE. *(On phone.)* God damn it, I said get Norton. Find him. Rough him if you have to. The Boss wants him, and he wants him now.

(She slams the phone to the rack, lifts her head toward the newcomers, blowing smoke out bitterly from her pursed lips.)

JACK. *(To her.)* What's up?

SADIE. Oh, nothing, just our dear Lieutenant Governor has decided to get rich quick.

STARK. *(Breaking in.)* Yeah, he — *(Whipping a forefinger toward DUFFY like a pistol.)* — he decided to run a little private graft on the sale of tax properties — yeah, Tiny, with Norton to help — yeah, a nice, little one-man, private bonanza —

TINY. *(Leaning toward the Boss, taking a step toward him.)* You got me wrong, Boss. It wasn't gonna be private — I was just working something up — you know, experimenting to get it sort of ship-shape — then I was gonna tell you — yeah, tell you — *(His words fade out under STARK's baleful gaze.)*

STARK. So you were going to tell me, huh?

TINY. Yeah, Boss — that's a God's fact, Boss. *(Leaning closer.)*

STARK. *(Softly.)* Now, Tiny, why were you going to tell me?

TINY. Well, Boss — you know, Boss — it takes money to run an organization, Boss — and sure, you got ways, Boss — but a little extra, I just figgered it never hurts and — *(As TINY is leaning closer and closer, explaining and justifying, STARK suddenly flings what whisky remains in his glass directly into TINY's face. TINY recoils from the shock, then seems about to plunge forward at the unmoving STARK. But SUGAR's right hand has slipped inside his coat to a shoulder-holster, and half withdrawn a revolver. SUGAR is rising from his chair.)*

SUGAR. No-no-no-no, y-y-you don't.

STARK. You may be tongue-tied, Sugar—but you're telling him.

(*Meanwhile* TINY *has stepped back, wiping his face with a large silk handkerchief, smiling a sickly, ingratiating smile, as though it were all a joke.*)

TINY. Now, Boss, you ought not to done that—now, Boss, what made you go and do that?

STARK. (*Soberly studying him.*) It just struck me as something I had sort of neglected for a long time.

TINY. (*Retreating a little.*) But you got me all wet—you got me all wet, Boss—

STARK. (*Suddenly sitting up in his chair.*) Tiny, you see that pen over there? (*Indicating a pen in a desk-set.*)

TINY. (*Staring at the pen in horrid fascination, making some sort of sound in his throat.*) Ye-yes.

STARK. Speak up! Say, yes, sir!

TINY. Yes, sir.

STARK. Say, yes, sir, I see it!

TINY. Yes, sir, I see it.

STARK. Well, God damn it, go and pick it up. (*TINY waits.*) Pick it up! (*He gingerly approaches the pen, and picks it up.*)

STARK. Now write. There's some paper there. Write what I say.

(*TINY leans over the desk.*)

STARK. (*Dictating.*) "Dear Governor Stark—because of ill health"—and boy, you don't know how sick you are!—"because of ill health I wish to offer my resignation as Lieutenant Governor—to take effect as soon after the above date as you can relieve me—Respectfully yours—"

(*TINY writes, sweating, occasionally wiping his brow, while STARK eyes him. Having finished, TINY straightens up.*)

STARK. Did you sign it?

TINY. No—no, sir.

STARK. Well, God damn it, sign!

(*TINY leans and signs.*)

STARK. Bring it here.

(*TINY brings it, holding it gingerly out. STARK takes it, toys delicately with it, speaks musingly.*)

STARK. Yeah, and I'll fill in the date when and if I need to. Yeah, I'm going to save you this time, Tiny. I'm going to save you, instead of tromping you into one quivering oleaginous mass of screaming blubber. I'm going to save you.

But — (*He snaps a forefinger at* TINY.) — it is not because I love you. Is that clear?

TINY. Yes — yes, sir.

STARK. Yeah, Tiny — I'm going to save you — (*Meditatively.*) — and you want to know why? You remember, Tiny, when I first saw you? Well, you were a big-shot politico, right hand of MacMurfee, with a silk shirt and a diamond ring, and me — I was just a hick. Nothing but a hick, and fool enough to think maybe an honest hick could bust into politics. Yeah, Tiny, it must have been a scream. But I fooled you, didn't I, Tiny? (*TINY does not answer.*) Answer me. Say, yes, sir, you fooled me good.

TINY. Yes, sir, you fooled me good.

STARK. And then I started to bust in — me, the honest hick — and you were just smart enough to double-cross MacMurfee in time and join me, and I let you. You know why I let you, Tiny? (*TINY does not answer.*) Well, I'll tell you. It was just so I could look at you every day, Tiny, and remind myself what life is really like. Yeah, a man ought to keep in mind what life is really like, and you — you are a reminder, Tiny. (*STARK seems to fall into himself, brooding, then looks up, as though surprised to find* TINY *still there.*) Get out!

(*TINY seems about to say something, thinks better of it, and then, fixing his gaze on the refilled glass of whisky now in* STARK's *hand, retreats, and with the peculiar lightness of some fat men, as though on tiptoes, moves toward the door.* JACK *and* JUDGE IRWIN *draw aside and let him pass, all eyes following him. Just as* TINY's *hand is on the knob,* STARK *starts to speak.*)

STARK. And don't come around for a couple of days, you hear? Just for a couple of days maybe I want to forget what life is really like.

(*TINY slips out, and the door closes softly behind him. The room is in perfect silence for a moment as the eyes of all swing from the door toward the Boss, who has sunk again into himself.*)

JACK. Well, you gave yourself a good time.

STARK. Damn it, there is just something in their eyes that makes you do it.

JACK. He licked spit, all right.

STARK. He could have walked out. He could have dated the resignation. He could have told me to go to hell.

JACK. What did you call me for?

STARK. I want you to help the boys. They're picking up soreheads in the Legislature who might want to help MacMurfee make something of this. They brought in Jeff Hopkins. (*STARK brightens as at a happy recollection.*) And you ought to seen his face when he found out I knew his pappy was forging prescriptions out of that one-horse drug store.

(The door opens, and a highway patrolman, very natty in uniform and smart in manner — LIEUTENANT BOYD — enters and salutes.)

PATROLMAN. Governor, the boys have brought in Joe Norton.

STARK. Put him in the other room and let him stew.

(JUDGE IRWIN, who has been intently observing the whole scene, steps forward.)

IRWIN. Willie, are you going to save Norton's hide, too?

STARK. I haven't thought it through, Judge.

IRWIN. You saved Duffy's.

STARK. *(Fretfully, as at ignorance.)* I don't give a damn about Duffy's hide.

IRWIN. He's guilty.

STARK. *(Cheerfully.)* Guilty as hell. But he won't be guilty again. I fixed him. I fixed him so his unborn great-grand-children will wet their pants on the anniversary of this event.

IRWIN. You are saving his hide.

STARK. I am saving something else. If MacMurfee knocks off Duffy, he might think he can knock us all off. Do you think he likes anything we've done? The extraction tax on oil, the textbook bill, the public health bill?

IRWIN. No, he doesn't.

STARK. Do you like it, Judge?

IRWIN. Yes, I like it.

STARK. Well?

IRWIN. But I can't say I like some of the things around it. I can't say that I have learned to like the odor of corruption.

STARK. *(Detached and philosophical.)* Do you think I'm corrupt, Judge?

IRWIN. No, I do not think you are corrupt. If I thought so, I would not be here now. But I do not like the odor of corruption.

STARK. Have you tried holding your nose, Judge?

IRWIN. Now, look here, Willie —

STARK. *(Leaning back in his chair, eyeing IRWIN with friendly, philosophical candor.)* Judge, the trouble with you is, you are a lawyer. You are a damned fine Harvard Law School lawyer.

IRWIN. You're a lawyer.

STARK. Sure, I know me some law. Fact is, I know a lot of law, even if I did learn it sitting up nights in my pappy's broke-down house on his wash-out farm and the wind whistled right through the wall. Yeah, and I made me some money out of law. But I'm not a lawyer. That's why I can see what the law is like. The law is a single-bed blanket on a double bed and three folks in the bed and a cold night and shank-bones to the breeze. There ain't ever enough blanket to cover the case, and somebody is always nigh to catching pneumonia. What you got to do then is make up some law to cover the case. Do you think half the things we have done—you and me—were clear and distinct and simple in the Constitution of this State?

IRWIN. There's nothing in the Constitution that says Duffy can commit a felony with impunity.

STARK. *(Soft and reasonable.)* Duffy doesn't mean a thing. He is just something we use, Judge. You can't make bricks without straw, as the Good Book says, and half the time the straw is second-hand straw from the cow-pen.

IRWIN. I suppose, Governor, that that is your considered opinion.

STARK. Judge, it is the fruit of my meditations in the night.

IRWIN. I'm something like you, there, Governor. *(STARK looks IRWIN in the face, slowly nodding. IRWIN nods back.)* I am offering my resignation as Attorney General.

STARK. *(Leaning at him, speaking even more softly.)* What made you take such a long time, Judge? *(IRWIN doesn't answer.)* I'll tell you, Judge. You sat in your office for twenty-five years and watched the rich get richer and the poor get poorer. Oh, yeah, you are a rich man yourself—or sort of rich—but you had enough conscience to want to do something. And I came along and fixed it so you could do something. I whispered low, "You want to get in there and lay around you a little?" And you had a wonderful time. You made the fur fly. You got a lot of fine reforms, didn't you?

IRWIN. Yes, Willie, we *did* get a lot of fine reforms. But Willie, I have begun to wonder. I wonder if sometimes—just sometimes, mind you—the price isn't too big that a man has to pay to get even the good thing he wants.

STARK. *(Pauses.)* You mean, Judge, you got all sweaty and dirty? You mean you want to keep your hands clean? You just want to keep your little Harvard Law School hands clean. But dirt—dirt, Judge—you know, dirt is a funny thing. Come to think of it, there ain't a thing but dirt on this green God's globe except what's under the water, and that's dirt too. It's dirt makes the grass grow. A diamond ain't a thing in the world but dirt that got awful hot. And God-a-Mighty, He picked up a handful of dirt and blew on it and created you and me and George Washington and mankind blessed in faculty and apprehension. It all depends on what you do with dirt. And you know damned well what I mean to do.

IRWIN. And I know what I mean to do.

STARK. You mean to welch. Deep down in your heart you know you are welching if you pull out on me. And that is why it took you so long to resign.

IRWIN. My mind is made up.

STARK. *(Softly, soothingly.)* Yes, Judge, yes, Judge.

IRWIN. *(Turning to JACK.)* Are you coming with me, Jack? Or will you stay and help—help Governor Stark terrorize the Legislature?

STARK. Tut—tut—Judge. Watch your language.

IRWIN. *(Ignoring STARK.)* Are you coming, Jack?

STARK. Yes, Judge, yes—Jack is your kind of folks. Like they say, he was born a gentleman. But you know, I bet he stays.

(JACK does not move, looking IRWIN in the eye.)

IRWIN. *(To JACK.)* There's the possibility, Jack, that all this will lead to impeachment. Would you like to mix up in that?

STARK. Let 'em try an impeachment. I'll take care of that.

IRWIN. Are you sure, Governor? That's one thing you haven't had to try yet.

STARK. *(Softly.)* You aren't figuring on backing an impeachment, are you, Judge?

IRWIN. *(Ignoring STARK.)* Are you coming, Jack?

JACK. *(Shrugging.)* I reckon I'm staying.

IRWIN. *(Studying him.)* Well, shall I give your regards to your old friends back at Burden's Landing?

JACK. *(Shrugging.)* Suit yourself, Judge.

(As JUDGE IRWIN turns toward the door, STARK rises and, in his sock feet, starts after IRWIN.)

STARK. Judge—

(JUDGE IRWIN turns and hesitates.)

STARK. *(Coming up close to look IRWIN in the face, grinning.)* You know, Judge, we made quite a team, you and me. Your brains and my brawn. *(He offers his hand to IRWIN, who hesitates. Then, in accents of comic woe.)* You're leaving me all alone, Judge, alone with the sons-of-bitches. Mine and the other fellows. Aren't you even going to shake hands?

IRWIN. *(Looking down at the hand, then into STARK's face.)* No. *(Then, with a change of tone, emotion breaking through.)* Hell, Willie, I didn't want it this way.

(JUDGE IRWIN goes quickly out. STARK stares at the door, then turns back to JACK.)

STARK. He wouldn't shake hands with me.

JACK. To hell with it.

STARK. Would he back an impeachment?

JACK. I don't know.

STARK. He wouldn't shake hands. *(Pause.)* Would he back an impeachment?

JACK. *(Shrugging.)* How do I know?

STARK. He is your kind of folks. He was damned near a father to you. If you don't know about him, what the hell do you know?

JACK. *(Shrugging again.)* Nothing. Just say I don't know nothing from nothing and forget it. *(He turns away, lights a cigarette, blows a smoke ring ceilingward, and inspects it studiously.)*

STARK. What do you think I pay you for?

JACK. *(Indifferently, watching his smoke ring.)* You could always quit paying me.

STARK. So you think I ought to throw Duffy to the wolves?

JACK. Thinking is not my line.

STARK. Damn it, I thought you understood me.

JACK. I take orders, don't I? And collect my pay.

STARK. I thought you understood me. *(Goes and sits, pours himself a drink, speaks broodingly.)* I thought the Judge understood me. And Lucy — there was a time I thought she did. *(Drinks.)* But now — you know, Lucy is figuring on leaving me. She might get a divorce.

(At this, SADIE, who has been occupied with some papers at her table, looks sharply up. At the same moment, JACK, looking at STARK, jerks a finger in SADIE's direction.)

JACK. Her?

STARK. No, it's not Sadie.

SADIE. *(Cutting in, with savage, mincing mimicry.)* Oh, no, it's not Sadie. Not dear old Sadie, oh no, nothing worth getting excited about there, she just happens to be handy.

STARK. *(Ignoring SADIE's outburst.)* No, Lucy doesn't know about —

(Nodding sidewise toward SADIE, but not looking at her.)

JACK. Lucy is a woman and a woman can smell it.

STARK. No, she talks about a divorce if I cover up for Duffy.

JACK. It looks like everybody is trying to run your business.

STARK. They don't understand a thing! None of 'em! They like what you do but they spit on you for the way you do it.

JACK. Well, you seem to do things your way.

STARK. There's just one way. Do it any way you can and make it stick. *(Pause.)* And you know what I'm going to do? As soon as I bust MacMurfee and his gang?

SADIE. Yeah, and that will be some cold Sunday in Hell's August if you keep sitting on your can and griping because nobody understands you.

STARK. *(Lunging up from his chair, in the grip of an idea.)* I am going to build the God-damnedest, biggest, chromium-platedest, formaldehyde-stinkingest free hospital and health center the All-Father ever let live! Yeah, and anybody can come there — anybody — and not cost a dime, and —

SADIE. Yeah, and you'll be the first patient. To fix your head. *(She taps her brow and rolls her eyes.)*

STARK. (*Approaching JACK.*) And listen — listen here, Jack — I want you to get that Adam Stanton — that old pal of yours — that Doctor Stanton.

JACK. Adam — Adam Stanton — what?

STARK. For director. Director of my hospital. He's the best. Up in New York, they told me he was the best. Yeah, one of the best neuro-surgeons — tops, they said —

JACK. (*Shaking his head.*) Sadie is right. You build that hospital fast. And reserve yourself a bed they can strap you down on.

STARK. You get Stanton.

JACK. You are hearing voices.

STARK. He is your pal. You get him.

SADIE. Sure, he is Jack's old pal. But he is also Judge Irwin's nephew, and Judge Irwin just threw you over — in case you forgot that.

JACK. (*With weary reasonableness.*) Boss, Sadie is right. Adam Stanton hates your guts.

STARK. You figure a way.

JACK. (*Pedantic irony.*) Boss, let me remind you, there are three classic ways. Fear, money, ambition. You can't scare Adam Stanton. He doesn't give a damn about money. He doesn't care about reputation. He lives like a monk, and spends all his time cutting on people and putting 'em back together again, and he just cares about one simple plain, crazy, lunatic thing.

STARK. Yeah?

JACK. He is the sort of guy nobody believes can exist, but he does exist. He simply wants to do good. He just wants to do good.

STARK. That's why I want him.

JACK. There is the small difficulty aforementioned. He hates your guts.

STARK. I don't want him to love me. I'm not asking anybody to love me.

JACK. (*With nauseous mimicry.*) You know how all us boys feels about you, Boss.

STARK. (*Ignoring JACK's by-play.*) Listen, here's what I want you to do. You just get Stanton to see me. Just tell him the topic. I'll do the rest.

JACK. You think highly of your powers of persuasion.

STARK. I won't have to persuade him. I'll simply explain the facts of life. Listen, you just get him to see me — yeah, bring him up to the Mansion tomorrow night. For a drink.

JACK. He doesn't drink.

SADIE. Oh, no — and Willie didn't use to drink either, did you, Willie? Oh, no — for Lucy didn't favor drinking, so he never touched it. Did you, Willie? Not till you caught on. Not till I taught you that. That and a few other things.

STARK. (*Ignoring her, to JACK.*) Just get him to see me.

SADIE. (*Expansively.*) Oh, yes, get him to the Mansion. Get them all, get Judge Irwin, too, get him in for a toddy, and all those silk-hat sons-of-bitches from

Burden's Landing that make me want to puke—yeah, and get that sister of Dr. Stanton—that Anne Stanton—yeah, get her in. Yeah, she's been hanging around the good Governor— *(JACK looks sharply at SADIE, but as she continues he relaxes.)* —yeah, trying to get State money for her orphans' home or something—yeah, she's hanging around like she was going to have something herself to put in an orphans' home if she's not careful, and—

STARK. Shut up!

SADIE. *(Rising, coming to STARK, facing him.)* You are a bastard. Yes, I saw you looking at her. I heard the way you talked to her. Yeah, you love orphans. In a pig's twat, and you think you are so all-fired smart. You forget it was me taught you half you know, it was me got you started—you were just a hick, and I mean a real hick, and now you want to ask 'em all to the Mansion— *(Mimicking.)* — oh, yes, to the Mansion—and you know what they'll do? *(She leans at him, whispering. JACK is watching with fascinated attention.)* They'll ruin you, that's what they'll do. They'll sweet-talk you and sell you out. They are silk-hat and they'll give you the sugar-tit just as long as you're some use to 'em, then they'll spit on you, for you are a hick. You are a red-neck. Yeah, didn't Irwin spit on you? Well, the next thing is, you'll read he's backing an impeachment, and—

STARK. *(Turns to JACK, speaks in a business-like fashion.)* I want you to dig.

JACK. *(For an instant puzzled.)* Dig?

STARK. On Judge Irwin. Get the dirt on him. Just in case.

JACK. Look here, Boss, I just don't reckon there is any dirt on him.

STARK. There is always something.

JACK. Maybe not on the Judge.

STARK. Man is conceived in sin and born in corruption, and he passeth from the stink of the didie to the stench of the shroud. There is always something.

SADIE. Oh, no, not the Judge, for he is one of Jack's silk-hat pals.

(As JACK stands there, not speaking, STARK leans slowly at him, staring into his face.)

STARK. *(Softly.)* What's the matter, Jack? You afraid you'll find something?

JACK. Oh, for Christ's sake.

STARK. Well, if there isn't anything, then it won't matter. It's my time you are digging on.

JACK. Sure, it's your time.

STARK. *(Grinning, slapping JACK on the shoulder.)* Sure, and maybe we won't need it anyway. Maybe there won't be any impeachment—

SADIE. Oh, no, they'd never impeach Little Willie.

STARK. Let 'em impeach. I'll fix those fice-faced, belly-dragging hounds. Let 'em try—but now you, you Jack, you go get Adam Stanton for me and—

SADIE. *(Again sitting sourly at her table.)* And don't forget little sister.

STARK.—and I'm going to build that hospital, Boy. There wasn't ever anything like it—

(STARK begins to move from JACK, looking out over the heads of the audience, in a kind of half-comic, half-serious fantasia. The facade of the hospital appears above.)

—yeah, and Boy, I tell you, I'm going to have a cage of canaries in every room that can sing Italian grand opera and there ain't going to be a nurse hasn't won a beauty contest at Atlantic City, and every bed-pan will be eighteen-caret gold, and every bed-pan will have a Swiss music box attachment to play "Turkey in the Straw" or "The Sextet from Lucia," take your choice.

JACK. That will be swell.

(The lights fade and come back up on JACK revealed at Stage Right, bending over a filing cabinet, perhaps a sign above, indicating files of mortgage records, etc. JACK is riffling the contents of a file. At the sound of a voice from the darkness, at Stage Left, he lifts his head.)

VOICE OF IRWIN. You have to lead a duck more, Jack. You have to lead 'em more, son! *(Sound of gunshot muffled.)* That's better, son. Now a duck flies fifty feet a second and your muzzle velocity is— *(Pause.)* Look! Look! *(Boom! Boom! Fading. As the sound fades, JACK bends over the filing case again, hunching his shoulders.)* Come about, Jack! Come about! Close in, close in on the island! Starboard, starboard it is! *(Sound of sail flapping, water slapping at bows. The VOICE is now quiet and explanatory, then rising to excitement.)* See, we got that eddy of air off the island. See, we're pulling away. By God, we've left 'em! The race is ours! By God, it's ours, Jack! *(Pause.)* Boy, I'll make you a sailor yet.

(JACK has been caught in the excitement of the recollection, drawn into physical participation, his hands moving with the old actions. He freezes as the VOICE OF STARK is heard whispering.)

VOICE OF STARK. Man is conceived in sin and born in corruption—

(The VOICE fades as JACK returns to the file.)

VOICE OF IRWIN. The boast of heraldry, the pomp of power
And all the beauty, all that wealth e'er gave,
Await alike the inevitable hour.
The paths of glory lead but to the grave.

(*At Stage Left the light reveals* JUDGE IRWIN, *seated, reading to* ANNE *on a hassock at his feet, and* ADAM *crouched beyond.* ANNE *has her hair in a girlish fashion, and* ADAM *has his collar open.* JACK *has lifted his head to listen, and has turned to see the group. Inaudibly the* JUDGE *is still reading, as* JACK *takes a couple of tentative steps toward the group. Then the* VOICE *again is audible.*)

Can storied urn or animated bust,
Back to its mansion call the fleeting breath?
Can Honor's voice provoke the silent dust?
JACK. Can honor's voice provoke —

(ANNE *lifts her head as at a sound behind her — but not in* JACK's *real direction on the stage.*)

ANNE. It must be Jack — oh, Jack, come on!
IRWIN. (*Lifting his head in the same direction, calling.*) Come on in, boy — come in!
JACK. (*Calling, but even as he calls,* IRWIN, ANNE, *and* ADAM *still face away from his direction.*) — Judge — Judge — I wanted to see you —
VOICE OF STARK. (*Whispering, harsh.*) Dig — I said dig!
JACK. (*Holding out hand toward group still facing away.*) Judge — I wanted —
VOICE OF STARK. (*Whispering.*) — There is always something — (JACK *fades backward, still facing the group, his hand still lifted toward them.*) There is always something — there is always —

(*The light has gone out on the group, and fades on* JACK *as he slowly retreats toward the filing cabinet, which is still illuminated. When* JACK *reaches the cabinet, blackout.*)

Scene 2

(*The scene is a sitting room in the Mansion.* LUCY *is very still, watching* STARK, *who paces back and forth, sunk in himself. Once or twice, as he passes a table where bottles, glasses, ice, etc. are set out, he almost stops, but controls the impulse. Then he stops, pours a drink, takes a sip, relishing the liquid on his tongue.*)

LUCY. I wish you wouldn't, Willie, not yet.
STARK. Well, I haven't had one all day. And what a day.
LUCY. I know, Willie, but I wish you wouldn't till after he — after he gets home.
STARK. Hell, I got to celebrate.
LUCY. Celebrate what, Willie?
STARK. (*Going to her, the drink still in his right hand, his face brightening, pat-*

ting her on the shoulder.) Sure, I admit I was worried a little, but it's over now. He'll be here any minute.

LUCY. *(After a pause.)* You've got to do something, Willie.

STARK. Sure, I'll do something. I'll do something he'll remember. Him the best quarterback in the Conference and the Stafford game four days off and he goes out and ties one on and gets in a fight in a roadhouse and gets jailed in some hick jail and won't give his name—you're tooting. I'll give him something to remember. I promised Coach Howes I'd give that boy something to remember. Howes was pretty sore, and I can't say I blame him. But Tom—he's all right. He'll pour it on 'em next Saturday. He'll be all right—

(STARK is being drawn away from the present into some vision of next Saturday, of Tom pouring it on 'em, of the excitement of the game before his eyes.)

LUCY. No, he isn't all right.

STARK. *(Angrily.)* What do you mean, he's not all right. Why, that boy, he's got real strategy, and when it comes to carrying the ball, well—

LUCY. *(Meditatively, bitterly.)* Carrying the ball. *(She lifts her head, rises from the chair, faces her husband.)* Oh, don't you see—don't you see!

STARK. See what?

LUCY. *(Bracing herself.)* Oh, it's not just football. That's bad enough, thinking he is a hero, that there's nothing else in the world—but it's everything that goes with it—he's wild and selfish and idle and—

STARK. No boy of mine is going to be a sissy. That's what you want!

LUCY. I had rather see him dead than what your vanity will make him.

STARK. Don't be a fool.

LUCY. *(Quiet now.)* You'll ruin him.

STARK. Now listen, all he did was take a couple of drinks and go out with a girl. Hell, that's what all boys do.

LUCY. *(Shaking her head.)* No, it's not. Not like this.

STARK. Damn it, let him have some fun. Look at me—you know the way I grew up, I never had any fun—twelve hours a day humped over the plow handles or chopping cotton and come home to slop the hogs—yeah, slop the hogs, and it looks like half the time right now that's what I'm still doing, pouring swill to hogs.

LUCY. Yes, Willie, and I wish things were different now with you, too. But I can't change that, Willie. I have tried, but I failed. But I can implore you to save Tom. I have to try, because he is my son.

STARK. *(Drawing back from her, a savage, disturbed belligerence growing on his face.)* Listen, he's my son, too. Mine, too, do you hear?—Mine!—*(Takes a drink, then stares defiantly at her.)* Yeah, because he's a chip off the old block—because he wades into things—you think it is just not nice. But if I hadn't been what I am, we'd be sitting back in Mason City right now in a slab-side shack and you'd be bending over the wash-tub and—

LUCY. *(Quietly.)* And I wouldn't mind, Willie—not if things could be like they used to be.

STARK. Listen. You know my father's house—yeah, a house bare as licked bone, set on that hill, on the rock-chunks, and the wind beat. Yeah, it was night, it was winter, and me—me a boy just coming on, yeah, with the sap rising— and I lay there and the house shook when the wind hit. I lay there in the dark and I shut my eyes and I saw how the snow and ice stretched away north a thousand—five thousand—miles—stretched away a million miles, and the moon was on the snow, and the wind riding down under the moon, and it hit the house. When I shut my eyes it was like that wind was in my head, it was like that million miles of wind was blowing through me—no, it was like it was me, and under the moon, and it was like wanting something and going near crazy and wanting it so bad you get near sick wanting it, and so full of wanting you forget what you are wanting. It was like something inside me just got so big I was going to die, it looked like my chest— *(A desperate pulling motion with both hands across his chest as though to rip it open.)* —it looked like it would bust open—it looked like it would—would— *(Suddenly withdrawing from her and his excitement in the effort to communicate, speaking now in a flat voice.)* —Lucy, Lucy, Lucy—but you wouldn't know. You wouldn't know.

LUCY. Oh, Willie, you think you are one thing, but you're another, and different. *(A burst of desperation, lifting her arms toward him.)* —But I know what you are, what you are deep inside. I know what the very bottom of your heart is, Willie, what you never see anymore, Willie—

(She approaches him, lifting her hands slowly to touch his cheeks lightly with her fingertips, to frame his face. He has been bemused by her approach, staring into her face, leaning at her, while longing grows on his face.)

LUCY. *(Touching his face, whispering.)* I see into the very bottom of your heart, Willie.

(SADIE BURKE has entered, catches sight of them, stops.)

SADIE. *(With a tinge of irony.)* Oh, excuse me, please.
STARK. *(Jerking back from LUCY.)* Yes?
SADIE. Lieutenant Boyd and your son are downstairs.
STARK. Thanks.

(He has stepped back from his wife. Now he takes a heavy drag from his glass, which he now seems to discover on the table beside him. SADIE has turned to LUCY.)

SADIE. *(In an ambiguous way, almost as an apology for the previous irony.)* Mrs. Stark, I'm — *(She stops.)*

LUCY. Yes?

SADIE. I'm glad they found him. I mean, I'm glad he's all right.

LUCY. Oh, yes, he's all right. *(She seems to drop into her own thoughts, then becomes aware of herself.)* — Oh, yes, he's fine. And thank you, Miss Burke.

(SADIE goes out. LUCY returns to her seat, waiting, not looking at her husband. STARK stands in the center of the floor, looking into his glass, taking an occasional sip, waiting, too. The door opens and SUGAR-BOY enters, followed by TOM STARK, disheveled, a cheek bruised, wearing a sweat shirt with STATE on it, a tweed jacket, nondescript slacks, dirty sneakers. Behind him is a patrolman, LIEUTEN-ANT BOYD, very military and severe, who salutes with his right hand, but keeps his left lightly on TOM's arm. TOM glances contemptuously at him, then down at the hand on his arm, then at his father. Meanwhile, LUCY has risen, utters some muffled greeting — TOM's name — and starts toward him. But she stops in her tracks as TOM speaks to his father.)

TOM. Now I'm here, maybe you can tell this — this Hessian of yours — to take his filthy hand off me.

(LIEUTENANT BOYD flushes, tenses murderously, but controls himself, and removes his hand from TOM's arm.)

STARK. I told him to club you over the ear if he had to do it to bring you in.

TOM. Yeah, him and how many more?

LUCY. *(Going to TOM, trying to put her hands on him, speaking with a mixture of reproach, grief, affection.)* Oh, Tom — Tom — don't talk like that!

(TOM stands rigid, suffering somehow, under her touch, his hands clenching. He is moved by her, but doesn't understand how or why. Meanwhile STARK has stepped toward the LIEUTENANT.)

STARK. You did a nice job, Lieutenant. *(He slips a bill into the officer's hand.)*

LIEUTENANT. Thanks, Boss. *(Glancing at the bill.)* — Thanks. *(Salutes and goes out.)*

STARK. *(Swinging toward TOM.)* Four days before the Stafford game, and you break training, miss two days of practice, and get boiled.

TOM. *(Shrugging.)* Wait till Saturday. I'll push over a few.

STARK. Maybe you won't ever push over any more. Not if you break training again. Coach Howes will fire you off. He has just about had a bellyful, and he —

TOM. He wants the championship, doesn't he?

STARK. Yeah, but he'll fire you off anyway. And I'll back him up.

TOM. Oh, yeah?

STARK. You're damned right, I'll back him. I don't care how hot you are on the field. I don't care if you are a cross between a locomotive and Pavlova. I don't care if you are Bonaparte at Marengo, I will see you never get your hands on a football again.

TOM. (*Shrugging, shaking his head, smiling sourly.*) No—no you won't.

STARK. What do you mean I won't? You know me well enough to—

TOM. I know you well enough to know that you want the championship. Worse than Howes ever did. Well enough to know you want me to shove 'em across every Saturday, so you can big-shot around. Yeah, it's my boy did it— (*Mimicking.*) —it's my boy Tom—

LUCY. (*Rushing to* TOM, *trying to put a hand over his mouth.*) Tom—Tom—don't!

STARK. (*Stepping toward* TOM, *lifting his arm as though to strike.*) Tom—you—

LUCY. Oh, Willie!

(STARK *regains control, sullenly takes a drink.* LUCY *holds* TOM *by the arm, and under her touch he begins to relax. They are standing thus as* SADIE *enters.*)

SADIE. They're here—Jack and Dr. Stanton and that— (*She twists her mouth in contempt.*)

STARK. Bring 'em up. (SADIE *goes.* LUCY *moves away.*) Why don't you stay, Lucy? It's not business, it's just—it's Dr. Stanton and his sister. I'd like for him—for them—to meet you. I think it might do some good and—

TOM. (*Heavy sarcasm.*) I thought you said it wasn't business.

LUCY. (*Laying her hand again on* TOM's *arm, soothingly.*) No, Willie, I just don't feel up to it, Willie.

STARK. Suit yourself. (LUCY *starts out, and* TOM *moves after her.* STARK *takes him by the arm.*) Hey, Tom, wait a minute—I want you to meet— (TOM *pulls away, and* STARK *stands there in an instant of hurt emptiness, even as the guests enter.* STARK *pulls himself together, and moves to greet them, first shaking hands with* ANNE. *His manner has a simple warmth and unpretending dignity.*) I'm awful glad you let Jack persuade you, Miss Stanton. (*Turning to* ADAM, *putting out his hand.*) And Dr. Stanton, I'm delighted to meet you. It's an honor. (*For a second* ADAM *does not take the hand, then manages to do so. In the middle of the handshake,* STARK *looks significantly down at the hands, then suddenly grins.*) See, boy, it's not nearly so bad as you figured. It won't kill you. (ADAM *is embarrassed an instant, then almost smiles.* STARK *has turned to* ANNE.) It didn't kill you, did it, Miss Stanton—the first time you ever shook hands with me?

ANNE. (*Blushing, embarrassed a little.*) Why—no. No, of course not—Governor Stark.

STARK. *(As though recollecting himself.)* Gosh, excuse me. Keeping you all standing around like this. Do have seats. Won't you sit here, Miss Stanton? *(He indicates a chair for her, readjusts its position to be a little more away from the light.)* And Doctor Stanton, would you be comfortable here? Do sit down. *(His manner has had an easy, natural courtesy, with dignity. Now turning to JACK, he slaps him on the shoulder, a gesture of confident friendliness.)* And you, old boy, you sprawl out in some quiet corner where the wind under the door won't get at your rheumatiz. *(STARK begins to serve drinks. ANNE takes a highball, as does JACK. DR. STANTON takes soda and ice, and sits somewhat self-consciously with it. Now, preparing his own drink, STARK goes casually back to the earlier topic, not even looking at ADAM meanwhile.)* Yes, you know, Dr. Stanton, your uncle resigned on me the other night.

ADAM. Yes, I know.

STARK. We'd been pretty thick, the Judge and I—we'd got a lot done in this State—but you know, when he quit, he didn't shake hands. *(He swings now to face ADAM, standing before him.)* Did he tell you that?

ADAM. No—why, no—

STARK. Well, he didn't. And I guess that was why I was sort of shy about it with you tonight. Even if you had done me the favor—no, I mean done Jack the favor—of dropping in tonight—*(Casually taking a drink.)* I suppose Jack gave you some background on why I wanted to see you?

ADAM. Yes. A health center and hospital.

STARK. *(Stops himself, turns sober.)* Dr. Stanton, it will be the best and most modern six million can buy, the finest facilities and staff. And it will be free—*(He stares directly, almost belligerently at ADAM.)* —What do you think of it?

ADAM. I think that it might do the people of this State some good. And it will get you more votes.

STARK. Forget about the votes, Doc. I don't have to build a hospital to get votes—*(Grinning, slyly, almost confidentially, taking ADAM into the secret.)* —Doc, I know lots of ways to skin a cat.

ADAM. So I understand.

STARK. *(Going dead earnest.)* Dr. Stanton, I want you as director. I want you to take over now, at the planning stage. I want you to build it right. I want you to—

ADAM. *(He gets up abruptly, to face STARK.)* You know what my views of your administration are.

STARK. *(Shaking his head in a kind of humorous pity.)* Yes. I know your views, Doc, and no offense, Doc, but I could run this State with you howling on every street corner like a pup with a sore tail. I wouldn't care what you thought, said, or did, so long as you ran that hospital right. *(Leaning at him, lowering his voice.)* You want to do good. *(ADAM sinks down into his chair, a little embarrassed by his show of violence.)* But boy, it's no disgrace. It's just eccentric. It's just you want to do good, Doc, and I am the man who can make it possible for you to do your kind of good in wholesale lots.

ADAM. Governor, a thing does not grow except in its proper climate.

STARK. You mean I'm not the proper climate, huh?

ADAM. I mean that good does not grow except in the proper climate for good.

STARK. What is the proper climate?

ADAM. It is not pressure and terror.

STARK. Those things are bad, aren't they, Doc?

ADAM. Yes, they are bad. But there's more —

STARK. Boy, you don't know the half of it. And some of it looks *awful* bad.

ADAM. Well.

STARK. Doc, there's a price tag on good. It's an awful big price tag. It is just knowing what good is. *(Pause.)* Do you know what good is?

ADAM. Certainly, I know.

STARK. Doc, that is one thing nobody knows for sure and certainly. But me — I got a pretty fair guess. Good is what you make out of bad. And the reason — *(Thrusting his head forward belligerently, his voice lowering.)* — the reason is that there isn't anything else to make it of.

ADAM. There is one question I'd like to ask you, Governor.

STARK. Shoot.

ADAM. If good is made from bad, then how do you ever get your notion of good? How do you recognize when you have made it?

STARK. Easy, Doc, easy.

ADAM. Well, tell me.

STARK. You make your notion up as you go along.

ADAM. *(Again with the air of a clincher.)* Well!

STARK. Oh, don't say *well* like that. When your great-great-grand-pappy first climbed down out of the tree he didn't find good blooming around his feet like primroses. How did he get the notion of good? *(Swinging to ANNE.)* Tell me, can you? Can you tell me, Miss Stanton? *(As she hesitates, he swings back to ADAM.)*

ADAM. Why do you ask her? What are you trying to do? Ask me.

STARK. Doc, I am asking you. Have you thought it through? Do you know the answer?

ADAM. *(Rising, taking a step toward STARK.)* What's that got to do with it? Every decent man knows what is good.

STARK. *(Dodging, as though to ward off a blow.)* Hey, Doc. Don't hit me! *(ADAM stops, again embarrassed by his own violent response.)* All I'm trying to do is make you examine your principles. To make you examine, as a matter of fact, the first principles of both of us.

ADAM. I know my principles.

STARK. No, son, you don't. Do you now? Do you? *(As ADAM hesitates, collecting himself, STARK steps to him, slaps him on the shoulder.)* You're a great boy, Doc, and don't let 'em tell you different! And when you get around to examining your first principles, just let me know. For all I'm trying to do is give you a nice six-million-dollar hospital to do good in. And I'll keep your little mitts clean. I'll keep you clean all over. I'll put you in that beautiful, antiseptic, sterile, six-million-dollar hospital, wrapped in cellophane, untouched by human hands. But me— *(He steps back, holding up his hands in comic woe.)* —look at my little mitts. *(He swings to ANNE, holding them out.)* —Potty black! *(ANNE laughs. ADAM looks sharply at her, then gets caught in her response, and smiles.)* See, Doc, you might even break out laughing if you tried. I caught you with your gloom slipping. But seriously, Doc, think of it this way. Whatever I am—me, Willie Stark, and he's got some rough edges—you just figure you are using me. You see, you know in your good conscience that I couldn't use you, not even if I tried. You just figure you are using me for your own good purposes, and nobody will ever believe different. The world knows you, and you are Adam Stanton—Dr. Stanton—and your motives are clear before the world. Now, think it over.

(ADAM rises from his chair.)

ADAM. Governor—

STARK. *(Stepping to him, laying a soothing hand on his shoulder.)* Now, boy— don't say it. Count to ten first. You just think it over. That's all I'm asking. You aren't afraid to think over my wisdom in the night, are you? Promise me you'll think it over. *(Suddenly grinning, putting out his hand.)* Honor bright!

(ADAM hesitates, then shrugs and grins sheepishly and puts out his hand.)

STARK. Atta-boy, Doc! Now we'll drop the subject. Sit down, sit down and I'll tell you about the hottest quarterback in the South. The Sophomore Thunderbird! All Southern for a cinch, and just a sophomore, and All American next year, and then—

(SADIE enters, obviously excited.)

SADIE. Listen, Boss— *(Then remembering the guests.)* —I mean, Governor, there's a call—

STARK. Tell 'em to call back.

SADIE. It's important.

STARK. Who is it?

SADIE. It's Duffy, he—

STARK. I told him I didn't want to see him. I told him that I—

SADIE. This is important.

STARK. What's it about?

SADIE. You better take the call.

STARK. *(Peevishly.)* What's it about? I asked you once.

(SADIE hesitates.)

STARK. Speak up, girlie, it's all friends here. No secrets here!

(SADIE looks around at the group, her eyes finally coming to rest on ANNE. Suddenly that seems to decide her.)

SADIE. Well, this secret wouldn't be a secret long. Your friends — *(She looks from STARK back at ANNE.)* — they can read it in the morning paper. *(Looks back to STARK.)* An impeachment resolution has just been introduced in the Legislature.

(For a moment, there is absolute silence. Then JACK jumps up. ANNE exhibits a deeply growing confusion and ADAM is staring intently at STARK, as though discovering something. Ignoring them all, even SADIE, STARK speaks quietly.)

STARK. So they're going to try it.

JACK. The lousy sons-of—

STARK. *(Shaking himself like a man waking from sleep, lifting his head, suddenly striking his right fist into the palm of his left hand.)* By God! By God, they've broke from cover, and I'll ride 'em down! All of 'em that were just waiting to sell out—well, now I'll know 'em—they're in the open and I'll ride 'em down. I'll—

ADAM. Governor Stark.

STARK. *(With the air of a man summoned back to trivial reality, turning to ADAM, almost not recognizing him.)* Yes—yes—

ADAM. Governor, I'll not be a front for you. I'll not be a glove you can put on to hide what your hand is. I'll not be used to fight the impeachment. Oh, yes, you were clever—to get me when you needed me most, when you—

STARK. *(Gradually paying attention to him, now stepping toward him, speaking almost irritably.)* I told you already, son. I don't need you. Except for one thing.

ADAM. Yes, the impeachment!

STARK. No, son, the hospital. And I need you bad. And listen, son— *(He comes very close, leaning at ADAM, speaking in almost a whisper.)* —do you know something?

ADAM. What?

STARK. You almost did it, son. Didn't you? *(ADAM stands quietly, staring at STARK.)* Come on, son, tell the truth. Didn't you?

ADAM. No!

STARK. I could see it in your eyes.

ADAM. But I didn't! (*Swinging away, as though triumphantly, taking a step, seeing* JACK, *speaking coldly.*) Goodnight, Jack. (*Seeing that* ANNE *has not moved, and is looking back at* STARK.) Come on, Anne. (ANNE, *with a backward look at* STARK, *moves after* ADAM, *who is now near the door.*)

STARK. Dr. Stanton!

ADAM. (*Turning back.*) Yes?

STARK. You need *me*, son. You need me in more ways than you ever reckoned.

ADAM. Need you!

STARK. A man like you always needs a man like me. (*During this speech of* STARK, ANNE *regards* STARK *with growing and disturbed attention. While* ADAM *is, apparently, hesitating for a reply,* ANNE *steps to* STARK *and offers him her hand. He looks down at the proffered hand, then into her face, then slowly takes the hand.*)

ANNE. Governor—

STARK. Yes— (*Staring into her face.*)

ANNE. I just wanted to say—

(*As she hesitates and* STARK *looks down at her,* JACK, SADIE, *and* ADAM *stare at them. There is a moment of total silence before* SADIE, *jerking her thumb toward* ADAM *at the door, speaks.*)

SADIE. Miss Stanton—your brother is waiting for you!

(*For the shade of an instant* ANNE *seems not to hear, then suddenly seems to come to herself, takes her hand, too hurriedly, from* STARK's *clasp, and speaks hurriedly, almost stuttering, even in the act of withdrawing from him.*)

ANNE. Good—goodnight.

(STARK *does not reply, standing with his hand still in the air as when it had held hers, looking after her.* ADAM *goes out and she hurries after him, and* STARK, *for an instant, stares at the empty space where they have disappeared.* SADIE *is watching him with fascinated attention. She speaks very softly.*)

SADIE. You *are* a bastard.

(STARK *is not listening.*)

End I

Act II

Scene 1

(ANNE near center of Forestage, speaking meditatively.)

ANNE. There was a time I was happy. I saw the sun on the sea, and I was happy. I saw the moon rise over the sea, and I was happy. Adam and Jack and I, and life was a promise, life was a promise and—

VOICE OF JACK. I'll race you to the raft!

(Sound of a dive.)

VOICE OF ANNE. I'll race you!

(ANNE has lifted her head to the VOICE OF JACK on one side, then toward the VOICE OF ADAM on the other side.)

VOICE OF ADAM. The net, Anne—cover the net! *(Sound of racket on tennis ball in quick rally.)* Atta-girl, Anne—oh, that was a beauty!

VOICE OF REFEREE. The set is now four all.

VOICE OF ADAM. Oh, that was a beauty.

(ANNE, with lifted head, is reliving the moment.)

VOICE OF JACK. *(Low and loverlike.)* Oh, you are my beauty—oh, you are my beauty, dear Anne—oh, Anne, see the moon come over the water—

ANNE. *(With a cradling gesture of her arms, murmuring.)* Oh, Jackie-Boy—oh, Jackie-Bird—oh, Jackie-Boy—

VOICE OF JACK. Oh, Anne, see the moon come over the water—

(As the voice fades, ANNE stands for an instant with her arms still in the cradling position, but not moving. Then she breaks the posture and speaks in a tense, cold tone.)

ANNE. And the water gets cold, it is cold, and the moon goes down, and life drives them past, flat and fast over the net, and it gets so life drives them past you and you see them coming, you see it happening, and oh, it is gone, fast and flat over the net, gone past you, and—

VOICE OF REFEREE. Game and set. It is game and set.

ANNE. And life slips through your fingers, like sand. It slips through your fingers, like wind. What you dream leaves you. Those whom you love leave you. They are withdrawing from you. *(During this speech light has revealed JACK at Stage Right and ADAM at Stage Left. JACK, as in Forestage between Scene 1 and Scene 2, is looking into a filing cabinet and taking notes, then picking up bound newspaper files, taking notes, or perhaps interviewing somebody in pantomime and taking notes.* ADAM, *wearing a white coat, is bent over a microscope.* ANNE *turns first to* ADAM, *then to* JACK. *They do not hear her.*) Oh, why do you leave me? Oh, why do you leave me? (*She pauses, touches herself on her breast, in a gesture of sad inculpation, whispering.*) Or is it my fault? Or is it my fault?

VOICE OF STARK. (*Distant and guttural.*) Come here! Come here! (ANNE *lifts her head to the voice, seems about to take a step.*) Jack!—Jack!—I said come here.—Jack—

(JACK *drops his occupation and moves toward the spot where the set will be revealed. He moves in a slow, dragging pace. As the lights on the Governor's office fade up, the lights on* ANNE *and* ADAM *fade out.* STARK *is revealed at his desk, papers in disorder before him.* JACK *arrives and stands before the desk, waiting.*)

STARK. Are you crippled? You move like Man-of-War in the stretch.

JACK. Just say I'm crippled.

STARK. Did you dig?

JACK. (*Lighting a cigarette, immensely casual.*) Dig what?

STARK. Boy, come off it. You know what Poppa means, and no matter how long it takes you to light that cigarette, it won't change it. Poppa means did you dig on Irwin? Did you stick the shovel in the pile? Did you find the dead pussy-cat?

JACK. (*Still very casual, sitting on the front of* STARK's *desk.*) He hasn't backed the impeachment, has he?

STARK. Not yet. ,

JACK. Well.

STARK. But I just want to know if you got the dead pussy?

JACK. What do you want it for if you don't need it?

STARK. Look here— (*Approaching* JACK.) —you did dig, didn't you? (JACK *shrugs off direct answer.*) You found something, didn't you? (JACK *shrugs.*) Yeah, you found something. And you're afraid of it. (*No answer.*) What the hell *did* you find?

JACK. To tell the truth, I don't know.

STARK. What do you mean, you don't know? (*Then, when* JACK *hesitates before answering, he rises from desk, coming around to* JACK, *a friendly hand on his shoulder.*) Look, Jack, either you found something or you didn't. If you found something, just remember it wasn't you killed the pussy-cat, it was Judge Irwin. Now, son—

(*The intercom on* STARK's *desk speaks.*)

VOICE. Governor, Mr. Duffy is here. He says it is very important. Urgent.

STARK. *(Into intercom.)* You tell him to —

JACK. I'll wait. I'm not in a hurry.

STARK. *(Leering up at JACK.)* Maybe I'm in a hurry. *(Hesitating, then to intercom.)* Send him in.

JACK. You want me out?

STARK. No, get the weight off.

(Motioning to a chair. JACK sits, just as TINY enters.)

TINY. *(Hearty.)* Hi, Boss.

STARK. *(Propped on the edge of his desk, rocking back and forth a second or two, regarding TINY before he speaks, very softly.)* Hi.

TINY. I didn't want to break in — not on you and Jack — but —

STARK. I got all the time in the world, Tiny. *(With mock graciousness.)* And Jack, he's got plenty of time, haven't you, Jack?

JACK. *(Not looking up from a picture magazine.)* You ought to know. It's your time.

TINY. Well, Boss, there's sort of a development. It is pretty important. Pretty important, if I say so myself. *(He swells a little, polishes the diamond.)* Boss, there's that fellow named Larsen, over in Bartonville. Well, Mr. Larsen, he —

STARK. Yeah, Larsen — Gummy Larsen.

TINY. Mr. Larsen, he's pretty important, you know, Boss. He's got a chunk of the Morton Bridge and Construction Company, he's got a —

STARK. He *is* the Morton Bridge and Construction and he is the First National Bank and he is also a big leg on MacMurfee's stool. Tiny, you think I been deaf, dumb, and stupid all my life?

TINY. Now, Boss — but Mr. Larsen, you know, he's a man that can sort of see how things shape up. I mean to say, he has got what they call vision and he can see an opportunity. You are right, Boss, sure Mr. Larsen has been a big thing for MacMurfee. You know, Boss, Mr. Larsen, he's not exactly satisfied. He don't think they're doing you exactly right, trying to impeach you, Boss. Now, he was saying to me how —

STARK. *(He has been leaning more and more forward studying TINY, assessing the situation.)* Just took you by the hand, Tiny, and poured out his little heart, huh? *(Wistfully.)* I wish Gummy would take me by the hand. *(He leans forward, directly into TINY's face.)* Am I to understand that the bastard is getting ready to sell out MacMurfee?

TINY. Mr. Larsen — now he's not exactly —

STARK. *Mr.* Larsen, my foot. I said, is the bastard getting ready to cross Mac-Murfee?

TINY. Boss, Mr. Larsen—I mean, he has eight votes in the Legislature, and eight votes right now—

STARK. (Quietly.) So he is a bastard. I mean, so he is that kind of a bastard, too.

TINY. Now, Boss, as I figger it—eight votes is—

STARK. (Even more quietly.) And what does the bastard want for eight votes?

TINY. (Obviously relieved.) Gee, Boss, I'm glad you see it that way. (Hesitating.) I'm mighty pleased, Boss, that I could sort of work something out. You know, sort of make it up—after you and me had our—our sort of misunderstanding, you might call it. Now, working with Mr. Larsen—you'll like it, Boss, he's—he's—he's—

STARK. (Gazing at TINY, letting him stutter; then suddenly.) Get the phlegm out!

TINY. Well—he—he—

STARK. What does he want?

TINY. (Bracing himself, managing to get out the words.) He wants— (Pause.) — the hospital contract.

(STARK doesn't move for a moment. There is complete silence. JACK is peering curiously at STARK around the edge of his picture magazine. Then as STARK rises slowly from the edge of the desk, TINY retreats a step, but STARK ignores him, turns his back on TINY, on the audience, and moves slowly around the desk, then comes and lets himself down in the desk chair. Leaning back. He acts like a man perfectly alone. He examines his nails, bending the fingers over his upward palms to scrutinize them; then spreads the fingers back, and for an instant he seems to be looking into the palms of his hand. Then he lifts his head and looks at TINY. He speaks very softly.)

STARK. You know, Tiny, I got to try harder to understand you. I've got to cultivate the understanding heart, Tiny. And you've got to bear with me, Tiny. You've got to try to understand me, too, Tiny.

TINY. (Wary and confused, but putting the best face on everything.) Sure, Boss, I understand you. I just know that you're Old Willie, Willie Stark—and you know how all the boys feel about you. And all.

STARK. (Sadly.) I've got my faults, Tiny. You've got to understand me. We got to try to understand each other. And you know why? (When TINY can't answer, STARK continues.) Because we got to live together, Tiny, you and me. You know, without charity and understanding, this room just wouldn't be big enough for you and me. You know, this State wouldn't. The world wouldn't. And right now— (He stands up, abruptly.) —right now—I feel as crowded as Daniel Boone wrastlin' a b'ar in a telephone booth.

TINY. (When the import has had time to sink in.) But, Boss—Boss—

STARK. (Soft, again.) I'm glad you figger out my meaning, Tiny.

TINY. But, Boss, it's slick—you never worked out a slicker one yourself, Boss—
and eight votes—

STARK. *(Moving around the far side of the desk, very slowly approaching* TINY.*)*
Remember something, Tiny. That hospital, it's mine— *(He taps himself on the*
chest with all his fingers, speaking very softly.) —it's mine— *(Taps again.)* —it's
mine— *(Taps again.)* —do you understand?— *(As he approaches* TINY, TINY
is backing away a little, toward the door. STARK *is leaning at him, making a*
quieting gesture with his right hand, fingers slightly cupped downward, a pat-
ting motion.) —and don't you ever—ever—lay a hand on it. Do you get me?
Do you get me? *(He looks at* TINY *with almost pitying solicitude, then suddenly*
wheels toward JACK, *and speaks loud, a timbre of pain and rage in his tone.)* —
Jack—God damn it—I'm feeling awful crowded! *(He is facing* JACK *for a*
moment, then slowly turns again toward the spot where TINY *had been.* TINY *is*
no longer there, and the door is shut. STARK *turns to* JACK.*)* You know what
Lincoln said?

JACK. What?

STARK. He said a house divided against itself cannot stand. Well, he was wrong.

JACK. Yeah?

STARK. Yeah, for this government is sure half slave and half son-of-a-bitch, and it
is standing.

JACK. Which is which?

STARK. Slaves down at the Legislature, and the sons-of-bitches up here. Only
sometimes they overlap.

JACK. What do you expect?

STARK. *(Lunging up.)* Can't you understand? Damn it, can't you understand
either?

JACK. I understand what I understand.

STARK. Can't you understand?—I'm building that place, the best in the country,
the best in the world, and a bugger like Tiny is not going to mess with it, and
I'm going to call it the Willie Stark Hospital, and it will be there a long time
after I'm dead and gone, and you are dead and gone, and all those sons-of-
bitches are dead and gone, and anybody, no matter he hasn't got a dime, can
go there—

JACK. *(Sardonically.)* Yeah.

STARK. —and I don't care whether he votes for me or not, he can go there—

JACK. Yeah.

STARK. What do you mean, yeah? *(Staring at* JACK, *trying to read his repudiation*
of the dream.) Can't you understand?

JACK. Yeah, I understand. I understand that you have to talk this way to keep on
operating.

STARK. Operating?

JACK. *(Shrugging.)* Living. Being Willie Stark. *(When STARK is hit by this, JACK goes on.)* Yeah, you have to talk that way for the same reason you have to spit on Tiny. And that's getting to be a habit.

STARK. *(Anger beginning.)* What the hell are you —

JACK. There was a man once who chewed tobacco, and he had a poodle he took everywhere with him, and somebody said how he sure must love that dog, and the man said, God, no, he did not love the son-of-a-bitch, but it was sure tidier than getting ambeer all over the floor.

STARK. What's eating on you? *(Looking with suspicion at JACK.)* You aren't in this with Tiny?

JACK. *(Shrugging.)* I am not in anything with Tiny, except the human predicament.

STARK. Tiny is not human.

JACK. Then maybe I am in the nonhuman predicament with Tiny.

STARK. What the hell are you talking about?

JACK. *(Pedantically.)* Is it not permitted that a man wonder if he is human?

STARK. *(Studying JACK, coming closer, leaning a little over him.)* You are sore about that Irwin stuff? *(When JACK does not answer, STARK leans nearer, slaps him on the shoulder.)* Damn it, boy, I told you it wasn't you killed the pussy-cat. Damn it, and you didn't make the world, did you? Now did you?

JACK. If I had, I wouldn't go around bragging about it.

STARK. Well, do you think your moping around will take the sins of the world away?

JACK. Men of action — such as you fancy yourself, Boss — have been known to confuse moping and philosophical reflection, and — *(He flings the picture magazine aside.)* —with your kind permission, I think I shall haul ass. *(He starts to rise from the chair.)*

STARK. *(Leaning, he puts a hand on JACK's shoulder, prevents his rising, then with the same hand makes a little gesture of "gimme," grinning confidentially the while.)* Gimme that pussy-cat. Did you think I was going to forget that pussy-cat? Gimme.

JACK. *(Pushing STARK's hand aside.)* No.

STARK. *(Almost petulantly.)* For Christ's sake, Jack, you go out and dig on Irwin and then when you find something you get sore. Come on, give it to me, and you'll feel better.

JACK. I don't want to feel better. I want to feel worse. Half the trouble is I don't feel as bad as I want to.

STARK. *(Grinning, putting out his hand in "gimme.")* Yeah, and I want the pussy-cat.

JACK. You could fire me. I have been fired from more jobs than I can count.

STARK. I'm not going to fire you.

JACK. I could just quit. I have quit more jobs than I can count.

STARK. (*Studying him, quizzically.*) No, boy, no. Boy, that is the one thing you just won't do. Not this job. And that's why it preys on your mind. It is why you take Tums for anti-acid. It is why you are always changing barbers. It is why you—

JACK. I might, you know. (*He starts toward the door, picks up his hat from the desk.*)

STARK. (*Unmoving, very quiet and friendly.*) Look here, Jack, I know you were thick with Irwin. You belonged to that gang. But you left 'em long back. (*As JACK starts to say something, STARK lifts his hand.*) Oh, I don't mean when you joined up with me. I mean long back before that, son. Something was eating on you and you couldn't stand it. So you were running a long time. Then— (*His voice sinks a little.*) —then you and me connected. Isn't that right? (*JACK seems about to answer, hesitating. Then STARK continues.*) Yes, that's right. But look here, you still got the old disease. You still got one thing just like that gang. You want things both ways. Yeah, when they want something mean, low, and reprehensible they want some good name for it, and when they want something good like Irwin did and like Adam Stanton, they want somebody else to do the dirty to get it.

JACK. (*Angrily.*) I told you in the first place I didn't know if there was anything on Irwin.

STARK. Are you afraid?

JACK. I told you I didn't know if there was anything.

STARK. The truth will make you free.

JACK. What the hell are you talking about?

STARK. Boy, we have come a long way, you and me. Since we connected.

JACK. (*We notice some reaction to this remark of STARK's, then a jerking away from it, a new tone of factuality.*) The truth. So you think I'm afraid of it. Well, I'll make you a proposition. I won't give you what I've got unless the heat gets on, and I won't give it to you then until after I've shown it to Irwin, and if he can convince me, then—

STARK. The son-of-a-bitch will claim he is washed in the Blood of the Lamb.

JACK. (*Turning away.*) Take it or leave it.

STARK. The son-of-a-bitch will be washed in whitewash.

JACK. (*Hotly.*) I'm not going to frame anybody.

STARK. (*Studying JACK.*) I never asked you to frame anybody. Did I?

JACK. No.

STARK. I never *did* ask you to frame anybody. And you know why?

JACK. No.

STARK. Because it ain't ever necessary. You don't ever have to frame anybody, because the truth is always sufficient.

JACK. Sufficient or not, I told you what I'm going to do. I'm going to show it to Irwin. Take it or leave it.

STARK. *(First studying JACK as if to discover his degree of stubbornness.)* I take it.

JACK. For once you haven't got much choice.

STARK. *(Watching JACK move toward the door.)* Jack —

JACK. *(Turning.)* What?

STARK. Adam Stanton, now — Doc Stanton — you know, I figure one thing might work on him. If you can't get him, well, that sister, she's the closest to him, she might sort of —

JACK. *(Sourly.)* Leave her out. Leave her out of the whole God-damned mess.

STARK. *(Studying him.)* You all — you and that Anne —

JACK. Leave her out of it.

STARK. You all were mighty sweet, weren't you?

JACK. *(Shrugging.)* We were kids.

STARK. *(Coming a step or two toward JACK, stopping.)* What happened? What made you blow out on her?

JACK. Who the hell said I blew out on her? *(He hesitates a moment.)* Nobody blew out on anybody. It was just the way it was.

STARK. So that's the way it was, huh? You mean you didn't blow out on her?

JACK. Damn it, it was just — it was just she wouldn't have me.

STARK. *(Coming to stand right in front of JACK.)* Why wouldn't she have you, huh? *(Pause.)* She had anybody else? Anybody since?

JACK. How do I know? She's been engaged a couple of times.

STARK. Engaged? Yeah, and what happened?

JACK. Oh, it busted up. She busted it up.

STARK. Christ, she busts engagements and fools with orphan homes. Built like she is, she busts engagements and fools with orphan homes. *(Pause.)* Boy, you sure must have made an impression. *(Pause.)* Maybe she'd have you now. Even if you haven't improved. Maybe she understands things better now. *(Leering at JACK, confidentially, insinuatingly.)* Are you sure she wouldn't have you now?

JACK. God damn it, it was a million years ago.

(Blackout, and lights up on Forestage.)

ANNE. Oh, Jack, why couldn't you remember?

JACK. Remember?

ANNE. We lay on the beach —

JACK. *(Taking a step toward her, his tone beginning to match hers.)* We lay on the beach —

ANNE. And sunlight glittered on the sea, and the fish-hawk rose. *(Lifting her hand upward to indicate the flight.)* He rose. He rose up. He was lost in the light. Our eyes burned after him. *(Hesitantly.)* Oh, Jack, we thought—we thought life might be like that.

JACK. Oh, darling—

ANNE. *(She lifts her hand to his face, and he begins to sink down.)* Oh, Jack—oh, Jackie-Boy, oh, Jackie-Bird—

JACK. *(Drawing suddenly from her.)* But—

ANNE. Oh, Jack—

JACK. We were kids.

ANNE. But Jack—oh, Jack, I loved you!

JACK. Why wouldn't you have me then?

ANNE. *(Quietly.)* I loved you. I loved you so much I felt sometimes I might just kiss you and hold you tight and jump off a cliff with you. But love—oh, Jack, it's not like jumping off a cliff. It's—oh, it's trying to live—

JACK. I'd have got a job—not with any of those rich bastards at the Landing but a job—enough money to live on.

ANNE. You know it wasn't that. I'd have lived in a shack with you, and eaten red beans, Jack. But a man's got to want to live in the world—to make his life mean something. Oh, Jack, you didn't want anything.

JACK. I wanted you.

ANNE. That wasn't enough. You couldn't want me, not really—unless you wanted something else—wanted life, life itself to mean something—oh, Jack, it could—it could—

JACK. *(Stepping toward her, arms out.)* Yes! Yes!

(ADAM suddenly appears between them, with a gesture to divide them, a rancorous fury.)

ADAM. Oh, yes, you wanted life to mean something! And is that why you did what you did? Is that why you betrayed me? Is that what you did those nights by the river?

(Meanwhile his accusatory finger seems to drive them back, step by step, to the set, where, under his finger, they begin their scene. The Forestage light cross fades to the light coming up on the wharf.)

Scene 2

(Scene, a wharf at night, the dark bulk of a warehouse beyond. JACK and ANNE are moving slowly the length of the wharf, finally stop and stand looking over the water, leaning on a coil of cable or other furniture of the place, etc.)

ANNE. *(Laying her hand on his arm.)* You can make him take it.

JACK. Look here, Adam's a grown man. He's—

ANNE. I want him to take it.

JACK. *(Staring meditatively at her.)* So you want him to take it? And you are the niece of Judge Irwin and the sister of Adam Stanton.

ANNE. *(With a sense of tensed-up, compulsive repetition.)* You've got to.

JACK. Why?

ANNE. He works like a slave. But it's not just being busy. It's something driving him — driving him. Sometimes I think that even his doing good — it's just a way of cutting himself off. From everything. From the world. From me — even from me. *(Her voice trails off, and she sinks into herself, then at the stab of a recollection, she turns to JACK.)* Oh, Jack, we had an awful row. You know how we've always been, and then to have an awful row. Don't you all see how awful it was?

JACK. Yes, sure.

ANNE. Oh, Jack — Jack — Adam just lives in his crazy cold pride-above-everything. What makes him that way?

JACK. Because he is Adam Stanton.

ANNE. Jack, you've got to save him.

JACK. Save him?

ANNE. Don't be a fool. You know what I mean. I mean, make him take that job. Swallow his foolish pride. Come out in the world — you know, not hide in himself — come out in the world — out where people are — we are — you are —

JACK. Yeah. I'm out in the world.

ANNE. *(Seizing him by the arm.)* Do it!

JACK. You don't have to tear my arm off. *(Staring soberly at her.)* So you really want that?

ANNE. *(Quietly.)* More than anything in the world.

JACK. There's just one way.

ANNE. What?

JACK. To change the picture in his head.

ANNE. The picture — what do you mean, the picture?

JACK. Adam Stanton is a romantic. A romantic is a guy who has a picture of the world in his head, and when the real world does not fit that picture in his head he wants to throw the real world away. That is Adam Stanton.

ANNE. *(Pointing forward and down, off wharf.)* Look out there, look at the river. What do you see?

JACK. Well, when the mist breaks I see a lot of black, greasy-looking river sliding by in the dark.

ANNE. That's what I mean. I can't bear it, Jack — I can't bear to think of life being nothing but that — just sliding by, under the mist, like that black water in the dark. Jack, it ought to mean something, to be something, to —

JACK. Well, do you want me to do it — to change the picture in his head?

ANNE. *(As though bracing herself.)* Do it!

(JACK turns away from her, looking at the water.)

ANNE. What are you going to do?

JACK. I'll give him a history lesson.

ANNE. A history lesson, what do you mean?

JACK. Way back—back in 1932 and '33—Judge Irwin was broke. His house—you know how proud he is of it, how his grandfather built it—you know. Well, it was mortgaged. And his plantation. *(Turning away again.)* Oh, to hell with it. Let's forget the whole thing.

ANNE. *(Seizing him.)* What? What? You've got to tell me!

JACK. Well, he was Attorney General back then, too.

ANNE. Are you implying—are you saying that he— *(She can't go on.)*

JACK. Oh, nothing vulgar. Oh, no! No greasy bills in a back alley. The State had a suit against the Southern Belle Coal Corporation. Royalty rates on State lands, and—

ANNE. I don't believe it.

JACK. *(Grimly continuing.)* —and the suit was killed and Judge Irwin got a block of stock in another corporation and got a sudden job with a hell of a salary and resigned as Attorney General and—

ANNE. I don't believe it!

JACK. Maybe I don't believe it, either. But there are the documents, the papers—

ANNE. Well, if you don't believe it, then why, why— *(She leans at him, scrutinizing his face, and speaks in a voice of dawning horror.)* Listen, why did you ever—why did you—

(She can't go on.)

JACK. You mean, why did I dig it up?

(She nods.)

JACK. I got paid for it.

(ANNE suddenly puts the back of her right hand against her mouth as though to cancel the words. JACK nods grimly.)

ANNE. *(Whispering, intensely.)* Oh, you are vile.

(JACK tries to put his arm around her shoulder.)

ANNE. Don't touch me! Don't! Oh, he loved you, he loved us all, he was like a father to you—to us all—and you—you are vile! *(She covers her face, and bursts into tears.)*

JACK. *(In a voice twisted by pain.)* Anne—oh, Anne!

(He tries to put his arm about her shoulders in comfort, but she jerks away, sobbing hysterically, and tries to run. He seizes her, and they are struggling together, when a POLICEMAN appears.)

COP. Hey, what you runnin' that dame for?

JACK. *(Collecting himself.)* I'm—I'm just trying to get her home.

COP. I'll git you home. I'll git you home in the wagon.

JACK. *(All his confusion of feeling finding an outlet.)* The hell you will! *(He is still holding ANNE by the arms.)*

COP. The hell I won't. I'm taking you right now. Both of you. March! *(He prods JACK with a stick.)*

JACK. *(Very cold.)* I'm giving you one chance. Beat it.

COP. Givin' me a chance! *(He jabs hard, with the stick.)*

JACK. Did you ever hear of Willie Stark?

COP. Yeah, and I heard of Jesus Christ, too. *(Jabs hard.)*

JACK. And you've heard of Jack Burden?

COP. Sure.

JACK. Well, if you take me in, I'll bust you off the force before day, and I'm not kidding. I'm Jack Burden.

COP. Yeah, and I'm Marilyn Monroe.

JACK. Listen, you cluck. I'm reaching for my wallet. Not a gun. I am going to show you my card.

(He reaches into his coat, but the COP taps his arm with the stick.)

COP. Naw, you don't.

(The COP reaches in, pulls out the wallet, and starts to open it.)

JACK. You open that wallet, and I'll bust you anyway. Whether you call the wagon or not. Give it here.

(In a somewhat dazed way the COP passes the wallet to JACK, who produces the card and, with a hint of ironical formality, passes it to the COP.)

COP. Jeez. Jeez. I did'n mean no harm. How was I to know you was on the payroll? How wuz I to—

JACK. Well, stop gargling, and call me a cab or I'll bust you anyway.

COP. Yes, sir—yes, sir— *(Exit.)*

ANNE. *(Flaring at JACK.)* Oh, you're so wonderful—oh, Jack Burden is so wonderful!

JACK. *(Shaking her.)* Shut up! Don't—

ANNE. *(With a mounting sense of hysteria.)* Oh, he's so wonderful—he bullies the bullies, he cops the cops—oh, he's so strong and clean—oh, he's

so clean—oh, everything is so wonderful and strong and clean—oh, everything—oh—everything—

*(Fast fade-out, a pause, and then at Stage Left, Forestage, in shadow a telephone
is ringing insistently. As JACK moves toward it, the instrument is revealed. JACK
picks it up.)*

JACK. Jack Burden.

VOICE OF ANNE. Those papers—those documents—the ones you said— *(Stops.)*

JACK. Oh, Anne—hello, Anne—listen, Anne, I want to see you—I—

VOICE. Those papers—send them to me.

JACK. I'll bring them—I'll—

VOICE. No. Send them.

JACK. I'll bring them.

VOICE. I don't want to see you.

JACK. All right. If that's it. I've got extra photostats.

VOICE. Photostats? So you don't trust me.

JACK. Oh, that's not the point—

VOICE. All right. Photostats.

JACK. All right. Photostats.

*(He slams the phone down, and as he does so, the light goes out on him, but
comes up at corresponding position, Stage Right, to reveal ANNE with a phone in
her hand. The voice from the phone is JACK's.)*

VOICE OF JACK. All right. Photostats.

ANNE. *(Desperately.)* Jack—oh, Jack—Jack—

*(She holds the silent phone for a moment, staring at it, as though she might
summon it back to life. As she stares at it, ADAM STANTON, just chest and face in
the light, appears close to her across her arm that holds the phone. She shrinks a
little from him, then he points an accusing forefinger at her.)*

ADAM. You!

(She lets the phone come to rest with exaggerated caution, her gaze still on him.)

ADAM. You!

ANNE. Adam, don't say it that way, you mustn't, you mustn't.

ADAM. Why?

ANNE. Because I love you—I love you—

*(He swings from her toward the audience. In his left hand he is clutching the
documents. Now he jerks them open, glances at them, lifts his face to the audience.)*

ADAM. They struck me where I was weak. My sister. My friend. And Stark. They
struck me at the point where what the future might be was joined to what I

thought the past was. It was the joint between what good I dreamed for the future and what good I dreamed the past had been. But the splice was imperfect, the nail was imperfect, the solder weak. At that point I broke. I was broken, and I was delivered into the hands of foulness.

ANNE. *(Confusion and pain.)* Foulness! No—

(STARK appears above, light showing only the upper half of his body, addressing the audience.)

STARK. —and I say that I see the need in your faces. I see the need in the face of Justice when she is deprived. I would answer that need. That no person aged or infirm shall beg for bread. That the man who produces something shall be able to take it to market without miring to the hub. And without toll. That no child shall lack for schooling and grow up ignorant like you—and, by God! like me. And I tell you what now I will do. I will build a hospital, the biggest and finest money can buy, and it will belong to you. Any man or woman or child who is sick or in pain can go in those doors and know that all will be done that man can do. To heal sickness. To ease pain. Free, but not as a charity. No, by God, as a right, as your human right. Do you hear me? And I have done and will do these things for Justice! And who will stop me? Let any man try, and I'll break him! *(He crashes his right fist into the palm of his left hand.)* Like that! I'll smite him. Hip and thigh, rabbit punch and kidney punch, shinbone and neckbone, uppercut and solar plexus, above the belt, below the belt, kick him in the eye, and his blood—his blood be on his head! Look! *(He flings up his right arm to point at the sky.)* Blood on the moon! Blood on the moon! *(Flinging up both arms as to grab something from the air.)* Gimme that meat-axe! Gimme that meat-axe! *(He stands in a frozen posture, then lets his arms slowly descend. He speaks quietly.)*

My study is the heart of the people.

Your will is my strength.

Your need is my law.

Your hope is my justification.

Your heart is my own.

(The light is fading on him during the last several sentences. But there is still light on the Forestage. SUGAR-BOY has come out and is looking raptly up at STARK.)

ADAM. Yes, that was the lie!

ANNE. *(Still staring up where STARK had been.)* Hush—oh, hush. If that was a lie, then where was any truth?

SUGAR. *(Staring upward.)* The Big B-B-B-Boss—he k-k-k-kin talk so good!

(Fade-out.)

Scene 3

(JACK at desk, occupied. SADIE bursts in, leans over front of desk, looks accusingly at him.)

SADIE. The bastard, the bastard!

JACK. *(Looking up, propping back with enormous casualness.)* Who?

SADIE. Oh, you know who—who would it be?

JACK. *(Getting his feet to the desk top.)* Oh, him.

SADIE. *(Leaning more over desk.)* I'll kill him! I swear I'll kill him.

JACK. You set a high valuation on something.

SADIE. I'll drive him out of this State, I swear to God. The son-of-a-bitch, to two-time me after all I've done for him. Listen— *(She comes around the desk and seizes JACK's lapels, shaking him.)* —listen—

JACK. *(Peevishly.)* Well, you needn't choke me. And I don't want to listen. I hear too damned much already.

SADIE. Listen—who made the s-o-b what he is today? Who made him Governor? Who took him when he was Sap of the Year and put him in the big time? Who gave it to him play by play?

JACK. I reckon you mean for me to say you did.

SADIE. Well, I did—I tell you I did and you know it, and—

JACK. I reckon you sort of showed him his strength. If that is what you mean.

SADIE. I mean I made him, and now he goes and two-times me and—

(JACK releases himself from her grip, slides out of the chair and around the desk.)

JACK. No, my sweeting, my chick. He was two-timing Lucy, so you need some other kind of arithmetic for what he's doing to you. Maybe he is four-timing you.

SADIE. Lucy! *(Contemptuously.)* She's had her chance.

JACK. You seem to think Lucy is on the way out.

SADIE. Lucy! Give him time, give him time, he'll ditch her, he'll ditch her.

JACK. You ought to know. *(She slaps him.)* Hey, I'm the wrong guy. I'm not the hero of the piece. This is me, your old friend, your old pal, Jack Burden.

(She stands looking sorrowfully at him, shaking her head slowly, seeming on the verge of tears; when she speaks, her voice is now small.)

SADIE. Oh, Jack—nobody cares. Nobody cares what happens.

JACK. Look here, what do you care? It's happened before. He is just that way. You know that.

SADIE. Look—look at my face. *(She leans toward JACK, prodding her cheeks with stiff fingers.)* I was a kid, lying up in a shack—and it was smallpox—and my father — oh, he was drunk, crying and drinking off in a saloon, crying and telling how his darling kiddie, his angel kiddie, was sick — oh, he was a lousy, drunk, warm-hearted, kid-beating Irishman — and I wish he had beat me to death sometime and now I could be dead and I wouldn't have a face like this so they can kick dirt up in it — yeah, the kind of a face my old man used to cry over, stinking of whisky, saying poor little face, poor little face, then he might look in my face and say, Jeez! Say, Jeez, and slap me. Yeah, Jack Burden — look at my face — they kick dirt in my face — Stark and that —

JACK. *(He is staring down at her as she speaks and prods her face. He tries to break in, awkwardly.)* Sadie, Sadie. *(Now he reaches to put his right hand under her chin and lifts her face to him.)* Sadie — Sadie Burke —

SADIE. *(For a moment responding to him, to his sympathy and comfort.)* Oh, Jack — if only —

JACK. It's a wonderful face, Sadie Burke. It's a wonderful face.

SADIE. *(Jerking back from him.)* Don't touch me! It's an awful face, but you can't touch it — not what you are —

JACK. What — what the hell?

SADIE. Oh, yeah, you brought your high-toned pals in — oh, yeah, you brought in the silk-hat ones and look what happened — look!

JACK. *(Some vague distrust in his voice.)* What the hell are you talking about?

SADIE. Oh, don't pretend with me! I know what you are like, and that's why you can't lay a finger on my face — you — you

JACK. *(Seizing SADIE's shoulders, shaking her.)* What are you saying?

SADIE. Yeah, what's he gonna make you director of?

JACK. What are you saying? Answer me! *(Shaking her.)*

SADIE. *(Lethally quiet.)* You're his pimp, aren't you? *(As JACK's hands fall from their grip on her arms, she steps back, looking into his face, still quiet.)* You just gave her to him, didn't you, Jack Burden?

(As JACK stands there looking at her, fascinated and stunned, the intercom box says, "Miss Stanton to see you, sir. Miss Stanton." JACK looks at the box, making some vague motion toward it. But the door opens, and there is ANNE.)

ANNE. *(Surprised.)* Oh, I'm sorry. I thought she said for me to go on in. Oh, excuse me, Jack, I'll wait, I'll —

(JACK is speechless, staring at ANNE now, making a sort of nod or gesture, to indicate that she go out. But SADIE cuts in.)

SADIE. Oh, no, Miss Stanton, you're just in time. You're just in time.

ANNE. *(Looking from one to the other.)* Just in time?

SADIE. Yeah. *(She moves quickly to ANNE's side, stares into her face, then turns to JACK.)* Look, Jack Burden — look. Look at that face. *(She reaches out a finger to touch* ANNE's *cheek.*) Look, Jack Burden, it's soft and smooth — did you ever feel that face — oh, they say you used to feel that face, Jack Burden — yeah, you used to, but — *(Venomously.)* — but you don't anymore! And you know why, Jack Burden? It's because he does — he! Just like this! *(She reaches out to caress* ANNE's *cheek; then to* ANNE.) But, oh, he'll fix you — he will fix you! Let him break your back and throw you out with the garbage. Let him break your back and throw you in swamp water to drown. Let him break your —

JACK. *(*JACK *seizes her by the arms, shaking her.)* Stop it! Stop it, do you hear!

SADIE. *(Going suddenly calm, facing him.)* You. You. And he'll fix you — you pimp. Yeah, he's fixed you already — just look at yourself, Jack Burden — and he — he'll fix everybody — *(Voice rising.)* — everybody — he'll fix the whole world — like he fixed me. Oh, God, I hope he does. *(She prods her face again, then with a gesture of grief or shame covers her face and rushes out.)*

JACK. *(Staring at* ANNE, *in a muffled, agonized voice demanding an answer.)* Anne — Anne?

(She nods slowly, then lifts her right hand to touch her cheek where SADIE's *hand had been, and she and* JACK *stand in long silence while the light fades.)*

Scene 4

*(*JACK *is backing down to the Forestage from the shadow that has concealed* ANNE, *staring at the place where she was last visible. As he turns to the audience, he speaks meditatively. As he names those whom* STARK *now "has," each one in turn appears above in a spotlight until they form a sort of arch over the stage. Each is in some characteristic pose or occupation:* LUCY *at a domestic task;* SADIE *at an invisible mirror, prodding her cheeks;* ANNE, *her arms out in a beseeching gesture turning from* JACK *Downstage to* VOICE OF STARK *Offstage;* TOM *in football uniform arrogant, chewing his gum;* ADAM, *in white coat, leaning with stethoscope over invisible patient;* SUGAR *cleaning his revolver with fondling care;* TINY *smoking a cigar, polishing and admiring his diamond ring. The arrangement of persons will be indicated.)*

ANNE (1)

SADIE (2)   LUCY (3)

TOM (4)   ADAM (5)

SUGAR (6)   TINY (7)

JACK. So he had us all now. Anne — yes, Anne. Sadie —

SADIE. *(Speaking in her spotlight.)* If he thinks he can do that to me. If the bastard thinks —

JACK. Lucy — no, she hadn't left him, after all, too decent to do it while he was under impeachment. Adam—for we had changed the picture in his head. Tom Stark—the Sophomore Thunderbird, the championship with just Alton University to come and that game in the bag. Sugar—and his .38 Special. Tiny—of course, Tiny—

TINY. (*Speaks in his spotlight.*) You know how us boys all feels about you, Boss.

JACK. And—and—(*Touching himself on the chest.*)—me.

VOICE OF STARK. (*Out of darkness to one side, hoarse and demanding.*) Jack! Jack!

JACK. (*Still to the audience.*) Yes—me.

TINY. (*Leaning down toward* STARK, *from his spot.*) Boss—Boss—it's just come through. Irwin has backed the impeachment—yeah, Boss, Irwin has endorsed the impeachment—

JACK. (*Looking up at figure of* TINY *with sudden excitement and elation.*) By God—by God—one thing—one thing at least—he didn't have Irwin!

(*All figures above are fading.*)

JACK. (*To audience.*) And we whirled through the swamp night, moon-bright and owl-anguished, 75 miles an hour, and a possum tried to make it out of the brush across the slab, but he didn't make it, for Sugar just shaded that wheel, and there was no possum, and back in the swamp the owls were moaning like sweet damnation, and we were whirling back to a land of bright beaches, where I had lain beside Anne Stanton, on the beach, and the fish hawk rose and rose, lost in the blaze of light. Back to the darkness of live oaks and the scent of myrtle and mimosa at night, and the white house beyond the shades, facing the moonlit sea. And Judge Irwin—who was not Stark's, at least not yet—would be sitting in his library, surrounded by those books, like masonry, which embodied the old utterances of honor and dignity and truth.

(*The light has just been coming up dim on set to show* JUDGE IRWIN *reading. As the light fades out on Forestage, leaving* JACK *in shadow, there is the sound of a motor suddenly cut off, the shutting of a car door; then* STARK, *followed by* SUGAR, *emerges from darkness to join* JACK. *They stare at the figure of the* JUDGE, *as through a window.*)

STARK. (*Nodding toward figure of* IRWIN.) Well, the light's on. There he is.

JACK. (*Absently.*) Yes, he always did read late.

STARK. (*Shrugging, taking a step forward.*) Well.

JACK. (*Not noticing* STARK's *movement.*) There—there—that's where Anne used to sit—

STARK. (*Moving.*) Come on—come on—

JACK.—we were kids and we sat there and he read to us. We sat there and he read to us.

STARK. You left that long back.

JACK. Yes, long back.

STARK. Yeah, you left it because there was a hole in you it couldn't fill up. *(Seizing JACK by the arm, as though to wake him.)* That was then. It was then, not now.

JACK. *(Not quite out of the entrapment of the past.)* Yes — yes — it was then.

STARK. *(Releasing his grip on the arm, laying his hand paternally, compassionately, on JACK's shoulder.)* Listen, son. There's one thing you got to learn, son. *Then* is always *then*, and *now* is always *now*, and every *then* was a *now* once — and the only time it was ever real was when it was a *now* and when it is not a *now* it is nothing, and — *(His hand clenches on JACK's shoulder.)* — and now is always now, and this is now. *(JACK stands silent for an instant. STARK leans at him.)* And you're with me. And it's now. *(Whispering.)* Do you get that? Do you get that?

JACK. *(Nodding.)* Yes. I get it.

STARK. *(Speaking even more softly.)* But you're afraid. You're afraid, aren't you, Jack?

JACK. *(Angrily.)* No. No, by God!

STARK. *(Putting a hand again on JACK's shoulder, again compassionate.)* All right, son. You go on in, son. *(JACK moves a step or two toward the house. STARK turns back to SUGAR.)* Come on, Sugar. Let's wait in the car. Till the bastard scares.

JACK. *(Wheeling angrily.)* Maybe he won't scare, Boss.

STARK. *(Across the distance, still compassionate.)* There's not any man, son, won't scare when the time comes.

(STARK turns heavily away, into shadow. JACK moves toward the set, very slowly. As JACK enters, IRWIN rises, his face showing pleasure.)

IRWIN. By George — by George, Jack — it's fine to see you!

JACK. *(Embarrassed.)* Well — it's sort of late — but —

IRWIN. Never too late, son — not for Jack Burden when he can find time to drop in to see this old coot. Come in, sit down, sit down and have a drink — I was just sitting here, reading Tacitus — you know, about that lousy scramble for power, before Vespasian — you know —

JACK. I used to know.

JUDGE. Well, it makes even our time look like — *(He stops, slaps JACK on the shoulder.)* To hell with politics, Jack, ours or the Romans'! Sit down and jaw.

JACK. *(Not sitting.)* Judge, there's — *(He can't go on.)*

JUDGE. There's what? — Hey, boy, sit down.

JACK. *(Bracing himself.)* Judge, you know who I work for.

JUDGE. Let's forget it. Right now, anyway. Let's be like old times.

JACK. We can't forget it, Judge.

JUDGE. Well, it's too bad it came out the way it did. I was for him. He was letting in some fresh air. Even if he broke a few window panes to do it. But I guess I was too old-fashioned. You know, his methods — (*He spreads his hands in a rueful gesture.*)

JACK. (*Hopefully.*) Listen, Judge, if I could convince you that MacMurfee is worse than Stark. If I could provide you —

(*JACK's words trail off as the JUDGE is slowly shaking his head.*)

JUDGE. My choice is made, son.

JACK. (*Desperately.*) It's not too late — not too late, Judge —

JUDGE. What are you driving at, Jack?

JACK. Did you ever hear of the American Electric Power Company?

JUDGE. Why, of course. I was their attorney for ten years.

JACK. Judge — Judge — I beg you, withdraw your endorsement of the impeachment.

JUDGE. (*Baffled.*) But — but, Jack —

JACK. Do you remember how you got the job?

JUDGE. (*Puzzling a little.*) Yes, I guess I do — yes, there was a man named — (*He apparently can't remember.*)

JACK. Named Littlepaugh. Do you remember now? (*Pause.*) Judge, you've got to reconsider. (*As the JUDGE stares at him with a dawning comprehension, JACK leans at him.*) I beg you, I beg you, Judge.

JUDGE. (*Drawing himself up a little, hardening.*) No.

(*With a sudden effort, JACK thrusts at IRWIN a leather attaché envelope. The JUDGE takes it, looks at the contents, sits down like a man whose strength is failing him, reexamines, more carefully, the documents.*)

JACK. (*Leaning over him, grasping him by the shoulder.*) Say it's a lie, Judge. Judge, for God's sake tell me it's a God-damned lie!

JUDGE. (*Looking up at JACK, marveling to himself.*) You know, I couldn't even remember his name. Littlepaugh. His name was Littlepaugh.

JACK. Just say it's a lie!

JUDGE. Don't you think it remarkable, I didn't even remember his name?

JACK. (*Reaching down to seize the documents.*) Just say it, Judge.

JUDGE. (*Holding on to the papers as though they were precious to him.*) You know — you know — for weeks, for months sometimes, for years even, I don't remember any of this. Not any. You live — you live and try to be honorable and do good in the world, and — and forget. Tell me, Jack — did I ever do any good in the world?

JACK. (*Anguished.*) Judge — Judge —

JUDGE. You know — it's as though this — (*He indicates the papers.*) — as though this never happened. At least, not to me. Not to me.

(STARK *has silently entered the room, with* SUGAR-BOY, *and has heard the last two exchanges. Now he steps forward.*)

STARK. But I just know it did, Judge. It happened to you.

JACK. You don't know a thing. Didn't you just hear him? Didn't you just hear him say it wasn't—

STARK. Didn't I tell you the son-of-a-bitch would claim to be washed in the Blood of the Lamb?

JACK. Yeah, and I told you I'd run this my own way—

STARK. Yeah, and you were running it in the ground, if you ask me. (STARK *walks across to a table, helps himself to a drink, salutes the* JUDGE, *and tosses off the drink.*) You know, Judge, I didn't ask your permission for that drink. I am a very impatient man. That is why I am not a gentleman. I didn't ask your permission, I just walked in and I poured myself a drink. And I want to know what the hell you are going to do about— (*Pointing to papers.*) —about that.

JUDGE. (*Grimly.*) I see the picture. (*To* JACK.) You were to come in and appeal to me. Then he— (*Indicating* STARK.) —was to come in and threaten and—

JACK. (*Breaking in, defending himself.*) No—it wasn't like that. He— (*Indicating* STARK.) —he doesn't even know what's here. I wasn't telling him, not till you had a chance, a chance to—

JUDGE. (*To* JACK.) You have very tender sensibilities for a—a blackmailer. (*Then, as though taking the offensive in practical terms, swinging to* STARK.) Your— your creature here has dug up some damaging material about me.

STARK. You are human, ain't you, Judge?

JUDGE. (*Ignoring him.*) But I am a lawyer, and I assure you that you have paid for something worthless. Nothing would stick in a court of law. It happened a generation ago. There is no testimony. Everybody is dead.

STARK. (*Leaning at him, pointing at him, speaking softly.*) Except you, Judge.

JUDGE. (*Shaken.*) It wouldn't stick!

STARK. You don't live in a court, Judge. You live in the world and the world thinks you are one kind of a man, and you couldn't bear them to think different, Judge.

JUDGE. They couldn't! I've done right. I've done my duty. I've—

STARK. (*Taking a step forward, standing over the* JUDGE, *pointing down at the papers.*) And you did that. (*Before* IRWIN *can recover,* STARK *continues in the tone of hard business.*) Listen, you. Make up your mind now. Revoke your endorsement or—

(JACK *leaps at* STARK, *as though to strike him, and* SUGAR-BOY *reaches for his revolver, half drawing it, before he sees that there will be no real violence, even though* JACK *has seized the wrist of the hand* STARK *points at* IRWIN.)

JACK. God damn it, you'll give him time. You'll give him a chance.

STARK. He's had time, and now I'm—

JACK. (With lethal quiet.) You will do what I say. You will get out. You will give him time. You—

JUDGE. (Rising from his chair, squaring his shoulders.) I want no time. I don't need any time to tell you, Stark, that I will not revoke my endorsement. I would see you hounded from office. I would see you hounded from—

STARK. (Swinging to JACK.) You see—you see, he doesn't need time, he—

JACK. (Still quiet, but with a gesture of command to STARK and SUGAR.) Get out. Now. Both of you.

(STARK studies JACK and a kind of sympathetic pitying softness comes over his face. He shrugs, jerks his thumb for SUGAR to follow, and without a word goes out. JACK watches the darkness after him, then turns slowly back to IRWIN. They stare at each other for a moment, very quiet. Then the JUDGE seems to be listening to a sound from beyond.)

IRWIN. You can hear the sea. There isn't any wind, but you can hear the sea just rippling on the sand out there.

JACK. You could still say it, Judge. You could say, Jack, you got the wrong number, and Judge—I'd believe you.

IRWIN. There is a half-moon and by now it's westering and the pines on the point across the bay are black against the sky. They are black and sharp, like cut-out tin.

JACK. Oh, Judge, I'd believe you!

IRWIN. (Looking at him slowly, incredulously, as though just discovering his presence.) So you thought you could blackmail me, Jack.

JACK. Damn it—no, damn it—it wasn't that!

IRWIN. Yes, Jack, you thought you could.

JACK. You might find a prettier word.

IRWIN. I don't care about pretty words anymore. You live with words a long time. Then all at once you are old, and there are the things, not the words, and the words don't matter anymore.

JACK. (Hurriedly.) Listen, Judge. I've got to go now. I'm going, and you just sleep over things. You sleep over it and—

IRWIN. My mind is made up.

JACK. (Angrily.) If you'd just say it's the wrong number. If you'd—

IRWIN. Goodnight, Jack.

(JACK moves toward the door, slowly, seems about to go.)

IRWIN. Jack!

JACK. You don't have to settle anything now—you just wait—wait until to-morrow—

(IRWIN crosses deliberately to JACK, putting out his hand as JACK's words trail off. Puzzled, JACK takes the hand.)

IRWIN. Thank you, Jack.

JACK. Take your time, Judge—

IRWIN. I don't need any time, Jack. *(Laying his hand paternally, affectionately, on JACK's shoulder.)* And thank you, boy. Thank you.

(IRWIN turns away, as though JACK weren't there, as though he had already gone. JACK watches as he walks away. Then JACK himself moves off. Light goes down on JUDGE, then up on STARK outside. JACK joins STARK on Forestage.)

STARK. *(Avidly.)* Yeah?—Yeah?

JACK. I told him I'd give him time.

STARK. The bastard is guilty and you know it.

JACK. I said we'd do it my way. Do you get me?

STARK. *(Taking a step toward the shadows away from the house.)* OK. OK. Well, you were right about one thing. The bastard don't scare easy.

(As JACK follows STARK off, there is the sound of a shot in the darkness behind, where the house is. JACK stiffens, listening. There is only silence. STARK is listening, too.)

JACK. *(With a kind of crazy elation in his voice.)* Did you hear that? Did you hear it?—He didn't scare—He didn't scare at all!

End II

Act III

Scene 1

(The scene is a ramp, presumably within the structure of a football stadium, leading to the GOVERNOR's box. TINY, JACK, and LARSEN are waiting, JACK dour and detached, GUMMY LARSEN, a thin, cold-faced man of middle years, TINY nervous and impatient. It is the half of the championship game with Alton University.

There is the noise of the crowd above. Snatches of college cheering, etc., through-out first part of scene.)

VOICE OF ANNOUNCER. The band is moving into the field. It is spectacular and colorful. It is really worth the price of admission. The biggest university band in the country moving out to spell that S — S for State — that's the school they love — and then they sing the Alma Mater.

For dear Old State we'd give our all

For dear Old State we'd hear the call

Hear the call,

Fight and fall,

For dear Old State!

TINY. *(Looking at his watch.)* Why don't he come on?

JACK. This is a football game. This is the game for the championship. This is important.

TINY. Well, he said to have Mr. Larsen here at the half, and Mr. Larsen is a mighty busy man. *(Turning to LARSEN.)* Yeah, Mr. Larsen, he said he'd be sure to see you at the half or I wouldn't caused you this inconvenience — no siree! *(Looks at watch again.)* Why don't he come on!

JACK. He did not calculate, you might say, on the mutability of human fortune. He did not calculate on trailing Alton University by ten points at the half. He did not calculate on the Sophomore Thunderbird being back-broke from night life. He did not calculate on the Thunderbird having lead in his pants.

TINY. Yeah, and I bet Stark never calculated on getting boo-ed. Oh, no, not him! Him the Governor, getting boo-ed right here in this stadium he built 'em. Well, if I was Governor of this State, and I got boo-ed in my own stadium, I sure wouldn't keep Mr. Larsen waiting, not when he's the only guy can fix it up. Yeah, if I was under impeachment, I would —

LARSEN. *(A weak, cold, detached voice.)* He will come, Governor Duffy.

JACK. I'll just point out that Mr. Duffy is not the Governor of this state. Not yet, anyway. He is the Lieutenant Governor.

TINY. Well, he won't be Governor forever, not if he keeps Mr. Larsen waiting. It's a disgrace.

LARSEN. Stark will come, Mr. Duffy. He will come, and he will do business. He has little choice, Mr. Duffy.

JACK. *(Drily.)* The Governor, you might remember, has been known to surprise people.

LARSEN. The Governor is in difficulties. The Governor is under impeachment. There is even some comment to the effect that Judge Irwin may not have committed suicide.

JACK. *(Flaring up.)* Look here — Gummy —

TINY. *(In horror.)* Gum—Gum—*(To JACK.)* Mr. Larsen—you mean Mr. Larsen—now Mr. Larsen, he didn't say—

JACK. *(Deliberately.)* I heard what *Gummy* said, and I will instruct *Gummy* that I was there and that I know what—

LARSEN. They say you were there and—

JACK. Yes, by God, I was there, and—*(Suddenly stops.)*

LARSEN. They say you were there.

(For a moment JACK is caught, anger and outrage and pain of recollection. Then TINY breaks in, wanting to smooth matters over.)

TINY. Now, look here, Mr. Larsen is not saying anything himself, Jack. People just will talk, and Mr. Larsen is just telling you like a friend, which is what Mr. Larsen is and wants to be. He is here to help out. He knows it is not doing the Boss any good, what people are saying, and—*(Looks at watch.)*—why, God damn it, don't he come on?

(Cross Fade to Locker Room. STARK haranguing the dejected team. TOM, arrogant, chewing gum, to one side. SUGAR-BOY in background.)

STARK.—yeah, that Alton University—yeah, a school where you have to be rich to go, and those pretty little pukes' poppas paying big tuition so the little bastards can play football, and you—you let 'em cut you down. Trailing ten points. And you—

(STARK turns to a hulking tackle who sits with head in hands, helmet on floor in front of him. STARK jerks him by the forelock to demand attention.)

STARK.—you, you Talley, you ought to be back chopping cotton. You a tackle! They barreled right over you like wild hogs over a buttercup. What you got on your chest? Hair or peach-fuzz? Let 'em barrel over you just once more and—

(Cross Fade to ramp.)

TINY. *(Fawning.)* Yeah, I always said Mr. Larsen was the man we needed. That's a fact, Mr. Larsen—jeez, Mr. Larsen—

(SADIE enters.)

TINY. *(To SADIE.)* Why don't he come on—he said he—

SADIE. How should I know? They don't let me in that place where they stall the cattle between what they call halves.

TINY. It's no time to be joking, Mr. Larsen is a mighty busy man and—

SADIE. *(Turning to LARSEN with an air of just seeing him.)* Why, hello, Gummy. *(Satirically.)* I mean, hello, Mr. Larsen.

TINY. Now look here, Stark can't just treat Mr. Larsen this a-way. Mr. Larsen is a mighty busy man, and if the Boss don't realize I think I better—

SADIE. Just better what, Tiny?

TINY. Well—what I mean is—

SADIE. Just better what, Tiny?

TINY. Well, I mean, if it was me got boo-ed—right in my own stadium—I mean I would—

SADIE. So you think he is dead? You think he is finished? So you are getting ready to kick the corpse? You start talking big, huh? Because he got boo-ed out there. And do you know what those lard-handed, lard-headed, pussel-gutted, retread college twirps up there waving little flags and booing are worth? Well, I'll tell you. Exactly nothing. You a big politico and you ought to know where the vote is. Down across the tracks where I came from. And out with the hicks. And was the Boss dead last week at Sill's Crossing?

JACK. *(To TINY.)* And was he dead last week at Hodgeville?

VOICE OF STARK.—yeah, and that Legislature—that gang of hyena-headed, fice-faced, belly-dragging sons of she-wolves—they would impeach me. They said I have betrayed you. But I ask you, have I? I have given you justice. I have built you roads. I have built you schools. I am going to build you a hospital—the finest, and it will be yours. Have I betrayed you? Have I? Have I? Have I?

(STARK's voice is lost in a roar of cheering—"Willie, Willie," etc.—then cheers fade as STARK enters, dour and preoccupied.)

TINY. *(Stepping to STARK, laying a hand on STARK's sleeve.)* Look here, boss— Mr. Larsen—he—he's been waiting and—

STARK. *(Looks down at hand on sleeve.)* Well, let him wait.

TINY. But—

STARK. *(To JACK.)* Jack, you bring Gummy up to the Mansion tonight. If he still wants to come.

TINY. But you said—

STARK. I don't give a damn what I said. Right now I am going to watch this football game. And if that team don't get the lead out— *(Stares down at the hand on his sleeve. TINY jerks it off.)* That's better. *(Turns away up the ramp.)*

ANNOUNCER. It is the kick-off. It is the kick-off!

(Off-stage cheers, etc.)

TINY. *(With disgust.)* The kick-off!

ANNOUNCER. State receives on the twenty—no, the eighteen—it is Stark—it is Tom Stark—it is that old number 27—it is Tom Stark—he is loose—no—no—down on the forty-five. It is the Alton forty-five—

TINY. But you just wait, Mr. Larsen, we'll get it all fixed up—

ANNOUNCER. —there's the snap —yes —yes —it is Stark again. Old Tom is carrying the ball. —It is the come-back trail —it is the old-time Tom Stark —he's loose —he's loose —it is a touchdown!

(Cheers and band.)

TINY. The Boss now —he don't mean nothing personal. It is just the way he is. You got to get used to him. Now, Mr. Larsen, you —
LARSEN. He is a very —difficult man.
TINY. He —it's not exactly that, Mr. Larsen. It's —
ANNOUNCER. No, it is not a touchdown —Tom Stark is hurt on the play —it is four feet to go. *(Pause.)* Tom Stark is still down. Here comes the doctor.

(JACK exits up the ramp to see.)

TINY. But you'll get used to him, Mr. Larsen, and —
SADIE. Yeah, Gummy, you'll get used to him. Everybody gets used to him.

(Follows up ramp. There is cheering, then sudden silence.)

ANNOUNCER. Here they come with the stretcher. Stark is still down.

(Cheering: "Tom! Tom! Tom!" STARK enters with JACK.)

ANNOUNCER. He has not regained consciousness.
STARK. It's just the breath knocked out. It's just the breath knocked out. A tough kid like him. I'll just go down and take a look and —
ANNOUNCER. There's the snap. Look! Oh, man, look. Look at that hole Talley is making —look at that hole! It is a touchdown! Those boys will not be denied. Tom Stark —he has fixed up the old spirit. He has blazed the trail. He —
STARK. *(Listening.)* Did you get that? It's a touchdown. And it was Tom —it was Tom set it up —those boys, they're made now —they'll do it now —and it was Tom who —
ANNOUNCER. They will not be denied. It was a straight power play. It was pure power. They boiled right over the goal line. Listen to the cheers, cheers for Tom Stark —

(Cheers.)

STARK. Yeah —it was Tom —it was Tom —
ANNOUNCER. We regret to report that Tom Stark has not regained consciousness. The Governor has left his box, presumably to go to the locker room.
STARK. He's going to be all right. He is tough.
JACK. Sure.
TINY. *(Coming forward.)* Sure, Boss, that boy is tough —sure, Boss —

STARK. Sure — sure — (*But he is edging down the ramp.*) — But I — I'll just take a look — sure, he's tough — he's —

(*STARK goes out. TINY and LARSEN stand looking after him. Then TINY looks connivingly, assessingly, at LARSEN as the light fades.*)

Scene 2

(*When the light comes back on, the scene is the Mansion. STARK, in shirt sleeves, is drunk but under control. SUGAR is in the background. TINY and LARSEN face STARK.*)

TINY. (*Rubbing his hands.*) Now that is fine. That is just fine, Boss. And Mr. Larsen, I know you are happy, too. We are all happy. I always knew you two guys would make out fine. Yeah, two of the finest guys a man could ever know and work with, and —

LARSEN. (*To STARK.*) If that is all now —

TINY. (*Slapping LARSEN on the shoulders.*) And it's quite a lot, eh, Mr. Larsen — that's a contract, that hospital, eh, Mr. Larsen?

LARSEN. If that is all, I'll say goodnight, Governor.

(*STARK takes drink, turns to LARSEN.*)

STARK. It is not all.

(*STARK approaches LARSEN, glass in left hand, stops before him, points right forefinger in his face.*)

STARK. So you sold out MacMurfee. So you sold out your best pal.

LARSEN. If you will excuse me, Governor, I'll say goodnight.

STARK. So you sold him out. Well, let me tell you I never wanted your dirty hands on my hospital. But one thing, get it straight. You leave one piece of iron out of that concrete, you put in one extra teaspoonful of sand, you leave off one window-latch, and I — (*Dropping the glass, he puts his hands together before his guest, then tears them apart.*) — I'll rip you, I'll rip you! (*Suddenly quiet.*) No, I never wanted your dirty hands on it, and you know — when it's all done, maybe I'll rip you anyway. Now get out. (*A drunken gesture of dismissal and repulsion.*) Get out before I — before I — (*To TINY.*) and you — you — get out. You — you too — (*TINY and LARSEN exit, TINY fearful, LARSEN with his cold, detached manner. STARK calls hoarsely after them.*) Get out! (*Wavering on his legs, suddenly weakened, turning to JACK.*) I never wanted his dirty hands on it. But they made me. I tell you, they made me. (*Seizing JACK's lapel.*) Do you understand? Do you understand?

JACK. Sure.

STARK. They made me. They all made me. Judge Irwin made me—I tell you, he made me do it. If he hadn't shot himself—if he hadn't—

JACK. But he did.

STARK. Yeah, and he made me do it—he made me—they made me—

(*STARK is wavering away from JACK, suddenly he collapses on the couch. SUGAR comes forward and stares down at the body.*)

JACK. He's drunk.

SUGAR. He ain't d-d-d-drunk. He's just d-d-d-disappointed.

JACK. (*Shrugging.*) He's got a right to be.

(*SUGAR takes off his own coat and spreads it over STARK.*)

JACK. Maybe you better get his shoes off.

SUGAR. Naw, I'll just let him r-r-r-rest a l-l-little, then get him to bed.

JACK. (*Turning away.*) Yeah, let him rest.

(*Slow Fade-out. Pause in total darkness, then telephone ringing. After a moment light on phone, then JACK's face visible, very dull and sleepy, as he answers.*)

JACK. Yes—yes—Burden—

VOICE OF SUGAR. M-M-M-Mister Burden—

JACK. Oh, it's you, Sugar.

VOICE OF SUGAR. G-g-g-get to the hos-hos-hos-pital fast. The B-B-Boss's boy. They gonna op-op-operate, now.

JACK. Yes—yes—

VOICE OF SUGAR. D-D-Doc Stanton gonna op-op-op-operate.

(*Blackout.*)

Scene 3

(*Hospital waiting room. STARK enters, disheveled, and sits in a chair, trying to look at a magazine. LUCY sits very stiff across from him, hands folded on her lap, looking straight before her, into the air. Occasionally her lips move, as in prayer. Finally STARK flings the magazine down, and stands up, staring almost angrily at her, at some distance.*)

STARK. What are you thinking?

LUCY. (*Quietly, distantly.*) Not anything. Not anything, Willie.

STARK. (*Approaching, anger breaking through.*) Yes, you were. You were thinking something.

LUCY. (*Sadly and distantly.*) Oh, Willie—Willie—

(Under that pitying, distant gaze, STARK slowly sits back down in his chair, leans heavily and picks up the magazine, thumbs it, staring at it with unseeing eyes. Suddenly he flings the magazine down, and stands.)

STARK. You were. You damned well were thinking something! *(She looks at him from the sad distance, and says nothing.)* I tell you he's going to be all right. That boy is young and strong and healthy. He is strong and tough. And Dr. Stanton, everybody knows he's the best. You couldn't get a better man to operate. Tom — he's — going to be all right. And I'll tell you what all right is, too. It is being just like he was — Tom Stark — yeah, young and strong and tough as whit-leather — yeah, and that grin — come on, admit it, he's quite a kid, isn't he — come on, Lucy — and the way he can use his hands — not like me, sort of clumsy from grabbing plow handles — not Tom — *(STARK lets his arms hang loose from the shoulders, hands a little forward, fingers spread for a grip, weaving them slightly, like a wrestler coming to the crouch.)* And on the field — when he comes on the field — *(STARK is like a man watching a spectacle, rapt. A nurse enters, carrying a vase of flowers. STARK, ignoring her obvious errand, steps to her, puts his hand timidly on her arm, beseechingly.)* Is there — is there any —

NURSE. *(Not unsympathetically, but coolly.)* I don't know anything, Governor. I'm sure they'll let you know as soon as Dr. Stanton comes from the operating room.

STARK. What did you come in for?

NURSE. Why — why, to change the flowers.

STARK. *(Looking at the vase in her hand, with surprise.)* Oh. *(Timidly, he reaches to the vase she carries and takes out a flower. He stands there, ridiculously holding it, while she exchanges vases, and goes out. He watches her out, stares down at the flowers, then at LUCY. He speaks darkly, suspiciously.)* What did she come in for? *(LUCY does not answer. She is staring beyond him, and her lips are moving. STARK crushes the flower in his hand, flings it down.)* You don't think he's going to get well.

LUCY. I don't know what to think, Willie.

STARK. You don't want him to get well.

LUCY. I never said that, Willie.

STARK. No — *(Stepping angrily a step toward her.)* No, but you said — you said — *(His voice gives out. He is standing there with one hand in the air, emptily, his lips moving, but no sound, while his face works. Suddenly, with something like an expression of surprise and marvel, he discovers his hand in the air, and examines it curiously. All at once he jerks it back, clenches it at his side, at the same time clenching his left hand in the same position, swings on his heel, turns to his chair, sits, stares at the floor, then leans forward and covers his face with his hands. He stays in this position a long time. After awhile, not lifting his head, he speaks.)* I don't know what happened. It happened a long time ago. It was like something happened at night, in the house, and you don't hear a sound in the dark, but you know something is happening.

LUCY. *(Distantly.)* Be quiet, Willie. Let's just sit and be quiet.

STARK. *(After a wait, still not looking up.)* It was like something happening in darkness. I don't know what happened between us.

LUCY. Let's be quiet, Willie.

STARK. *(After a delay.)* You used to love me. You loved me, once.

LUCY. *(Delay.)* I won't deny it. I loved you.

STARK. You don't now. I know you don't.

LUCY. *(With sudden weariness.)* Oh, let's don't talk. I don't feel anything now. I'm just numb, right now.

STARK. *(Delay, then suddenly rising, as though jerked to his feet by a discovery.)* Yeah—yeah—that's why! It's because you don't love me. That's why you want him to die! (LUCY *looks at him with dawning horror, seeming to draw back in her chair from him as he stands there, staring accusingly at her. After a moment, he begins to move his head almost imperceptibly from side to side, like a man coming out of a trance, trying to make things come clear. He moves his hands in an uncertain, weaving motion. When he speaks his voice is weak. He is not really speaking to her, but out of some inner depth.)* I don't know what's wrong with me. I don't know what makes me talk like that. Something makes me talk like that. *(He sits down, head again in hands. Picks up magazine again, then lays it down, and again puts head in hands. Finally he looks up with an air of false excitement.)* Listen! Listen here, Lucy, you know what I'm going to do?

LUCY. No.

STARK. *(Rising.)* I tell you what. I'm going to name my new hospital and medical center for him. It's going to be—it'll be the Tom Stark Hospital and Medical Center, and when they dedicate it, he'll be sitting up there on the platform, and— *(Seeing her begin to shake her head in an unutterable sadness, he stops, then questions her angrily.)* Didn't you hear me?

LUCY. Oh, Willie—

STARK. Don't you think it's a great idea?

LUCY. *(Staring up at him.)* Yes, that's what it will be. That's what it will all come to.

STARK. What? What are you talking about?

LUCY. Oh, can't you see? Can't you ever see?

STARK. See? See what?

LUCY. *(Rising, stepping toward him.)* Listen—I had a baby—I had a little boy— we had a boy, he was ours—but you, all you want is just the name being yelled, all you want is the name in the papers, all you want is—is his name cut in a piece of stone. But our boy— *(Desperately.)* Oh, where is our boy?

(STARK is frozen in a gesture of protest, staring at her. She slowly seems to sink away from her own words. She is in a posture of sad listening. When she speaks it is a voice gone very small, almost childlike, after her outburst.) It's raining. It looked like rain when we came in. It's raining outside, Willie —

(He stands in the same posture, unable to move for a moment, then slowly his hand sinks a little, and he begins to listen to the rain. A NURSE opens the door, and steps to one side. DR. STANTON enters. He is pale and withdrawn, simply standing there, as the eyes of the parents find him. Very slowly he shakes his head. Both parents make a movement toward him, then stop.)

ADAM. I'm sorry. I am very sorry.

STARK. *(Seizing ADAM's arm.)* What did you do? What did you do?

ADAM. There was a fracture of the fifth and sixth cervical vertebrae. With serious complications. We had no choice but the operation. Mrs. Stark took full responsibility when we could not get you. I am sorry for the outcome.

(During ADAM's speech, STARK has been staring into his face as though trying to read something beyond the words. He suddenly releases his grip on ADAM. LUCY sinks back into her chair, hands clenched on her knees, staring at the floor. STARK stands for a moment, then makes a gesture of anguish and anger. As he makes the gesture the light goes down on ADAM and NURSE, so that their withdrawal from the set is scarcely noticeable. STARK and LUCY are now seen as more isolated in the little area of light. STARK turns toward LUCY, tentatively, reaching out his hand.)

STARK. Lucy —

LUCY. *(Looking up, seeing the outstretched hand.)* I've been in the dark alone — by myself — and dark ticked like a watch, and I remembered —

STARK. *(A step closer.)* Lucy —

LUCY. — and I remembered you laughed and said he was *your* son — your son, not mine.

STARK. *(In a throttled, anguished tone.)* Oh, Lucy!

LUCY. And now you have your son, but you cannot have mine. *(She rises, steps toward him, an air of triumph coming over her.)* — You have your son now. Do with him what you want. You can use him the way you use everything, everything in the world. But you cannot have mine. For he — for he — *(She looks away, groping toward an elated truth.)* — for he is going to live where the yelling and cheering doesn't matter. He's going to live where the newspapers just don't come. He's going to live — with me. With me, in my heart. *(She waits again for her knowledge, then suddenly puts her hand to her heart.)* And be safe — be safe from —

(*STARK reaches out, but she recoils from him.*)

STARK. Stop — stop, Lucy — you talk like I had — like I had killed him, Lucy.

LUCY. (*Coming out of her elation, growing aware of him, shaking her head a little.*) No, you didn't mean to. But you — you, Willie — you ruin everything you touch.

STARK. (*Reaching out his hand.*) Give me your hand, Lucy.

LUCY. (*Shrinking.*) No — no, you can't touch him.

STARK. Oh, Lucy — I love you!

LUCY. No, Willie. You don't, Willie.

STARK. But I do, I do! You've got to believe me.

LUCY. If you had loved me, you would have made things all different.

STARK. Different? Different? What do you mean — different?

LUCY. If you had loved me — if you had loved anything — oh, love would have made a world that love could live in.

STARK. But I do love you!

LUCY. Oh, if you had, all the world would be different. Different — yes, different — not everything ruined when you touch it.

STARK. (*Again groping.*) Oh, Lucy — give me your hand.

LUCY. Whatever you touched, Willie, you ruined. You ruined it.

STARK. (*Hand groping for her.*) Are you afraid? Are you afraid?

LUCY. (*She backs from him, then sinks into her chair.*) If I could only believe — if it were not dark, if it were not dark, Willie — if I could only believe now —

(*STARK drops to his knees before her, his hand out but not touching her yet.*)

STARK. I have come a long way, and I didn't see the way, and — oh, Lucy, I have horrors in my head — they lurch and grind, like street cars.

(*He seizes her hand, and lets his head sink into her lap. She is perfectly passive for a time, not even looking down at him, her eyes fixed across the room. But after a little she lays her free hand on his head and begins, slowly, to stroke his hair. When she speaks her voice is that of distant reverie.*)

LUCY. He was a good baby when he was little. He never cried.

(*Fade-out*)

(*Out of the shadow to the Forestage comes TALLEY, the tackle who had been with STARK in the locker room scene. Crepe is on his arm, a long flowing streamer. His uniform is a new one, untarnished, and his hair is neatly combed and slicked down. But as he speaks he will rumple it in agitation and embarrassment. There is music of a football band — the last of the alma mater —*

Give our all
Fight and fall
For dear Old State.)

TALLEY. I didn't give a durn. I didn't give one durn who saw me cryin. Marchin along behind that coffin — Ole Tom's coffin — and Tom's dirty jersey — the one he played in that last time — ole number 27 — that jersey layin there on the coffin —

(Interruption of band:

For dear Old State we'd give our all
For dear Old State we'd fight and fall.)

TALLEY. Yeah, and when we come to the grave, we throwed our helmets in the grave — it was a tribute to Ole Tom — and then I thought — it ain't no lie, I thought my heart was gonna break. Throwed our helmets on Ole Thunderbird. Yeah, my heart was breakin', but we did'n let Ole Tom down. We had chawed up that Alton team, and the Boss — Boss — naw, we ain't never gonna let you down. *(STARK appears quietly out of the shadows. TALLEY sees him, rushes to him.)* Let you and Ole Tom down. Naw, Boss. Naw —

(TALLEY has seized STARK's hand, jerking it like a child. STARK is gazing pityingly down at him as he half crouches, like a tackle dropping into the line.)

STARK. You're a good boy, Talley. It's all right, Talley.

TALLEY. Durn, Boss — durn — you called me a buttercup, Boss —

STARK. That was a long time ago, Talley. It was a thousand years ago, fellow. It's all over, Talley. *(Pause.)* If anything is ever over.

TALLEY. You said they come barreling over me like I was a buttercup. But they ain't gonna do it. Never no more, Boss. Not even if it's the whole durn world coming.

(He has crouched down, ready for the play, tears down his cheeks now.)

STARK. *(Putting a hand paternally, almost pityingly on his shoulders.)* Atta-boy, Talley. Don't you ever let 'em come barreling over you.

TALLEY. *(Digging his toes in, shaking his head to get rid of the tears, wiping his nose quickly on a sleeve.)* Naw, Boss, they ain't barreling over me. It ain't peach-fuzz on my chest, Boss — naw —

STARK. *(Quietly.)* No, son, don't let 'em barrel over you.

(Fade-out on Forestage.)

Scene 4

(STARK's office in the Capitol, JACK and SADIE present. TINY, wearing a histrionically doleful expression, followed by two men, enters, sees that STARK is not present, and dismisses his gloom.)

TINY. How's tricks?

JACK. *(Dourly.)* Tricks is OK.

TINY. The Boss—you seen the Boss?

JACK. Not yet.

TINY. *(Assuming his doleful expression, shaking his head.)* Jeez, it is sure tough. It is what I always call tragic. A good clean square-shooting kid like that. It is what I call tragic.

JACK. You needn't practice your gloom on me.

MAN. *(To JACK.)* Is he coming?

TINY. Sure, he'll come. He'll take it on the chin. He won't let it prey on his mind. Not the Boss, he's tough.

SADIE. Oh, no, it's just his boy died. *(Pause.)* Even if he was a little bastard.

TINY. *(Readjusting his face to the doleful subject.)* Yeah, yeah, it was sad. But that preacher—at the funeral—he sure said a beautiful sentiment. And the flowers. Take those flowers from the Fifth Ward! And the telegrams— *(He prods a great pile on the desk.)* —telegrams of condolence and sympathy. The money that has been spent on flowers and telegrams. It just goes to show how folks love the Boss. I was just saying to the boys here— *(Hooking his thumb at the men who had entered with him.)* —yeah, I was just saying—

SADIE. You better save it for the Boss where it will help your case.

(SADIE has seen STARK enter, even at the last words of TINY's speech. Now he stands there behind the others, who one by one become aware of his presence. He is gray in the face, but in command of himself.)

TINY. *(Trying to take charge of the situation.)* Good morning, Boss. How you making it, Boss? We want you to know how us boys all feel for you, Boss. And look, Boss— *(Indicating the pile of telegrams.)* —condolence and sympathy, Boss. Now I was just saying, it goes to show how folks love Old Willie.

(STARK goes to the desk, not listening, prods the pile, then sweeps them to the floor, and turns to SADIE.)

STARK. Get this muck out of here.

(TINY and the politicians begin to edge out of the office, sensing that the occasion has gone sour.)

STARK. Tiny, you wait.

(TINY waits uneasily. STARK turns to SADIE.)

STARK. Get me my files on the Morton Bridge and Construction Company and— *(TINY perks up, shows puzzlement and apprehension.)* —and the tax records of the American Electric — *(Swinging to TINY.)* —yeah, that is Gummy Larsen, too.

TINY. But, Boss —

STARK. *(To JACK, very calmly.)* And while it is on my mind, you might do a complete job on Gummy. If you understand what I mean.

(TINY is making some gesture of stunned protest, but can't speak.)

SADIE. I thought you were buddies with Gummy these days.

STARK. I love old Gummy. But will he love me when he hears the news?

TINY. But, Boss —

STARK. Yes, Tiny, I love Gummy, but it's you he feels closest to. And it's only proper that his nearest and dearest should break the news to him. You can lay your arm on his shoulder. Like this, Tiny. *(And STARK demonstrates the gesture of manly comfort.)*

TINY. *(Agitated.)* Huh, Boss? Huh?

STARK. *(Jerking his arm off TINY's shoulder, speaking almost gaily.)* Tiny — the deal is off!

TINY. But, Boss — Mr. Larsen, he's got it all fixed — fixed to deliver and —

STARK. Maybe he won't want to unfix it either —

TINY. But the deal, Boss —

STARK. Maybe he won't want to unfix it when I've worked over the tax records of Morton Bridge and American Electric. You know, Tiny, I had just forgotten something there, maybe. And when Jack gets through digging. Yeah, maybe Gummy won't want to unfix.

TINY. *(Pulling himself together.)* Listen, Boss, you got to remember that Mr. Larsen is a very, very big man. He has a lot of this State sewed up, and has a —

STARK. Larsen may think, and you may think, that he owns a piece of the Legislature. Yeah, and MacMurfee may think he owns a piece. But it won't stick. He may give 'em fifty bucks, but I am going to give 'em galloping paralysis. Come the next election, there is going to be a bear market on farmhands and barbers, for if there's anything cheap around here it is statesmen and sweet potatoes. They both grow on pore ground. And as for you — *(He whips his forefinger at TINY, like a pistol.)* — if you don't quit fooling with Larsen —

TINY. Boss — Boss — I wouldn't cross you — I —

STARK. —you may be wearing a three-hundred-dollar suit and a diamond ring, but on the hoof you are crow-bait, and boy, I can strip you to the blast.

TINY. You got me wrong, Boss — you got me wrong —

STARK. Now get out.

(TINY goes out. STARK stands heavily in the middle of the floor. JACK moves toward the exit.)

JACK. I'll be getting on it.

(*STARK makes some slight signal of recognition, and good-bye, and continues to stand there after JACK has gone out. SADIE is watching him curiously. STARK moves heavily, almost like an aging man, to sit down.*)

STARK. Yeah. (*Broodingly.*) Yeah.

SADIE. Yeah, what?

STARK. You got to start somewhere.

SADIE. What?

STARK. Skip it.

SADIE. Skip what?

STARK. (*Not noticing her.*) Yeah —you start, and then you find it is just the same.

SADIE. What? What's the same?

STARK. (*Not even looking at her.*) You find you're just heaving yourself around like you did. You find yourself saying the same things. You find yourself heaving your weight around just like you did. You find yourself just —

SADIE. (*With sour solicitude.*) Boss —you sick, Boss?

STARK. (*Still not looking at her.*) Anne Stanton, she —

SADIE. That bag.

STARK. It's over. Over between us.

SADIE. (*Tensing, taking a step forward, her face lighting up.*) Yeah —yeah —

STARK. Yes, it's over.

SADIE. (*Joyously, at him now, leaning over him.*) Boss —Boss, I always knew —I knew you'd —

STARK. (*Swinging in his chair to face her, lifting a hand to stay her outburst, rising from his chair, very deliberately.*) Sadie, I want to tell you something.

SADIE. (*Still excited, but a little confused.*) Willie —

STARK. I'm going back to my wife, Sadie.

SADIE. To that screwball! To that sewing circle! Hah, don't make me laugh.

STARK. I'm going back to her. For good.

SADIE. (*Slowly, incredulously.*) To that sewing circle? And dump me? (*Suddenly bursting out.*) Oh, I'll be damned if you —

STARK. (*Lifting his hand again.*) If she will have me.

SADIE. (*Slowly and venomously.*) I wish to Christ I had never had you. Yeah, and where would you be now? Back slopping the hogs, where you came from. And what did I ever get? A couple of hand-me-down kisses and a pinch on the ear and — (*Mimicking.*) "That's a good girl, Sadie," and —yeah, on a wet night or when you're too tired to go on the prowl. Yeah, and what you were when I took you in hand!

STARK. I don't know what I was, Sadie. It's been a long time, Sadie. But whatever it was that I was then, it was better —

SADIE. I'll tell you what it was. It was a crummy little wide-eyed hick that didn't know cow-patties from porridge and was going to save the world and was wearing Lucy's Christmas tie—yeah, "Love to Darling Willie from his loving wife."

STARK. Whatever it was, Sadie, I'm going to try to find him again. You've got to start somewhere, Sadie. But, Sadie— *(He takes a step toward her.)* —I know you did your best for me, and I want— *(He takes her face between his hands and looks down at her.)* —I want to be your friend.

(She has stood for an instant with her face between his hands as though expecting a kiss, as though believing his gesture more than his words, her own arms lifting a little as though about to go around him in an embrace. Now she jerks back.)

SADIE. You—oh, you—

(She slaps him, stares at him in surprise at her act, as he stands there unmoved, looking sadly at her. She takes another step back, and another. The light is fading on STARK. She has begun to press her fingertips into the flesh of her face, as though finding there the explanation of all. In the same backing motion she is moving to the Forestage, staring at the darkness where STARK has been. As the light fades on SADIE, it comes up on ANNE to one side of the Forestage. She too is staring after the vanished form of STARK.)

ANNE. Oh, I understand now. I understand now, and would not have it otherwise. And what I had loved in Willie was what, in the end, made him leave me. I had loved him because I knew there was a truth in him, and if, in the end, he found that truth, why should I complain that the truth had no place for me? But oh, it was hard, it was hard.

Scene 5

(On another part of the stage SADIE has become visible leaning toward TINY, whispering to him.)

SADIE. Sure, he'll ruin us. He'll ruin you. Yes, for Larsen will blame you. Then what? Then what?

TINY. *(Breathless with alarm.)* Yeah—yeah—

SADIE. But do you know what he's done?

TINY. Huh?

SADIE. He's going back to his wife.

TINY. Sweet Jesus!

SADIE. Listen, do you think Dr. Stanton knows he rolled Little Sister in the hay?

TINY. *(Surprised.)* Don't he? I figgered he got that hospital job just to shut up and —

SADIE. Listen, you fool, he doesn't know it. But if he knew it — the kind of man he is, if he knew it, and knew Little Sister is getting her spare chemise cleaned out of the Boss's bureau drawer because —

TINY. Huh?

SADIE. —because Stanton killed his boy. Operated on him and killed him. And knew that the Boss is going to fire Stanton himself and —

TINY. Is that a fact? Is it all a fact?

SADIE. Hell, no, it's not a fact. But Stanton will think so when — *(She seizes* TINY *by his lapel, drawing him.)* —when you tell him!

TINY. *(Drawing back in alarm.)* Me tell him!

SADIE. *(Not releasing her grip on the lapels.)* When *you* tell him.

TINY. Sure — sure, I'll get one of the boys.

SADIE. Put it in the paper, you fool.

TINY. Well, now —

SADIE. Sure, you're afraid when you tell him. I don't blame you. Not if he's what I figure — and pray to Christ — he is. But maybe you'll escape with your life. And then — *(She jerks the lapels, releases them, and steps back.* TINY *seems paralyzed, wetting his lips but not speaking.)* Can't you for once be human? Can't you for once be haf-himan? Sucking around all your life, letting somebody spit on you and grin when they spit for the money in it. Couldn't you for once forget you're a coward — just one time do something because you're sick of being spit on? Couldn't you once be just half-human?

TINY. *(With dry lips.)* Yeah. Yeah.

SADIE. Just half-human, for all you do is tell Stanton. He does it.

TINY. Yeah. Yeah.

SADIE. *(Turning away indifferently.)* Take it or leave it. It's all your funeral.

TINY. All right. All right.

SADIE. *(Wearily.)* All right.

TINY. *(Enthusiasm growing.)* Yeah, all right. *(Pause.)* And gee, Sadie, you got something on the ball. You'll get something out of this, bet your bottom dollar.

SADIE. *(Wearily.)* I could have been rich, long back, paddling in this muck.

TINY. *(Stepping to her, putting his right hand between her shoulder blades, gently massaging the area.)* Now, Baby, money ain't everything. I didn't mean just money. I meant I—

SADIE. *(Through tight lips.)* Take your God-damn greasy hands off me.

(Light out on SADIE *and* TINY. *Comes up on* ADAM *at a desk. The only light is from a reading lamp on the desk.* ADAM's *hands are spread out under the lamp on the desk. He is staring down at them, and speaking in a harsh whisper.)*

ADAM. — and I had thought there was something to live by. And I had thought there was something to live for —

ANNE. *(Approaching, imploring.)* Oh, Adam — *(He retreats from her.)* Oh, can't you see? Oh, can't you understand?

ADAM. *(With tense quietness.)* Oh, yes, oh, yes, I understand. *(Spreading his hands as though they were gummed in some sticky substance.)* Listen — don't you remember — remember when we were children —

ANNE. *(Hopefully.)* Yes — oh, yes — I remember —

ADAM. Well. Remember there was that foul old cripple, the hunchback living down in the swamp, and the sharecropper children, they called him Dirty Dan and they rubbed his hump? Remember? They rubbed the hump for luck. Well, you — *(A mirthless, painful laugh.)* — well, you have found something fouler. Oh yes, and you rubbed the hump for luck — for luck — yes, you —

ANNE. *(Again imploring.)* Oh, Adam — remember what we were — what we used to be — I'm Anne — I'm Anne — oh, help me!

(As she lays hands on him he jerks away.)

ADAM. Don't touch me!

ANNE. *(Again laying hands on him.)* Oh, Adam —

ADAM. Oh, I'll not be the happy pimp. Oh, no — *(He flings her from him.)* No — no — and I — and I — *(With an air of dawning, joyous discovery.)* why, I'll — I'll —

ANNE. Oh, Adam.

ADAM. *(Coming out of the trance of discovery, staring into her face, then turning, ready to rush out.)* Oh, now I see! Oh, now!

(ADAM rushes out. ANNE hangs a moment on the back of a chair as the light is fading; she jerks herself up, and tries to follow, calling.)

ANNE. Adam! Adam!

(Blackout.)
(Voices in total darkness.)

VOICE OF ANNE. — Jack — Jack — you've got to find him — find him —

VOICE OF JACK. What? What?

VOICE OF ANNE. Find Adam — find him — oh, it was awful — find him before he does something awful — find him so I can tell him — can try to explain — he's run out somewhere — somewhere — it's raining — oh, Jack — oh, find him —

(Sound of rain, running steps, etc.)

VOICE OF JACK. Taxi! Taxi! *(Slamming door, motor, brakes.)* Dr. Stanton—I said, has Dr. Stanton been here—

VOICE OF NURSE. No—no—he has an operation in the morning, but—

VOICE OF JACK. Taxi! Taxi! Taxi!

(Spotlight up on ADAM on stage alone.)

VOICE OF ADAM. If they had known me. If they had known me as they should have known me through all the years, they would have known where to find me. They would have known my last necessity.

(With the last sentence, ADAM is making motions of a man trying to clean his hands of a sticky foulness.)
(Again blackout.)

Scene 6

(The scene is the lobby of the Capitol—an indicated arch, the statue of some statesman rising in shadow, etc. ADAM, his raincoat dripping, his hair disheveled, is standing to Stage Right. For a moment there is silence, then the faint, distant hum of voices, shouts, cheers, occasionally, "WILLIE, WILLIE! WE WANT WILLIE!" Figures begin to pass and repass in the shadowy back area of the stage. One of the figures stops, peers toward ADAM, comes forward.)

FIRST MAN. *(Excited.)* Great God, hear that! Boy, there's a million folks out there in front of this Capitol—they done come in from everywhere—come in from somewhere—back up in the creeks where you can't get mail—back in the hills. Great God, they have come in for the Boss!

ADAM. Yes.

SECOND MAN. Boy, I tell you, if that Legislature votes tonight to impeach the Boss, that crowd will tear 'em apart. Boy, you wouldn't catch me voting wrong, not tonight with that crowd out there.

ADAM. Yes.

SECOND MAN. Boy, I'm here to state, if I was voting, I would be durn sure to vote right.

ADAM. Yes.

(This MAN, too, begins to realize that ADAM is not attending. He studies him a second, shakes his head embarrassed, turns to go.)

SECOND MAN. Well—well, so long.

(Goes.)

ADAM. You labor all your life for it, but learn in the end that innocence is easy. It is as easy and unsought as the childhood recollection. It is as easy as the most casual farewell. It is as easy—

(There is a roar from beyond, then the voice of STARK out of the darkness high up at Center Stage. Then the light comes on STARK from the waist up, addressing the audience as though it were the crowd before the capitol dome of the building. Behind STARK is the impression of the great dome of the building. Below, the light is now low on ADAM, who after lifting his head to the first roar has sunk back into the flow of his being.)

STARK'S VOICE AND THEN STARK. *(The voice has started low, as in the distance, now, with the light, rising to fullness.)* —and my enemies say that what I have done has not been done for love of you but for love of power. Do you believe that?

VOICE OF CROWD. No! No! No!

STARK. *(Lifting his arms as to still the shouts.)* What man knows the truth of his heart? But I shall look in my heart, and I hope to find some love for you. Some little, at least. *(He waits as there is a stunned silence from the crowd.)* There is something else I must tell you. My enemies say that I have used pressure. Threats. Deals. Bribery. Corruption. That I have preyed on the weaknesses of men. Do you believe it?

VOICE OF CROWD. *(A little less promptly than before.)* No! No! No!

STARK. *(Lifting his arms again for silence.)* It is true. *(Then in silence, he continues, more quietly.)* I will say this, but not to excuse myself. I will say that I had thought it the only way. But now I ask you: Is it the only way? Now from the bottom of my heart, from the secrecy of my soul, I ask you. Is it the only way?

VOICE OF CROWD. *(After a longer silence.)* Willie! Willie! We want Willie!

STARK. *(Lifting his arms for silence.)* You must give me an answer. You must give me an answer to live by. They are now in there voting on me, but, however that vote comes out, I will have that thing. No vote can stop me, for I will have one thing, and no man can stop me from having that thing. No man can stop me, for— *(Here there is a lift of the arms, the flash of the old oratorical savagery.)* —there's blood on the moon. Blood on the moon! *(There is an answering roar from the crowd, guttural and savage. STARK goes suddenly quiet, slowly lowering his arms.)* And I must tell you what that one thing is that I would have, and no man may deny me. I want to be able to stand and look you in the eye. I want to be able to stand and look you in the eye. I want that much innocence.

(The light has been fading out on STARK, and his last words are in darkness. The light comes up now on ADAM, who resumes his soliloquy.)

ADAM. I have lived to learn now that innocence is as easy as the late tide's turn. It is as easy as the late light of a spring afternoon on the yellow jonquils under the maples. I remember what delight was. I remember how thin and far in summer, on a summer afternoon, a shout would come across the bay. I remember how—I remember—yes, I remember—

(*STARK has entered at Stage Left, rear, with* SUGAR *and others,* JACK *among them. There is a good deal of ad lib congratulations to* STARK: *"Boss—Boss, you done it!"—"Boss, they'd die for you now, Boss"—"Ain't nobody gonna dare impeach you now, Boss, not with that crowd worked up like you done"—"Yeah, Boss, folks crying like kids"—"Hear that yelling." Distant shouts of "Willie! Willie! Willie!" Messengers come and go with messages.* ADAM *has been so bemused that he does not notice* STARK's *approach. He looks up just as* STARK *sees him and comes toward him with his hand out.*)

STARK. Doc—Dr. Stanton—you're the very man I—

(ADAM *takes a step toward* STARK, *and seems to be putting out his hand in greeting, but suddenly there is a revolver in it.* ADAM *fires twice.* STARK *stands for an instant, wavering, surprise on his face.*)

STARK. But, Doc—Doc—it's me,—it's me—

(SUGAR *has leaped forward, revolver in hand, and as* STARK *falls he shoots* ADAM, *and after* ADAM *is down continues to fire into the body. Then he flings down the weapon and leans over* STARK. *Meanwhile,* JACK *has raised* STARK's *head, and the crowd is gathering from the shadows.*)

SUGAR. D-d-d-does it h-hurt much, B-B-Boss? Does it hurt much?

(STARK *is trying to lift his head.*)

STARK. It was the—Doc, Jack. It was the Doc—
SUGAR. D-d-d-does it hurt much? Does it h-h-hurt?
STARK. The Doc—what did he—shoot me—for—Jack?
JACK. God damn it—God damn it—I don't know—
STARK. Jack—Jack—there's something you got—got to believe—
JACK. Boss—
STARK. It might—have been different—Jack. Everything might have been—different.

(STARK's *head sags.*)

JACK. Boss—Boss—can you hear me?
STARK. (*Slightly reviving.*) You got to believe that—Jack—we might have done

different — everything might have been — different — you — got — to believe that —

(Light is fading off STARK's *body as* JACK *rises and swings around Forestage.)*

Epilogue

*(*JACK *swings forward from* STARK's *body to the Forestage as the light goes down on the group behind him and up again on the rostrum where* SHIPWORTH, *with* DUFFY *and the others in the background, is continuing his speech, as in the Prologue.)*

JACK. *(Vehemently.)* I believe it, Boss — Boss, I believe it! *(Catching himself, as though just becoming aware of the audience.)* I believe it, because if we do not believe it —

SHIPWORTH. *(Pantomime becomes words.)* — as I was saying, in the great pattern of cause and effect, the past could not have been different from what it was. Therefore, it does not matter how this hospital came to be, and —

JACK. Stop! — Oh, it matters, it matters! It matters because everything is part of everything else. All the past — the past is part of —

SHIPWORTH. *(Unaware of* JACK's *interruption.)* Let us accept this hospital for what good it is and not disturb ourselves with metaphysical speculation.

JACK. Fool! Fool! I have told you how it happened. I have told you how —

SHIPWORTH. For it is not important what manner of man Willie Stark was, nor should we —

*(*STARK *appears above, as in the Prologue, grave and composed, speaking above the heads of the audience, as though into distance.)*

STARK. I was a man and I lived in the world of men. And being a man, I did not know what I was, nor what might be the fullness of man. But being a man, I yearned toward that definition, even in the dark night of my ignorance.

(As in the Prologue, LUCY, SADIE, *etc., appear on the Forestage with characteristic posture and gesture —* LUCY *with arms lifting toward* WILLIE, SADIE *first prodding her cheeks, as she stares up at him, then covering her face with shame and guilt,* ADAM *in a gesture of denunciation,* ANNE *with face lifted and expectant,* SUGAR *rapt.)*

STARK. *(Continuing.)* I say this not for extenuation or for forgiveness, for I have no need now for those things. All I need now is truth. Whatever its name, or face.

JACK. (*Still looking up at* STARK, *speaking in meditative echo.*) Whatever its name, or face. (*Turning toward* ANNE.) Oh, Anne — oh, Anne —

ANNE. (*Still looking at* STARK.) Whatever its name, or face.

JACK. Oh, Anne, if we can understand the truth — if we can understand the truth of the past — (*Lifting his arms toward her.*) — the awful truth that the past might have been different — if we believe that, then we may create the future.

ANNE. (*A step toward him tentatively.*) Do you believe it — oh, Jack, do you believe it?

JACK. Yes, I believe it. For if we don't believe it — (*He takes a step toward her, again lifting his arms.*) Oh, Anne — (*Another step.*) — for if we don't believe it, how can we bear to watch the living and the dying. We could not bear to be men. Oh, Anne!

(*She comes to his arms, and in his embrace, she looks up at him and speaks quietly.*)

ANNE. I believe it, for if I had not come to believe it, I could not have lived.

(*As they stand there, embracing, the light begins to fade on them and on the other figures on the Forestage. It is still on* STARK, *above.*)

SUGAR. (*Taking a step to come closer to* STARK, *as the light begins to fade on him too.*) The B-B-B-Big B-B-Boss — he k-k-kin talk so good!

(*Dim out.*)

End

All the King's Men

(A PLAY)

BY

ROBERT PENN WARREN

All the King's Men *was presented by Michel Bouché, Arnold M. Brockman, and Iris Michaels at the East 74th Street Theatre, New York City, on October 16, 1959, with the following cast:*

(in order of appearance)

PROFESSOR   Stan Watt
TINY DUFFY   Roger C. Carmel
WILLIAM LARSEN   Jay Kobler
TOM STARK   Donald Quine
A MAN   Stephen J. Hall
JACK BURDEN   John Ragin
ANNE STANTON   Joan Harvey
LUCY STARK   Mary Van Fleet
DR. ADAM STANTON   Richard Kneeland
JUDGE IRWIN   Alex Reed
SUGAR-BOY   Will Corry
SADIE BURKE   Marian Reardon
WILLIE STARK   Clifton James
MOTHER OF JACK BURDEN Allyn Monroe
SLADE   Jay Kobler
A SECOND MAN   Stephen J. Hall
FREY   Stephen J. Hall
A THIRD MAN   Stephen J. Hall
THE CROWD
Elizabeth Farley
Edna Jean Lundy
Ralph Mauer
Jay Kobler
Patricia Doyle
Alfred de Graaff

Directed by Mark Schoenberg
Production designed by Gary Smith
Costumes by Sue Spector
Lighting by Jules Fisher
Technical direction by Ivor Balding
Associate producers: Eugene Koblents [and] Gerald Marks

The action takes place in a state of the deep South.

There are a prologue and three acts. [*Editors' note:* This play has an untitled epilogue; it begins when JACK turns toward the audience after WILLIE dies. Everything after that is connected to the prologue—same scene, same characters, same time frame.]

Dedication:
"To Francis Fergusson
and the memory of
Marion Crowne Fergusson."

A Note on Production

An open stage is envisaged for this play. No set changes are required, for the story is devised to move by a fluid shifting of light from one playing area to another. Some indication of a structure to the rear — girders perhaps — would be helpful. A low platform is required toward stage center, and a balcony, or small, high platform, a little to either side and back. A permanent group of blocks, one in each of the four main playing areas, may be used for furniture, supplemented, as needed, by simple props. One group of blocks, low and benchlike, is at the center, extreme downstage. One group is at each side of the stage, and one on the platform. Special attention should be given to the creation of mood, and the feeling of locale, through the imaginative use of light and sound effects.

Prologue

(At a lectern on the platform, addressing the audience, the PROFESSOR appears, a man of early middle age, incisive and somewhat ironical in manner, with an air of authority. On the platform sit TINY DUFFY, the Governor, and WILLIAM LARSEN.)

PROFESSOR. Ladies and gentlemen, we are gathered together today to dedicate this great hospital, which will mean so much to every citizen of this state — and so much, I may add, to the cause of science, to which my colleagues and I are humbly dedicated. As director of this institution, it is my privilege to welcome you all here, and to welcome our distinguished guests and speakers. The Honorable Aloysius Duffy, Governor of this state. *(TINY, overdressed and self-important, rises and bows, with oleaginous dignity)* And Mr. William Larsen, builder, financier, philanthropist. *(LARSEN rises and bows — a gray-faced, quiet, watchful man, with some trace yet on him of his years as a gambler and racketeer)* This beautiful structure — *(Gesturing toward the structure behind him)* — bears the name of a young man who several years ago received a mortal injury in that great football stadium across the Mall. The Tom Stark Memorial Hospital. Tom Stark — *(On the balcony above, in a spotlight, TOM STARK has appeared. He is a handsome, strong, sullen-faced boy, wearing a football uniform, and carrying his helmet. He stands there, impassive, until just before the appearance of JACK BURDEN)* —who was he? And why should this hospital be named for him? He was an All-American quarterback, one of the finest athletes this state — no, the entire South — has ever produced. Tom Stark's father, as Governor of this state —

MAN. *(Rising from the audience)* Say it! Can't you even say his name? Damn it — it was Willie Stark!

PROFESSOR. Yes — well, yes — Willie Stark. As Governor of this state, he projected the institution which today we dedicate.

MAN. He was a crook! He built the hospital to fight impeachment!

(The GOVERNOR has risen and is making gestures toward the rear of the audience. The MAN is seized and ejected, as the PROFESSOR continues.)

PROFESSOR. He was, let us admit, a controversial figure. But let us not dwell on that. What matters is that the hospital exists. We must remember that historical evolution concerns itself only with the total society, and that individual names do not matter. The hospital is here. In one sense, and in my belief, the deepest and only important sense, it does not matter how it came to be. It does not matter why Governor Stark — Willie Stark — conceived it —

JACK. *(Rising from the audience, a youngish man, darkly handsome and somewhat saturnine, given to withdrawal)* Crap.

PROFESSOR. I beg your pardon!

JACK. I beg *your* pardon. But you are talking crap, you know.

PROFESSOR. Who are you?

JACK. Burden. Jack Burden. And may I again remark that you are talking crap?

PROFESSOR. I was merely referring to a verifiable phenomenon — a fact. *(Pointing to the structure behind him)* That hospital is a fact.

JACK. I should like to know the truth behind that fact.

PROFESSOR. Truth? A name for excuses. Or, to use your word — crap. That — *(Indicating the hospital)* — is a fact. It does not matter who observes it. It does not matter how it came to be. It doesn't matter why it was conceived — whether as a political expedient to fight an impeachment or as a —

JACK. Stark conceived it because he owed it to something he was.

(He has now come upon the stage, followed by ANNE STANTON, his wife.)

PROFESSOR. *(Coming down from the platform, approaching JACK)* Excuse me, Mr. Burden. I must impress upon you that it does not matter what he was.

JACK. If Stark hadn't been what he was, that hospital wouldn't exist at all.

PROFESSOR. What if he was a starry-eyed idealist? Or what if, on the other hand, he was, as he appeared to be by ordinary standards, a cheap demagogue, a ruffian, hag-ridden by vanity, a drunkard — but, no, I don't want to allow my personal feelings to intrude, for as I've already said, in the long view those things do not matter, the hospital is what —

LUCY. *(Appearing at stage left, a woman of middle age, handsome in a spare, countrified way, with feeling and dignity, now making a gesture of anguished protest)* Oh, but Willie wasn't like that!

JACK. Yes, ask Lucy — ask his wife if it matters what Willie Stark was!

ADAM. *(Appearing at stage right, an intense, finely grained man of JACK's age, speaking directly to the audience, out of a painful urgency)* It mattered that my best hope was fouled —

JACK. Yes, ask Dr. Adam Stanton!

ADAM. I did what I did because he breathed the air I breathed. Because he —

ANNE. *(Leaving JACK's side, and moving in protest toward ADAM)* Oh, Adam, no — don't say it!

JACK. Yes, ask her, Prof — ask Adam's sister, my wife — ask Anne.

IRWIN. *(Appearing near ADAM. He is a man of some sixty-five or seventy years, dignified, handsome, well dressed in a severe fashion)* Ask me.

JACK. *(Taking a step toward him, lifting his hand in excited greeting)* Judge — Judge Irwin!

IRWIN. *(Ignoring JACK, addressing the PROFESSOR)* Yes, ask me, for the dead have a long time to think. Stark was —

SUGAR-BOY. *(Appearing at stage left, a runty Irish youth, nondescript in dress, a shoulder holster visible under his left arm. He speaks with a stutter, made worse by his present excitement)* The B-B-B-Big B-B-Boss—he was the Big B-B-B-Boss.

JACK. Ask Sugar-Boy!—Ask Sadie Burke! *(The light is up on a youngish woman with a pocked face, dark burning eyes, and a vital intensity)* Ask Tiny Duffy— that bag of guts yonder— *(Pointing to* TINY, *who, angry, confused, and defensive, comes down from the platform)* —ask him if it matters what Stark was— *(Waving his arm in an inclusive gesture)* —yes, ask them all!

(As all draw closer toward the PROFESSOR, *babbling for an instant, impelled by a communal need to define themselves and their relations to* STARK, *the* PROFESSOR *lifts his hand, and they are suddenly still.)*

PROFESSOR. What could their sick compulsions mean? Nothing more than your own, Mr. Burden—mere froth, shall we say, on the stream of history. What Willie Stark was— *(With irony)* —now really, Mr. Burden.

STARK. *(Picked out in a spotlight on the balcony is a powerful man of about forty-five, somewhat gone to seed, but handsome in a rural way, untidy, but wearing a good dark suit. He does not look down at the stage, but out over the audience, speaking almost as though to himself, in a tone of painful meditation)* You live in the world and you try to know the truth of the world. You live, and you try to know the truth that is in you.

PROFESSOR. The truth!

SUGAR-BOY. *(Staring up at* STARK, *raptly)* It's the B-B-Big B-B-Boss—he c-c-can talk s-s-s-so good!

STARK. The truth is there. But you walk in the darkness of the world. You walk in the darkness of yourself. The darkness whirls. And in the sick hour before dawn, you are sick of the world. You are sick of yourself. And you say, "If only—if only—"

PROFESSOR. My dear Governor, in the texture of reality, there is no "If only"— no "What might have been." At one time I thought you understood such matters.

(The light is down on STARK.)

JACK. *(With a surge of excitement, interrupting the* PROFESSOR) Hold it! I'll tell you how that hospital came to be built.

PROFESSOR. All right. Tell me. *(Withdrawing a little to stage left)* If you can.

(He retreats further, and leans against a girder. During the entire play he is always present, watching, from one point of vantage or another, the course of the action.)

The Light Dims

Act One

(In the central area of the stage, now lighted, JACK moves back toward the plat-form. The lectern has been removed; a bench is visible toward the rear.)

JACK. Once upon a time, I was in my mother's house, the big white house a man named Burden had walked out of and left my mother and me—and never said why. He had left my beautiful mother, whom I loved and hated. Who had married all those men after he left her—and tonight—now, now—lies up there behind the jalousies with a taffy-haired bastard named Murrell, nearly ten years younger than she.

(At the clink of glasses, he swings back and quickly lies down on the bench, as though sleeping. His MOTHER enters into the light, a handsome woman of inde-terminate years, wearing a robe, carrying a tray with a bottle of whiskey, a siphon, and glasses with drinks already mixed.)

MOTHER. I heard you moving—I thought I'd bring you a cold drink.

JACK. *(Rising)* I heard you, too. I heard the cork pop. I heard the gurgle.

MOTHER. Oh, son, son—don't be like that. I didn't touch it. I just heard you moving around and thought you might have a nightcap. *(Having set down the tray, she offers a drink to him)* A nightcap with me.

JACK. Why don't you have it with that beautiful, taffy-headed, new, cretin hus-band of yours?

MOTHER. He's asleep—Be nice to him, son. Be nice, just a little. You're not nice to anyone here at the Landing anymore. You didn't even call Judge Irwin when you got in today, to say hello. *(As he takes the glass and drinks from it)* What's the matter? You're not like you used to be. Not like yourself.

JACK. Before I'll be like I used to be, I'll shoot myself.

MOTHER. And Judge Irwin was like a father to you when you were a boy. Didn't you have a good time with him, son? When he took you hunting? When he taught you how to sail? When he—

JACK. Oh, cut it out!

MOTHER. *(Sitting down, drawing him down beside her, then making him lie with his head in her lap, his glass still in his hand)* Listen, don't leave in the morn-ing. I'm having dinner with Judge Irwin tomorrow. Stay, son—he'd adore it. You like the Judge, don't you?

JACK. *(Jerking himself away, rising)* Like I like booze! *(He drinks.)*

MOTHER. He loves you, son. *(The phone rings and she answers)* Hello. *(She cov-ers the mouthpiece, turning to JACK)* It's those people! Those voices. You can always tell those voices. Why don't you stay here? You belong here. You don't belong with that kind of people—that scum off the human pot, that canai—

JACK. (*Mimicking, picking up the phrase out of old familiarity*) —that scum off the human pot, that canaille—but, oh, they love me. (*Seizing the phone*) Hi, Boss.

(*The light comes up on* SADIE, *stage left.*)

SADIE. (*Speaking into the phone*) Listen, you patrician poop. Hell has popped. MacMurfee's boys in the Legislature are starting impeachment proceedings tomorrow. On the Boss.

JACK. Has MacMurfee got anything?

SADIE. It doesn't matter what he's got. It matters how many bastards he's bought. Or scared.

JACK. Well, the Boss wasn't born yesterday.

SADIE. Oh, he's playing rough. The boys are out and they're dragging in the sore-tails and wobblies in the Legislature. Lot of 'em here right now, weeping and praying. They are strictly crying for Mother. The Boss has something on most of 'em.

JACK. Don't tell me the Boss would use any of those undated resignations.

SADIE. Shut up, Educated, and listen. The Boss is coming down there. Now.

JACK. To the Landing? Here? What the Christ-sake for?

SADIE. Plenty. One of your high-toned pals down there—Judge Irwin—has knifed the Boss.

JACK. He has?

SADIE. Endorsed the impeachment.

JACK. For God's sake.

SADIE. Yeah, it's a fact. In the morning paper tomorrow. We got a leak.

JACK. What do I do?

SADIE. Be standing out in front of Judge Irwin's house in half an hour.

JACK. Okay. And then what?

(*As the light goes down on* SADIE, JACK *stands with the phone in his hand, staring at it. There is a repeated offstage echo, "And then what?" over and over, like the rhythm of anesthesia, fading. As* JACK *stands there, the* PROFESSOR *approaches from a point of vantage.*)

PROFESSOR. Don't you remember, Mr. Burden? You took Stark to your old friend Irwin in the middle of the night. Stark and his little stuttering pathological gunman.

JACK. Sugar-Boy wasn't a gunman. He was just a little Irish runt that had bad teeth from sucking cube sugar, and that got kicked around and never had a dime till the Boss found him.

PROFESSOR. And made him his gunman.

JACK. Oh, he could shoot. I won't deny that.

PROFESSOR. Or deny that you took them—him and Stark—to Irwin in the middle of the night.

JACK. No, I don't deny it. Sure, I was reluctant to take Stark to Irwin. I had been happy there with Irwin, years back. I had been happy at Burden's Landing with Adam Stanton and his little sister Anne.—Anne Stanton, oh, she was the night and day, and she sang to me of what innocence and love I have known.

ANNE. (*ANNE appears at stage right, in a girlish dress. ADAM is near her, further forward, in a tennis rig, with a racket, looking toward the audience. Throughout the following, the characters are not speaking to each other, but forward toward the audience*) I was happy there once. I saw the moon rise over the sea, and I was happy. There were Adam and Jack and I, and life was a bright promise. Life was a promise, and—

JACK. (*With a gesture forward, as though calling*) I'll race you to the raft!

ANNE. (*Facing forward*) I'll race you!

(*There is a sound of laughter, offstage, and the splash.*)

ADAM. (*Facing forward*) The net, Anne—cover the net!

REFEREE'S VOICE. (*Offstage*) The games are now four-all.

ADAM. (*Still speaking forward*) Atta girl, Anne—oh, that was a beauty!

JACK. (*Still speaking forward*) You are my beauty, dear Anne—oh, Anne, see the moon come over the water—

ANNE. (*In her own dream, with a cradling gesture of her arms, singing*) Oh, Jackie-Boy—oh, Jackie-Bird—sweet Jackie-Boy—

JACK. (*Singing*) Oh, darling Anne, see the moon rise over the water—

ANNE. But the water gets cold, it is cold, and the moon goes down, and life drives them past, flat and fast over the net, and life drives them past you and you see them coming but oh, it is gone, flat and fast over the net—

REFEREE'S VOICE. Game and set. It is game and set.

ANNE. And life slips through your fingers like wind. It leaves you—and what you dream leaves you. Those whom you love leave you. They withdraw from you and you are alone.

(*The lights are down on ANNE and ADAM.*)

JACK. And it is all flown away.

PROFESSOR. (*Moving into the area of light*) So there you are, waiting in the middle of the night.

(*There are the lights of an approaching car, the sound of brakes, and the slam of the car door. STARK enters from the shadow at stage left, wearing a light topcoat, fawn-colored, and a homburg. He seems gay and confident. JACK turns toward him in alarm.*)

JACK. Hey, Boss—what—

STARK. Easy boy, it had to come. And now, by God, it's here! I've got 'em out of the brush, I got 'em out in the open now, and I'll ride 'em down!

SUGAR-BOY. R-R-R-Ride 'em down, Boss! Ride 'em d-d-d-down!

STARK. (*Mussing* SUGAR'S *hair with an affectionate gesture; turning to* JACK) By God, they'll remember this day. MacMurfee—MacMurfee—his unborn great-grandchildren will wet their pants on this anniversary and not know why. It will be the sins of the father and wet pants unto the tenth generation.

JACK. Judge Irwin—what are you going to say to him?

STARK. (*Gaily*) You never know till you look 'em in the eye. I just want to look him in the eye.

JACK. Look here, Boss—the Judge won't scare.

STARK. I just want to look him in the eye.

JACK. God damn it, the Judge won't scare.

STARK. Let's get him out, Jack. (*As* JACK *hesitates*) Get the bastard out.

(*As* JACK *moves toward stage left, the light is up on* IRWIN, *seated under a desk lamp, reading. There is a bust of Thomas Jefferson, on a plinth, profile to the audience. As* JACK *enters,* IRWIN *rises cordially, placing a hand on* JACK'S *shoulder.*)

IRWIN. Well, Jack—Jack my boy! Come in. What can I do for you? (*As* JACK *seems disturbed, unable to speak*) You're not in any—in any—trouble?

JACK. No, Judge, I'm not in any—

STARK. (*Suddenly stepping into the light of the* JUDGE'S *study*) No, Judge, Jack's not in any trouble. Nor me. (*As* IRWIN *seems taken aback*) Ain't you asking me in, Judge?

IRWIN. I beg your pardon, I was about to retire.

STARK. Not yet, Judge.

IRWIN. (*As* STARK *pushes past him, followed by* SUGAR-BOY) You—you even bring your—your bodyguard.

STARK. Hell, Judge, Sugar's just a pal.

IRWIN. If you think the presence of a hired gunman can intimidate me—

STARK. Hell, Judge, Sugar wouldn't hurt a fly. He's just a pal. A pal that drives my car for me. Ain't you my pal, Sugar?

SUGAR-BOY. Sh-Sh-Sh-Sure, I'm j-j-j-just a—

STARK. Swallow it, Sugar.

IRWIN. If you have any business, make it brief.

STARK. (*Discovering a tray with a bottle and glasses*) Judge, the best business I got on my mind is what's in that bottle there. I trust you don't mind if Jack pours me a slug.

IRWIN. I did not realize, Jack, that your duties include those of a body servant. But of course, if I'm mistaken—

STARK. Nuts, Judge. Sometimes Jack pours me a slug and sometimes I pour Jack a slug. And sometimes I pour myself a slug— *(Pouring a drink, then sitting in the JUDGE's chair)* —whether I'm asked or not. For I am a very impatient man, Judge, and there are a lot of things you never get if you wait till you are asked. That is why I am not what you would term a gentleman, Judge.

IRWIN. Really?

STARK. Yeah, but you—you're a gentleman, Judge. Is that why you endorsed my impeachment?

IRWIN. I owe you no explanation.

STARK. Oh, you said this state needed better roads and decent schools and an income tax. I did those things. By God, I did 'em!

IRWIN. You accomplished certain necessary reforms, but the Supreme Court of this state ruled—

STARK. —that my income tax was illegal, that my extraction tax was illegal. They ruled it. But the court reversed itself, didn't it?

IRWIN. After you had packed the court.

STARK. Hell, all courts are packed from the start. It just came my turn to pack it.

IRWIN. You have flouted the Constitution, you have flouted the rule of law—

STARK. You know, Judge, the trouble with you is, you're a lawyer. You're a damned fine Harvard Law School lawyer.

IRWIN. You're a lawyer, and you ought—

STARK. Hold it, I'm not your kind of lawyer. Oh, I know me some law. Fact is, I know me a lot of law, even if I never went to any silk-hat law school. I can see what the law is like. The law is like a single-bed blanket on a double bed and three folks in bed on a cold night. There ain't ever enough blanket to cover the case, and somebody is always nigh to catch pneumonia. Hell, the law is like the pants you bought last year for a growing boy, but it is always this year and the seams are popped and the shank bones to the breeze. The law is always too short or too tight for growing humankind. And that, Judge, is why I made me up some law. To protect folks from the kind of law you and your kind make up, and by God—

IRWIN. I do not care to discuss the matter with you.

STARK. You ain't discussing it, Judge. I am. And while I'm at it, I'll just tell you why you want to impeach me. *(He rises from the chair, facing IRWIN)*

IRWIN. I followed the dictates of my conscience.

STARK. Which ain't a thing but the conscience of every corporation and bank in this state. Oh, you were a friend to the common man. Oh, you talked about sweet reform until you saw I meant business. Real business. And then something happened inside you, Judge, and you call that something your conscience.

IRWIN. If you mean to imply that I've been dictated to—

STARK. Oh, the silk hats didn't have to buy you, Judge, for you are one of them. And that's why I'm telling you right now that I'm just getting started. And nothing will stop me — nothing —

IRWIN. That is precisely the point. You will stop at nothing. Some of your personal methods have come to my attention.

STARK. Oh, somebody's been digging up some dirt, huh? Some of the sweet-smelling?

IRWIN. If you choose to call it that.

STARK. Now dirt is a funny thing, Judge. (*Going back to the chair, settling himself comfortably*) Come to think of it, there ain't anything but dirt on this green God's globe. It's dirt makes the grass grow. A diamond ain't a thing in the world but a piece of dirt that got awful hot. And God-A-Mighty picked up a handful of dirt and blew on it and made you and me and George Washington and mankind, blessed in faculty and apprehension. It all depends on what you do with dirt, ain't that right, Judge?

IRWIN. The facts are clear. What you say makes no difference.

STARK. No difference, huh? Well, this makes a difference. I can run this state. I'll run it any way I can, and that can make a big difference to you.

IRWIN. I'll take my chances.

STARK. Judge, you ain't got but one chance, and this is the last one. You been sitting back in this fine room, and nigger boys been single-footing in here bringing you toddies, and you been guessing right. Oh, you took a little time off from duck hunting and corporation law to do a hitch as Attorney General. You been playing at being a judge for a long time. How would it feel not to be a judge anymore?

IRWIN. No man has ever been able to intimidate me.

STARK. And I'm not trying to, Judge. Not yet. I'm just telling you that you don't know a thing about politics. Not my kind, Judge. I'm just telling you the facts of life.

IRWIN. I'll thank you, sir, to get out of that chair and to get out of this house.

STARK. Jack, you were right. The Judge don't scare easy.

IRWIN. Get out.

STARK. Those old bones don't move so fast, but now I've done my bounden duty, let me rise and go. (*Spying the bust of Jefferson, greeting it like an old friend, slapping it on the shoulder*) Damned if it ain't old Tom Jefferson. Hello, Thomas! (*Studying the face of the bust, his hand still patronizingly on its shoulder, then speaking in the serious tone of a school elocution class*)
"Can storied urn or animated bust
Back to its mansion call the fleeting breath?
Can Honor's voice provoke the silent dust,
Or Flatt'ry soothe the dull cold ear — of Death?"

(Shaking his head, he pats the bust on the shoulder, and turns to IRWIN*)* Well, Judge, more in pain than wrath I go. And if you and your conscience ever see the light—in a reasonable time, of course—

IRWIN. Get out.

STARK. Let's haul ass, Jack. *(He starts toward the center of the stage.)*

IRWIN. Your employer has called you, Mr. Burden.

JACK. I don't use an ear trumpet yet.

IRWIN. I'm dining with your mother this week. Shall I tell her you like your work?

JACK. Sure, Judge. You tell her that. But if I were you I wouldn't go advertising this visit. Someone might think you had stooped to a low political deal in the middle of the night. With the Boss.

IRWIN. Boss!

(The light is down on IRWIN *as* JACK *joins* STARK *at stage center.)*

STARK. You were right, Jack. The Judge didn't scare. *(Chewing his cigar meditatively, then taking it from his mouth and twisting it in his finger)* But why can't he understand me? Why can't he, now? You know, there was a time I figgered he understood me. Damn it, he's just like Lucy.

JACK. Lucy?

STARK. Yeah. She might leave me. Separate.

JACK. Sadie—is it Sadie?

STARK. No. She don't know about that.

JACK. Lucy's a woman, isn't she. And they can smell it. *(He sits on a block, his back to the audience.)*

STARK. No, it's not Sadie. It's just that Lucy don't like the way I do things. Like the Judge, she don't like my methods.

JACK. It looks like everybody is trying to run your business.

STARK. God damn 'em. Damn 'em all. Oh, they like what you do. They think it's great. But they don't like the way you do it. They want to spit on you. But there's just one way. And by God, I know the way.

JACK. And you do things that way.

STARK. Even you.

JACK. I didn't say a word.

STARK. Gimme a slug.

JACK. You know where it lives.

(STARK lifts JACK's coat, takes a flask from his hip pocket, and drinks.)

STARK. This sure ain't as good as Irwin's. *(Hands JACK the flask)* You know—you know what I'm going to do? As soon as I beat this impeachment.

JACK. Sure, take a long rest. Make a novena. Get drunk.

STARK. Nope. I'm going to build me a hospital. I'm going to build the God-damnedest, biggest, chromium-platedest, formaldehyde-stinkingest free hospital and health center the All-Father ever let live. Boy, I tell you, I'm going to have a cage of canaries in every room that can sing Italian Grand Opera and there ain't going to be a nurse hasn't won a beauty contest at Atlantic City, and every bedpan will be eighteen-carat gold, and, by God, every bedpan will have a Swiss music-box attachment to play "Turkey in the Straw," or the Sextet from *Lucia*, take your choice.

JACK. You'd better bust MacMurfee first.

STARK. Oh, I'll bust him, I'll — (*Angry, as an idea strikes him*) Listen, Jack, you get in there and dig. Get the dirt on the Judge.

JACK. Look here, Boss, there isn't any dirt. Not on the Judge.

STARK. There's always something.

JACK. Maybe not on the Judge.

STARK. Listen, Jack. Man is conceived in sin and born in corruption, and he passeth from the stink of the didie to the stench of the shroud. There is always something.

JACK. But, Boss — the Judge —

STARK. He's a man, ain't he? And if he's a man — (*STARK turns abruptly and goes.*)

PROFESSOR. (*Moving from the shadows, where he has been watching*) So, Mr. Burden, in the midst of your "inner struggle," you thought you could have it both ways — that you could dig as Stark commanded, but in the end, prove that Irwin was the man you had always thought. That was terribly unrealistic. But Stark, he was a realist. The hospital proves it. He conceived it to assure the public of his good faith while he was under impeachment. And it was tactically necessary that he do so.

JACK. Stark conceived it because he wanted to do something for the people of this state, pure and simple.

PROFESSOR. That is merely a justification. I tell you I am not concerned with justification. I am concerned with the ultimate end, and what that end delivers to society. Not with your sugar-coated justification of the means to that end.

JACK. But the reasons for an action must be justified. For that is what makes a man. If man cannot justify —

PROFESSOR. My dear fellow, can't you see that your whole point of view is irrelevant? All this moralistic moonshine about personal justification. But even in your own deluded terms, what sense are you making? How would you justify Stark when he set out to terrorize a legislature — blackmail, thuggery, conspiracy — he carried his appeals from one end of the state to the other — he inflamed the lawless and illiterate —

JACK. He went to the people and he inflamed them with hope.

PROFESSOR. A blind mob, fed on promises —

JACK. He promised them only their right. They were the ordinary people of this state — the society of this state. If they are worth nothing, then how can this hospital be a "good"? It is for them.

STARK'S VOICE. (*Offstage, addressing a crowd*)

Your will is my strength.

Your hope is my justification.

Your need is my law.

Your heart is my own.

JACK. (*Moving to stage left to challenge the* PROFESSOR) What if that were true? Yes, Prof — what if it is true?

PROFESSOR. The hospital is here. It is a "good." No matter if the particular society it serves is, at the moment, illiterate and decadent. And that, Mr. Burden, is what you must understand.

TOM. (*In a spotlight, on the platform, wearing his football uniform*) I tried to understand him and what it was I was supposed to be. But all that mattered was that I watch the ball arch toward me through the hot sun and that I take it and cradle it to me and run for the glory of the Great God Willie. That was what I had to do in order to be called "Son." Oh, but I tried, I held out my hand to him and said, "Father, Father, help me, love me." But he never heard, and so, in the silence, there was nothing left.

LUCY. (*Appearing in a spotlight, stage right*) But he wanted to know you, Tom. He never meant to —

TOM. Mother, I was your son. Why couldn't that have been enough?

LUCY. Oh, I wish you could have known him as I did. For then you would have known that there was in him something to love.

JACK. (*To the* PROFESSOR, *as the light goes down on* LUCY *and* TOM) Yes. Lucy knew him, and I knew him too. I'll tell you what he was, back when I first saw him. And if you can understand that, you will understand what you must understand. It was back in 1930, and I was in the back room of Slade's speakeasy with Tiny Duffy, who was city assessor, a city hall swell with a hard straw hat and a diamond ring and lard oozing sweetly from every pore. (*JACK moves to the platform, stage center, where the light comes up on* DUFFY, *reading a paper, in shirt sleeves, on his head a hard straw hat with a garish band. A table with a red-check cloth is before him.* SLADE, *a waiter, is in the background. To* DUFFY) Who's this guy you waiting for?

DUFFY. Name of Stark. From the sticks. Hey, Slade, will you turn that damned thing down? Name of Stark. County Treasurer up in Mason County. Some hick. I never laid eyes on him. A guy's bringing him to me to see about some school bonds they're trying to float up there. Just to get the benefit of my advice, my experience.

MAN. *(Entering, escorting* STARK, *in a tight seersucker coat, loud tie, hair slicked down, full of rural diffidence)* This is Willie Stark, gents. From up home in Mason City. And this—this is Mr. Duffy. Yes sir, this is Mr. Duffy. Just like I told you.

STARK. *(Shaking hands)* Mr. Duffy.

MAN. This is Jack Burden—he's a newspaperman.

STARK. *(Shaking hands scrupulously)* How'do, Mr. Burden.

JACK. How'do.

MAN. Yeah, Willie here is from up home, at Mason City. Me and Willie went to school together. Yeah, and Willie was a bookworm. He was the teacher's pet. Wasn't you, Willie? And he's still the teacher's pet, damned if he ain't, ain't you, Willie? Willie married a schoolteacher.

DUFFY. *(With ponderous humor)* Well, they tells me that schoolteachers are made with it in the same place.

MAN. Gawd, Mr. Duffy, you sure are a card! Now ain't Mr. Duffy a card, Willie?

STARK. Yeah, Mr. Duffy is a card.

SLADE. What'll it be, Mr. Duffy?

DUFFY. Beer all around.

STARK. Not for me, thank you kindly.

DUFFY. Beer all around.

STARK. Not for me, thank you kindly.

DUFFY. You bring him a beer.

STARK. No, thank you.

MAN. Maybe the schoolteacher don't let him drink nothing.

STARK. Lucy don't favor drinking, for a fact.

DUFFY. Well, what Lucy don't know don't hurt Lucy, does it? Give him a beer.

STARK. No, thanks.

MAN. Maybe she lets him drink orange pop. Hey, Slade, you got any orange pop?

SLADE. I got orange pop for them as wants it.

STARK. I reckon I'll have me a orange drink.

SLADE. *(Giving pop to* STARK*)* Pop.

MAN. Yeah, Willie's County Treasurer for two years now up in Mason City. He's getting into politics.

DUFFY. Politics! *(Staring incredulously at* STARK *as he drinks the pop, soberly like a child)* My God.

JACK. *(Moving to stage right as the light goes down on the others)* "My God," Duffy said, and you couldn't blame him. Willie was in politics, but not for long. The Commissioner wanted to give the school contract to a gentleman who happened to be his brother-in-law and who, by the way, did not offer the lowest bid. But Willie wouldn't sign. So they threw Willie out. He knew they would throw him out and throw out Lucy, who was teaching school, but he didn't sign.

LUCY. (*Appearing on the platform, stage center*) No, he wouldn't. And one day they had a fire drill at the school. The fire escape pulled loose, because the schoolhouse was built of politics-rotten bricks, and eight poor little scholars hit the concrete walk and were killed. We went to the funeral—the big funeral for all eight of them. We stood in the back, and Willie was just standing there when old Mr. Sandeen saw him and shouted, "It's God's judgment on me for not listening to an honest man. May God bless Willie Stark who tried to save my little Sallie!" And I was proud that he had done what was right, Willie had. And he always wanted to—he wanted to do what was right—you must believe it—you must—

(*The light is down on her, cutting off her urgency.*)

PROFESSOR. (*Moving toward JACK*) But that accident, it was fortunate, wasn't it, for Willie Stark? For Stark's connection with the accident made one faction of the Democratic Party try to use him in the primary.

JACK. Sure, the Harrison gang wanted a stooge. So Willie was picked for the sucker. I was along covering the campaign, for the *Chronicle*, what there was to cover, with Tiny Duffy, and Sadie Burke, who was one very tough cookie, from up in the Yankee North. Just the night before what was supposed to be the big barbecue and rally, Sadie was sitting in my hotel room, gloomy as a constipated owl. (*The light is up on SADIE, as JACK takes a chair*) It's no go, Sadie.

SADIE. What's no go?

JACK. You know what I'm talking about. Willie is no go.

SADIE. Maybe he'll pick up.

JACK. Listen, Sadie, that guy couldn't steal a vote from Lincoln in the Cradle of Confederacy. Those speeches.

SADIE. (*Wearily*) Yeah, ain't it awful?

JACK. Why don't you tell the big boys back in town it's no go? Get the sap out of his misery.

SADIE. What do you mean?

JACK. Come on, Sadie. We are old pals. I won't print it, but I know it's a frame-up. Willie is a dummy candidate to split MacMurfee's cocklebur vote.

SADIE. Look here, now.

JACK. It's a frame-up. Anybody could see that. Anybody, but Willie.

SADIE. Okay. It's a frame-up.

JACK. Why don't you tell the big boys it won't work? Get the guy out of his misery.

SADIE. I told 'em a long time back. I told 'em it wouldn't work. Let 'em spend their money. They wouldn't listen to me.

JACK. I'm not worried about their money. It's the sap.

SADIE. You know, suppose they told him. He might go on making those speeches. Even if he found out he was a sucker.

JACK. Maybe.

SADIE. God, aren't they awful?

(STARK, in shirt sleeves, enters, and hesitates in embarrassment.)

JACK. Hey, look. It's Willie. Come on in, Willie. Give Willie a drink.

SADIE. He don't take it.

JACK. Oh, yeah. Have a seat, Willie.

STARK. No, thanks, Jack. No, thanks.

JACK. What's on your mind?

STARK. *(Standing aimlessly)* Nothing. Nothing special.

JACK. Come on, spill it.

STARK. It's just — it's just I wondered.

JACK. Wondered what?

STARK. How do you think it's going?

JACK. What's going?

STARK. My campaign.

JACK. Fine. I think it's going fine, Willie.

STARK. They didn't seem to be listening so good yesterday.

JACK. You tell 'em too much. It breaks down their brain cells.

STARK. Looks like they'd want to hear about my road program. And my tax program.

JACK. Just say you're going to soak the rich.

STARK. What this state needs is a balanced tax program. Now, the ratio between income and —

JACK. We heard the speech.

SADIE. *(Speaking to him over her shoulder as she refills her glass)* Hell, make 'em laugh. Make 'em cry. Stir 'em up. They aren't alive, most of them and haven't been in twenty years. *(Moving toward him, warming to the topic)* Hell, their wives have lost their shape, likker won't set on their stomach, and they've lost their religion, so it's up to you to stir 'em up. Make 'em feel alive again. For half an hour. They'll love you for it. Hell, heat 'em up.

STARK. I've heard that kind of talk.

SADIE. It's no secret. It gets around.

STARK. Maybe I can't talk that way.

JACK. That's the only way you'll ever be Governor.

STARK. A man don't have to be Governor. *(Hesitating, gulping)* I'm not denying I wanted it. I wanted it. A man can lie there at night and just be so full of wanting something that he just plain forgets what it is he wants. Like when you are a boy, and the sap first rises good in you, and you think you will go crazy some night just wanting something — Gee, Miss Burke — I apologize — talking that way before a lady —

SADIE. I ain't a lady.

STARK. I could have made a pretty good Governor, too. By God — by God, better'n Joe Harrison — better'n MacMurfee. I know what people need. You know why? I know because I never had 'em. Look at me — I never had a day's decent schooling in my life. I *know* what people need. I would have made a pretty good Governor —

JACK. Hell, the votes haven't been counted yet.

STARK. No, Jack, I won't make it.

SADIE. If you don't stop talking like that — oh, you make me sick.

STARK. I'm sorry, Miss Burke. But it's just the way I feel. And I'm sorry to be telling you what I'm going to tell you. After you've worked so hard to help me and been so nice. It ain't that I don't appreciate it and all, but —

SADIE. What — what are you trying to say?

STARK. It's just that I'm quitting, Miss Burke. I'm not man enough, and I know it. I'm going back home to Mason City, and farm and practice me a little law. That's all I know how to do.

SADIE. You mean that you're resigning?

STARK. I mean it. I won't ever be Governor.

SADIE. Listen to him! He won't be Governor. Whatever made you think you could be Governor? Look at yourself. *(A vindictive edge coming into her tone)* Whatever made you think it? You were framed. Do you get it? Framed.

STARK. Framed?

SADIE. And how! Oh, you decoy, you dummy, you woodenhead, and you let 'em because you thought you were the little white lamb of God — Baa aa — But you know what you are? You are the goat. The sacrificial goat. Oh, you sap!

STARK. Why did they frame me?

SADIE. Oh, my God. Listen to him. He wants to know why. I'll tell you why. If you can get it through your thick skull. To split MacMurfee's vote in the sticks.

STARK. Jack, is that true?

JACK. That's what they tell me, Willie. *(As STARK sits with a stricken look, SADIE thrusts her drink into his hands, and he desperately gulps the whole glassful)* Hey, take it easy, you aren't used to that stuff.

SADIE. He ain't used to a lot of things. Are you, Willie? You ain't used to the idea of not being Governor.

STARK. I was used to it. To not being Governor.

SADIE. Well, you better stay used to it.

STARK. I was used to it, but not now.

SADIE. Not what?

STARK. Not used to it now.

SADIE. Not used to it now. My God! He says he's not used to it now.

STARK. *(Rising from his chair, seizing SADIE by the shoulders, shaking her)* I'll kill 'em. I'll kill 'em. I'll—

SADIE. Sit down and shut up. *(She shoves him so that he falls back into the chair.)*

STARK. I'll kill 'em.

SADIE. Oh, you won't do a Goddamned thing. Not you, you tin-plated, one-gallus sap, you.

JACK. I don't know what kind of games you play. But I'm not going to stay here and watch. *(He exits.)*

SADIE. *(She fills a tumbler half full of whiskey)* Take it, you sap. Take it, it's all you got left.

STARK. I'll kill 'em.

SADIE. *(Crouching on the floor before him, a hand on one of his knees, thrusting the glass up at him)* Take this and shut up, you — Come on, drink it.

(STARK gulps the drink, as SADIE, fascinated, stares at him. He shudders with the drink, then finds her staring up at him, as the light dims out and comes up again on JACK, downstage.)

JACK. I couldn't stay and watch it. So I walked out, and put the town to bed. When I got back Willie was out cold. He didn't look like a winner. The next morning either, when I tried to get him on his feet for the big political barbecue. He was Weary Willie and his face was pale and pure. He couldn't keep a thing on his stomach. Not even water. But I finally tried the hair of the dog, and he had near a pint of whiskey in him by the time I got him to the fairgrounds.

(People—rural types—begin to move around the platform as the entire stage is lit. DUFFY takes a seat on the platform, fanning himself with his hat. We hear the band playing "Hail, Hail, the Gang's All Here." STARK unsteadily mounts the platform. JACK and SADIE appear stage left.)

DUFFY. *(Rising)* And now friends, I give you our next Governor, Willie Stark.

STARK. Friends, I have a speech here. It is a speech about what this state needs. But you wouldn't listen to it. And you're right not to listen to it. You are right not to listen, because you already know what you need. Look at your pants. Have they got holes in the knees? Listen to your belly. Does it ever rumble for emptiness? Look at your kids. Are they growing up ignorant as dirt? No, I'm not going to read you any speech. No, folks, I'm going to tell you a story.

JACK. *(To SADIE)* What's that booger up to?

SADIE. *(Engrossed)* Shut up.

STARK. It's a funny story. Get ready to bust out laughing. It's about a hick. A red-neck hick like you.

MAN. Who you calling a hick?

STARK. Yeah, you heard me! A red-neck hick like you. He knew what it was to get up before day and slop and feed, with cowdung between his toes, and then walk six miles to a slab-side schoolhouse. He knew about red-clay roads so gully-washed they'd string-halt his mules. Oh, he knew what it was to be a hick—summer or winter.

MAN. Summer *and* winter.

STARK. And he figured he'd have to help himself. For nobody ever helps a hick.

MAN. God's truth!

STARK. So he sat up nights studying law. Not in any man's college, but at night after a hard day in the field. He sweated so he could change things. For himself. I'm not lying to you. He wasn't any Tin Jesus. He was out for number one—himself.

MAN. Every time!

STARK. But something came to him on the way. How he couldn't help himself without helping other hicks. That came to him. And it came to him with the power of God-A-Mighty's own lightning on the day when back in his home county the first brick school ever built there collapsed because it was built with politics-rotten brick and killed eight pore little scholars. Oh, you know what happened, and how he tried to stop it.

MAN. Yeah, he tried.

WOMAN. Willie tried!

STARK. And the big boys in the city knew it, too. So they came riding up in a fine automobile. Up to his Pappy's red-clay farm, and said how they wanted him to run for Governor. Because he was an honest man. Oh, they sweet-talked him. But you know what they wanted, those crooks in the striped pants? What they never told him. They wanted to use that little hick to split the hick vote for MacMurfee and help elect their secret boss, Joe Harrison. Joe Harrison, that deadhead!

MAN. How do you know that?

STARK. *(DUFFY has risen in alarm)* How do I know? I know because that fine woman right there— *(Pointing to SADIE)* —she told me the truth. The truth that stinks in the nostrils of the Most High!

DUFFY. *(Toward stage right)* Play the "Star-Spangled Banner"!

STARK. *(Pointing to* DUFFY*)* And there he is! The man that fooled that hick. There is the Judas Iscariot, the lick-spittle for Joe Harrison.

DUFFY. *(Desperately)* Play the Goddamned "Star-Spangled Banner"!

(As DUFFY *leans toward the band,* STARK *boots him on the behind so that he falls off the platform.)*

STARK. *(As the crowd starts angrily toward* TINY*)* Let the hog lie! Let him lie, and listen to me, you hicks. I'm resigning from this race. In favor of MacMurfee. That's not because I love him. But to beat Joe Harrison. So vote. Vote to beat Harrison. And next time — next time, you hicks — I'm coming back. For I have got me a gospel. Oh, Lord, I've got me a word. Take this state for it is yours! Oh, Lord, I have seen a sign! Oh, Lord, you have given a sign to Gideon! Dew on the ground and fleece dry! *(The crowd chants, "Gideon, Gideon, and the fleece dry!")* Oh, Lord, I am coming back and under God's holy hand no man will stop me. I will smite him. Hip and thigh, shinbone and neckbone. Kidney punch, rabbit punch, and solar plexus. For, oh, Lord, I have seen a sign. Blood on the moon! It'll be their blood. Gimme that meat ax. *(Leaning toward the crowd, holding out his hands. The crowd lift up their hands as though passing the ax up to him)* Blood on the moon! *(The crowd roars.)*

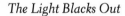

The Light Blacks Out

Act Two

STARK. *(Offstage)*

Your will is my strength.

Your hope is my justification.

Your need is my law.

Your heart is my own.

JACK. *(In the light, stage center)* In 1938, Willie Stark came back, and it was hell among the yearlings, and when the smoke cleared away not a picture hung on the walls. And in the midst of the steaming carnage, there wasn't anything but Willie.

PROFESSOR. *(Moving toward* JACK*)* Oh, yes, there was. There was. There was Sadie Burke. By that time the Boss's mistress.

JACK. All right, she came along. But she paid her own fare, for she was a smart fixer. But it was Willie had the gospel. For the people.

PROFESSOR. And there was you, Mr. Burden — there was you —

JACK. All right. I came. I came because —

PROFESSOR. Because being incapable of action in your own confused and wasted life, you had a romantic admiration for action. Oh, you fancied the role of the cynical observer, but deep inside —

JACK. All right, all right —

PROFESSOR. All right, and there was Duffy. Don't forget him, Mr. Burden, the crook Stark made his Lieutenant Governor.

JACK. Sure, he used him. And if you are the scientific realist you fancy yourself, you ought to know why. Willie had been wised up and knew what he had to do. He had to use Duffy.

PROFESSOR. Oh, I don't object. It was historically necessary to use Duffy. I merely want to keep the record straight.

JACK. Well, to keep the record straight, had you thought of this? That Stark had Duffy because Duffy was another self — the self the Boss could give every insult to and contempt — what one self of Stark did to the other self as a tribute to what Stark wanted to be?

PROFESSOR. That is amateur psychology, Mr. Burden. He wanted Duffy because Duffy was a crook, plain and simple. And it was Duffy who, when Stark was under impeachment, fixed up the rotten contract with Larsen for the hospital, and who —

JACK. That was exactly what Stark did not want. Duffy had tried for a long time to make Stark do it —

(STARK is shown at the left, in his office area, seated, with a bottle of pop. SUGAR-BOY is at one side, cleaning his revolver. DUFFY is standing, leaning toward STARK. JACK moves into the scene, waiting.)

DUFFY. Boss, I got a neat little trick, Boss. It'll sure kill the impeachment. It'll make MacMurfee get down and say "Uncle."

STARK. Spill it, Tiny, spill it.

DUFFY. Well, you know Larsen — Mr. Larsen —

STARK. Sure, I know Gummy. He's a crook. Just like you, Tiny.

DUFFY. *(Grinning feebly)* Now, Boss, I wouldn't say that. And Boss — Mr. Larsen, he's a pretty important man, you know. He's got a chunk of the Morton Bridge and Construction Company, he has a —

STARK. He *is* the Morton Bridge and Construction Company.

DUFFY. Well, Boss, I just happened to run into him on the street the other day and we sort of got to talking —

STARK. Hey, Tiny, will you get off the pot?

DUFFY. Well, now, you know how it's Mr. Larsen sort of calls the tune for MacMurfee — he puts up the jack —

STARK. Yeah? You don't tell me.

DUFFY. Well, you know he ain't so satisfied with MacMurfee anymore, he—

STARK. You mean he wants to sell his pal out?

DUFFY. Now, Boss, I wouldn't put it that way. Mr. Larsen admires you, Boss. He was just saying—how he admires you and—

STARK. Gummy Larsen admires a dollar bill.

DUFFY. Oh, he admires you, Boss. He knows what's going on. He's seen how you got the goods on lots of them guys in the Legislature. He's seen you handling the impeachment, Boss, and he admires you for it. He figures how you and him might work together and he could fix things up all smooth, Boss, no trouble.

STARK. What does he want?

DUFFY. Well, you know he's got that fine construction company. Mighty fine.

STARK. What does he want?

DUFFY. Well, now, that hospital—you know this hospital of yours—

STARK. (Rising, sadly) You know, Tiny, I got to try harder to understand you. I got to cultivate me an understanding heart, Tiny. And you got to try to understand me, too.

DUFFY. (Laying his hand on STARK's shoulder) Sure, Boss, I understand you. You—you're old Willie—and you know how all us boys feel about you.

STARK. (With manly sweetness) Yeah, Tiny, I know how you feel.

DUFFY. I know you know, Boss. And, Boss— (Pawing STARK's shoulder) —this business with Larsen would be slick— (Delighted with himself) —it'll be slick. And, Boss, I got a surprise for you! (Gesturing to stage left, rear, LARSEN appears, composed and watchful. STARK stares at him an instant, dumbfounded, as DUFFY continues) Yeah, Boss, I knew you'd want to see Mr. Larsen. I just knew you'd want to talk a little turkey with Mr. Larsen, I knew—

STARK. (Moving on DUFFY, but speaking in a low, grating, controlled voice) Say it again, and I'll strangle you. Larsen won't touch my hospital—Larsen or nobody like him. And you—you hyena-headed, feist-faced, belly-dragging son of a slack-gutted she-wolf— (With an anguished look at LARSEN, DUFFY flees. STARK turns on LARSEN) And as for you, Gummy—

(LARSEN, completely calm and cold, confronts him, rolling a cigarette between a thumb and forefinger.)

LARSEN. My dear Governor, it is all a matter of timing. The timing was bad. It seems you aren't ready to do business with me. (He turns calmly to go, then looks back over his shoulder at STARK) But you will, Governor.

(Before STARK can collect himself, LARSEN is gone, leaving STARK to swallow his rage.)

STARK. That Duffy—that Tiny—if he thinks he can—*(Turning to JACK)* You know what Lincoln said?

JACK. What?

STARK. He said a house divided against itself cannot stand. Well, he was wrong. This house is standing, and it's half slave and half son-of-a-bitch.

JACK. Yeah—and which is which?

STARK. Slaves down in the Legislature, and sons-of-bitches up here. *(STARK sits at the desk, brooding a moment)* Damn it, nobody understands me, not even you. *(After a pause)* I'm gonna build the biggest and best hospital money can buy. And any man or woman or child, in sickness or in pain, can walk through those doors, and know that all man can do will be done to cure sickness and ease pain. Free. Not as a charity, but as a right. And I don't care if he votes for me or not. You hear me? *(Rising, with a sudden idea)* Adam Stanton—Dr. Stanton—he is one of your high-toned pals, isn't he?

JACK. He's my friend.

STARK. I want him.

JACK. What for?

STARK. The hospital—what else would I want him for? I want him to be the director. He's the best. I want the best.

JACK. You'd better take the Keeley cure. He hates your guts.

STARK. I don't care what he hates. I want him.

JACK. You are dreaming dreams.

STARK. I dream lots of dreams. But, by God, I can make 'em walk. Get him.

(As STARK withdraws, the PROFESSOR approaches.)

PROFESSOR. So you believed Stark, and tried to deliver your friend over to him.

JACK. Why shouldn't I have believed him?

PROFESSOR. Ha, ha. If you want reasons, which one of a dozen would you like to hear?

JACK. All right, all right. *(The light comes up on ADAM in his office, stage right; an x-ray plate is in his hands. JACK enters the office. To ADAM)* Still don't lock your door?

ADAM. Well, Jack! Gee, I'm glad to see you.

JACK. I'm sorry to bust in on you when you're so busy and—

ADAM. Never too busy for you, boy. What's on your mind?

JACK. Well, Adam, Stark wants you to be the director of that hospital he's planning.

ADAM. Jack, you know what I think of Stark. You know me.

JACK. Oh, sure, Stark is a tough baby. Sure, he plays rough, but this thing—why, this hospital is going to be the nuts—the biggest thing ever. Why, I've heard you say a thousand times that what this state needed was a decent health program — hospitals — clinics — and, boy —

ADAM. It will be an instrument for power — a tool for graft.

JACK. Not this time. Why, this thing is his baby. Any crook tries to lay a finger on it, and he'll tear him limb from limb. And — he expects you to write your own ticket.

ADAM. Did you come here to buy me? Does Willie Stark think he can buy me?

JACK. He knows he couldn't buy you, Adam.

ADAM. Or threaten me? That would be next.

JACK. No, he couldn't scare you.

ADAM. That's what he seems to depend on. The bribe or the threat.

JACK. Guess again.

ADAM. Well, I'll not be flattered by —

JACK. By any man, Adam. Oh, no — you're too proud for that. For you *are* proud, aren't you, Adam?

ADAM. I'm too proud to be any man's tool, and if that is pride —

JACK. Not a bribe, not a threat, not flattery — guess again.

ADAM. What are you driving at?

JACK. He knows your little secret.

ADAM. You go back and tell your boss that I've got no "little secret."

JACK. He knows your little secret — and I'll tell you what it is.

ADAM. What?

JACK. You want to do good. (*As* ADAM *turns away in confusion*) Well, it's no disgrace. It may be eccentric, but it's no disgrace. You want to heal the sick. And the Boss — he —

ADAM. I told you I'll do nothing for him.

JACK. But, Adam, a ten-million-dollar hospital, every facility you have ever dreamed of. We know you're respected, but aside from that, what have you got now? A one-horse practice in a small town, and a batch of research papers that might get read someday. You take that directorship and people will listen.

ADAM. I told you I will do nothing for him.

JACK. Not even good?

ADAM. Good — that's a hell of a word to use around him — the Boss!

JACK. If a thing is good, it is good in itself.

ADAM. A thing does not grow except in its proper climate, and you know what climate Stark creates.

JACK. A good is a good, pal. Is the rose less of a rose for the dung in the ground? Is a love sonnet any worse because the guy who wrote it had hot pants? Is a —

ADAM. You are completely irrelevant.

JACK. That's what you always used to say when we were kids, pal, and I won the argument. Could a lion whip a tiger? Is Keats better than Shelley? Is there a God? I always won the argument, and you always said I was irrelevant— But Little Jackie is never irrelevant, and I leave you with that thought. 'Bye, Adam. *(Reappearing near stage center as the light is down on* ADAM*)* And I might have left him alone forever to be whatever he was, to do what good he could do, sunk in his world and his isolation, and not have bothered him about the hospital anymore. If Anne had not asked me. But even then I could not have persuaded Adam, if when I dug on Judge Irwin I had not found something I never expected to find. *(*ANNE *is revealed in a spotlight.* JACK *continues talking as he approaches to take her arm)* And I had the documents in my pocket as Anne and I walked the streets that night and came to the docks on the river.

ANNE. All right, Jack, why is he so against it?

JACK. *(Stepping back from her)* I don't know, I tried.

ANNE. But you can make him do it. You're the only person he loves.

JACK. Anne, it's impossible.

ANNE. Then try harder.

JACK. Listen, Anne, I think the best thing for Adam is to let Adam alone.

ANNE. Alone, that's the trouble. He's alone—he has withdrawn from me, from us, from the world—and it's killing him and it's killing me.

JACK. Yeah, I know.

ANNE. Please, Jack.

JACK. Anne, it's impossible.

ANNE. I can't believe there's no way to make him.

JACK. There's no way to make him because, to be perfectly brutal, he is the son of Governor Stanton, the grandson of Judge Peyton Stanton, and the great-grandson of General Morgan Stanton. It is because he is a romantic, and has a picture of the world in his head, and when the world doesn't conform in the slightest particular to that picture, he wants to throw the world away. Even if it means throwing out the baby with the bath.

ANNE. Make him do it.

JACK. It means changing the picture in his head. *(With a dawning idea)* It would be like an operation—like cutting a chunk out of what makes Adam Adam.

ANNE. I don't care. I want him to do it.

JACK. How much do you want that?

ANNE. *(Embracing him with sudden lover-like intensity)* More than anything in the world.

JACK. *(As she releases him)* Are you sure?

ANNE. Sure.

JACK. Okay. Okay. But I couldn't ever do this if you hadn't asked me.

ANNE. Do what?

JACK. What I am going to do. Damn it, there's only one way.

ANNE. What way?

JACK. By giving him a history lesson. What we students of history always learn is that man is not good or bad, but bad *and* good —

ANNE. Tell me.

JACK. — and the good comes out of the bad — and the bad comes out of the good, and —

ANNE. Oh, stop it and tell me.

JACK. Remember, you asked me.

ANNE. Damn it, Jack. You're just talking so you won't tell me.

JACK. Back in 1928 Judge Irwin was broke. His house and his plantation were mortgaged. But he was State Attorney General.

ANNE. Oh, Jack, I know all that. Back when Father was Governor.

JACK. Yes. Irwin was State Attorney General. The state had a suit against the Southern Belle Coal Corporation. Well, Irwin killed the suit.

ANNE. Irwin — Judge Irwin — took a bribe?

JACK. No greasy bills in a back alley. Just some stock in one corporation to help pay off the mortgage. And a nice job as attorney to take care of the debts.

ANNE. Tell me, what has this got to do with it? With me — with Adam?

JACK. *(Coming to put an arm around her shoulder)* There was a man named Littlepaugh who had been attorney for the corporation that took Irwin. They threw Littlepaugh out to make a place for Irwin. But Littlepaugh raised a kick. And they laughed in his face. So he went to the capital to see your father, and to demand an investigation of Irwin and the Southern Belle —

ANNE. *(As JACK withdraws from her)* Jack, was my father — You *are* a coward! God, you're a coward. You won't tell me. Did they buy him too? Did they, did they?

JACK. It's not that bad.

ANNE. Well, if it's not that bad, then how bad is it?

JACK. Your father threw Littlepaugh out. Unfortunately, Littlepaugh killed himself. Jumped out of a window.

ANNE. Not that bad! *(Collecting herself)* I don't believe it.

JACK. Anne, I don't like it any better than you do. But it's true. I have the proof. Littlepaugh wrote a death letter to his sister. I got it. I have the stock transactions. Oh, I have all the documents. *(He takes some papers from a pocket.)*

ANNE. *(Withdrawing from him, she sits down, leaning forward, sick and weak)* I don't want to see them.

JACK. Anne, I'm sorry.

ANNE. *(Numbly)* If you were sorry, why did you get them? *(Jerking up)* Yes, why did you get them?

JACK. Damn it — if you must know, I got them for Stark.

ANNE. So you got them for Stark. *(Leaning forward weakly again, laughing, shaking her head at the sad humor)* So that's what it all comes to. So that's what our lives have all come to. You had to go dig it all up. For Stark.

JACK. I didn't want to tell you. But it's the only way.

ANNE. For what?

JACK. To make Adam do what you want—

ANNE. Oh—oh— *(Rising with sudden decision)* Give me those papers!

JACK. What? What are you going to do?

ANNE. Show them to Adam. *(She seizes the papers from his hand)* Yes, isn't that what Stark would want? Isn't that what you would want—since Stark would want it?

(The light is down on ANNE, and, as JACK stands listening, we hear an echo— offstage—over and over:

    Stark would want
    Stark would want
    Stark would want—

Then the light is down on JACK.)

ANNE. *(Reappearing at stage right, the papers no longer in her hand, speaking toward the audience)* No, not for that. Not for Stark. It was to save Adam, to bring him back to the world—

ADAM. *(Appearing at stage right, further forward than ANNE, with the papers in his hand, staring at them)* And she put them in my hand, and she said—

ANNE. *(Toward the audience)* Can't you see you are living a lie? Can't you see you can't live in the past, for the past was not what you think—

ADAM. And she said—

ANNE. Even our father, Adam. Even our father—

ADAM. God damn his soul to hell. *(Pausing, as he stares at the papers)* They struck me where I was weak. My friend, my sister—

ANNE. Oh, do what good you can—and forget the way it's done—

ADAM. They struck me at the point where what I was, was joined to what the past had been. It was the joint between what good I dreamed and what good I dreamed the past had been. The splice was imperfect, the nail was rusted, the solder weak. And at that point, I broke.

PROFESSOR. *(Approaching from stage left, where he has been watching)* For all your scientific training, Doctor, you were as romantically deluded as all the rest.

ADAM. Deluded? My God, he came to my office—even to my office Stark came!

(JACK ushers STARK and SUGAR-BOY into ADAM's office.)

JACK. Governor Stark, this is Dr. Stanton. You've already met his sister, Anne.

STARK. *(Standing solidly before ANNE, who is seated, then turning toward ADAM)* Yes, I've had the pleasure. Nice to meet you, Doc.

ADAM. *(Very reluctantly taking* STARK's *hand)* How do you do.

STARK. *(Looking down at the clasped hands)* See, boy, it's not nearly as bad as you thought. It didn't kill you. *(As* ADAM *jerks his hand away,* STARK *turns to* ANNE*)* It didn't kill you, Miss Stanton, the first time you shook hands with me?

ANNE. Why, no, Governor. Of course not.

ADAM. Won't you be seated?

STARK. Well, Doc, what do you think of it?

ADAM. Of what?

STARK. Of my hospital, boy.

ADAM. I think it will do the people of this state some good. And will get you some votes.

STARK. Forget about the votes, Doc. I don't have to build a hospital to get votes. I know lots of ways to skin a cat.

ADAM. So I understand.

STARK. Yeah, it'll do some good. But not too much good unless you take over. You're the man for it. And Jack here says you've agreed.

ADAM. I won't tolerate any interference.

STARK. Don't worry. I might fire you, boy, but I won't interfere —

ADAM. If that is a threat —

STARK. Boy, I wouldn't threaten you.

ADAM. I believe you know my views of your administration. They are no secret. They will be no secret in the future. Do you understand?

STARK. No offense, Doc, but I could run this state with you howling on every street corner like a pup with a sore tail. All I want is for you to run that hospital and run it right. Do you understand?

ADAM. I understand that you think my name will be useful to you politically.

STARK. You just don't understand politics, Doc. You don't understand what makes the mare go. *(Rising, casual and amiable)* You're just like a lot of folks. You want certain things that are nice and right. For instance, you want this hospital and you want the bricks, but don't you know that somebody has got to get down in the mud to make 'em? You are just like everybody who loves a big juicy steak but just can't bear to go down to the slaughterhouse because there are some mean men down there who aren't kind to animals. Maybe it is all right for me to be down in the mud, huh? Or down at the slaughter-house. *(Crossing to stand over* ANNE *and speak challengingly down to her)* I mean no offense, Miss Stanton, but do you think it's honorable to want something and not be willing to pay the price for it?

ANNE. Why — why — I don't know —

STARK. Now, if you think that is honorable, just tell your brother here —

ADAM. If you came here for the purpose of —

ANNE. Adam, please.

STARK. (*Gaily*) Easy, Doc, easy. It's just that folks like you think you can inherit everything. Just because you inherited your father's name, his brains, and a little money, you think you can inherit everything. But there's one thing you can't inherit. And do you know what that is?

ADAM. No, what?

STARK. Goodness, Doc. Just plain, simple goodness. You want it, but you can't inherit it. You've got to make it out of badness. And do you know why?

ADAM. Why?

STARK. Because there's nothing else to make it out of. Did you know that, Doc?

ADAM. What are you trying to convince me of?

STARK. Nothing. I'm just telling you the facts of life.

ADAM. You don't have to tell me anything. I said I'd take your job. That's all. I'll take the job. And my reasons are my own.

STARK. Yeah, your reasons are your own. But I just thought you'd want to know something about mine.

ADAM. I'm not interested.

STARK. Not even if we're going to do business together?

ADAM. I'm going to run the hospital. If you call that doing business together.

STARK. Doc, just don't worry. You don't have to get mixed up in my business. I'll keep your little mitts clean. I'll put you in that beautiful ten-million-dollar hospital, and wrap you in cellophane, untouched by human hands. But look at my hands, Doc. (*Cheerfully holding his hands out*) Pitch-black. But don't you worry. I'll take care of you, Doc.

ADAM. I can take care of myself.

STARK. Sure you can, Doc. (*With a sudden change of tone, dignified and businesslike*) You will no doubt want to see all the plans that have been drawn up. We have the most reputable architects in the state. Mr. Todd, of Todd and Waters, will call on you. Start picking your staff. It is your baby. Jack'll stay and fill you in on some of the details. (*Suddenly slapping* ADAM *on the shoulder*) You're a great boy, Doc. And don't let them tell you different. (*Turning to* ANNE) May I drop you somewhere, Miss Stanton?

ANNE. Why, yes — Thank you, Governor.

(ANNE *rises and precedes* STARK's *exit from the office.* ADAM *and* JACK *stare at her, and then, as the light begins to dim, their eyes meet. Meanwhile, the light comes up on* SUGAR-BOY, *who is near center stage, waiting as* ANNE *crosses slowly, followed by* STARK. *He makes a gesture of dismissal to* SUGAR, *who disappears; there is the sound of a car starting and driving off.* ANNE *is standing with her back to* STARK, *some distance from him.*)

STARK. Miss Stanton — Miss Stanton — (*She does not turn*) Do you think it's honorable to want something and not be willing to pay the price?

(STARK steps forward and lays a hand on her shoulder and she stiffens, as the light is down. In the office area, the light comes up on ADAM.)

ADAM. *(Toward the audience)* He laid his hand on me, and smiled. "You're a great boy," he said. I was weak. But I came to see. I saw. I saw. And I—

PROFESSOR. *(Approaching)* And what you saw, or thought you saw, made you perform the final romantic act. For you could not understand the nature of things. You repudiated the world which you could not understand. It proves that what you would call your ideal had no reference to reality, but was, as your sister said, only a self-indulgent dream.

ADAM. I should have struck him where he stood.

JACK. You would have if you had known. You would have done it, for you are Adam. But you didn't know. And neither did I. But I—

(JACK moves across to stage left, and occupies himself, leaning over the desk, as SADIE bursts in.)

SADIE. The son-of-a-bitch, I'll kill him.

JACK. You having woman trouble with him again?

SADIE. I'll kill him, I swear it. After what I did for him. After I made him. After I took him when he was the Sap of the Year and put him in the Big Time. He can't two-time me, he—

JACK. Look here, my pet, he can't be two-timing you. He was two-timing Lucy with you. Whatever he's doing to you ain't two-timing—it may be four-timing. It may be six-timing. Your arithmetic—

SADIE. I'll kill him. He can't chuck me. Not after I made him. And every time he sees some tart with a pretty face— *(Prodding her face)* Look, look at my face—is it so bad?

JACK. Look here, Sadie, it's not worth the grief. You know him, he—

SADIE. Look at my face—look at it, Jack—did the smallpox make it so bad? And he—

JACK. Come on, Sadie, it's a swell face. Forget about him, forget . . . *(He tries to comfort her.)*

SADIE. Don't touch me, don't touch me. For it's all your fault. Your fault, do you hear? You had to bring your high-toned friends—oh, I didn't mind those common tarts, he always came back, he came back—but your high-toned friends—oh, it's all your fault!

JACK. What the hell are you talking about?

SADIE. You know what I'm talking about, you pimp. If you were a man you'd go in there and knock him down. I thought she was yours. Or maybe he's fixing you up, too.

JACK. What are you saying?

SADIE. Maybe he's fixed you up like he fixed that doctor—that Stanton. Oh, yeah—maybe he'll make you the director of a hospital to keep you quiet.

JACK. Are you implying that—that—that she—

SADIE. Implying—implying—I'm telling you. That Stanton girl—that high-toned whore—that whore!

JACK. *(Putting the heel of his right hand to his brow, with a low, painful utterance)* Oh—oh.

PROFESSOR. So, unable to face that fact, you got in a car and drove blind for two thousand miles to Long Beach, California.

JACK. But the past rode with me all the way. It followed me like a flood. For I loved her. I loved her.

ANNE. *(Appearing at stage center, facing him)* You loved me, yes. But you were lost in the world, and so was I. And the years were lost, like sand in the fingers, or wind. For I had needed someone to say, "See, this is the way." *(Holding out her hands)* But you did not.

JACK. Anne, I remembered.

ANNE. And I remember, too. I was eighteen. It was back at Burden's Landing. *(JACK moves forward to take her in his arms. They sink to the platform)* Jack, what are you doing? Let me go! No, Jack, no!

JACK. Don't you love me anymore?

ANNE. Oh, Jack, you know I love you—I'll always love you—Just you.

JACK. All right. If you love me—now, now.

ANNE. No—Jack—no.

JACK. You would have, last week. You almost did. If my mother hadn't come back that night you would have—wouldn't you?

ANNE. It's true. I almost did.

JACK. All right.

ANNE. But, Jack—it's horrible to say, Jack—but I'm glad I didn't.

JACK. I knew it. You don't love me now.

ANNE. I love you. I'll always love you. I love you more than the world. For you are the world—the whole green, beautiful world—you are the whole world—Jackie-Boy. You're older than the world.

JACK. Don't you call me Jackie-Boy. Not after what you said. That you were glad you didn't. That night with me.

ANNE. Don't you understand? Can't you understand? I do love you. I want you. But—

JACK. But what?

ANNE. Oh, don't you understand?

JACK. Damn it, I'm not trying to steal your virginity. If that's what's on your mind. I've tried to make you marry me a dozen times. Right now, will you marry me? Tonight? Tomorrow?

ANNE. Oh, Jack, I love you. And I feel sometimes I might just kiss you and hold you tight and close my eyes and jump off a cliff with you. Or like the time we dived down deep, deep, and kissed in the water. Don't you remember, Jack?

JACK. But now, what about now?

ANNE. I love you now, but it's different.

JACK. How, different?

ANNE. Jack, you don't understand that love isn't like jumping off a cliff. Or getting drowned. It's — oh, it's trying to live, Jack.

JACK. Money — if it's money — I'll get a job. But not with any of these rich bastards here at the Landing. Or through them. Not even Irwin. If it's money you want —

ANNE. You idiot, you silly Jackie-Boy. It's not money and you know it. I'd love you and live in a shack with you and eat red beans, if you'd only understand. If you only knew what you wanted, if you only —

JACK. I want you.

ANNE. That isn't enough. It isn't enough, darling. You've got to want — oh, I don't know how to say it, but you've got to want to live, to live in the world, to do something — something that means something. Oh, Jack — it's just the way you are, you don't want anything.

JACK. *(Jerking away as the light is down on* ANNE*)* God damn it. God damn it all.

PROFESSOR. *(Moving into view)* So, Mr. Burden, you left her. Alone to face the world. Although you knew Stark was the opposite of everything she had been brought up to esteem, still he was the opposite of you. For he could act. He was sure of himself. So when Sadie Burke, somewhat indelicately, informed you of the fact, you, unable to face that fact, ran away.

JACK. Oh, the past rode with me all the way, to Long Beach, California, and it lay with me when I lay naked, at night, on my hotel bed. And lying there, I thought that nothing mattered, nothing, and then I had a vision of bodies, and naked, detached limbs heaving and bleeding from inexhaustible wounds. And that was my picture of the world.

PROFESSOR. You should have hunted up a good psychiatrist.

JACK. No, I didn't need one. For, suddenly, it was funny. For I saw that even that vision didn't matter. For everything in the world was only the dark heave of blood and the twitch of nerve, like the twitch of the nerve in the dead frog's leg in the experiment, when you run the electric current through it. And I laughed, I laughed out loud, for if that is true, then everything is like everything else, and it does not matter what happens to anybody — not to Anne Stanton, or Willie Stark, or Jack Burden. And there is no God but the Great Twitch. *(Approaching the* PROFESSOR*)* You see, back then I was like you. I worshiped the Great Twitch. Which is the God of your age.

PROFESSOR. I suppose that what you are trying to say is that you somewhat tardily recognized the physical basis of life.

JACK. Oh, I recognized it, and it made everything look like everything else.

PROFESSOR. But can't you see, that was sentimental, too? For Nature prescribes her own values. Adjustment, balance, health — a sound mind in a sound body — a well-organized society — a —

JACK. Oh, I know your line, pal, and since I used to agree with it, I came back. I came back to Willie Stark. Oh, he was well adjusted. He was on top of the world. He had Anne. He had the opposition licked. It looked as if the hospital was going to be built his own way. And to top it all, Tom Stark, his son, was a hero. All-American quarterback — and the crowd roared! Oh, the Boss was crazy about that boy. The crummy little cock-of-the-walk. Not yet hurt by the likker and the girls.

LUCY. *(Appearing stage right)* He was a good boy. If they had let him be. But they gave him a ball and they cheered and their spittle was on him — Oh, I did what I could.

JACK. Yeah, Lucy was separated from the Boss, and Tom was the Boss's boy. But she tried. Like the time Tom got in a brawl in a roadhouse, a fight over a girl, and got thrown in the jug, and it hits the papers. Lucy went to see Stark at the Mansion.

(JACK and the PROFESSOR withdraw as STARK is revealed brooding alone in his office. LUCY enters to surprise him, with a newspaper in her hand.)

STARK. Lucy! What are you doing here?

LUCY. It's about Tom. It's in the papers. You've got to put a stop to it.

STARK. If you mean stop playing football, I told you —

LUCY. It's not just football. That's bad enough, thinking he's a hero, that there's nothing else in the world — but it's what he has become — he's wild and selfish and idle — and last night, last night, Willie, he was in jail — our boy, Willie — in jail —

STARK. No son of mine is going to be a sissy.

LUCY. If you won't think of him, think of yourself — what a thing like this means to you, what —

STARK. I can take care of myself.

LUCY. You will ruin him.

STARK. Ruin him, ruin him! Hell, let him have some fun growing up. I never had any fun when I was a kid.

LUCY. I'd rather see him dead at my feet than what your vanity will make him.

STARK. Don't be a damned fool, Lucy.

LUCY. Oh, Willie, you loved me once — and he's our son — our son.

STARK. Our son — *our* son? I tell you, he's *my* son. *Mine*, do you hear?

LUCY. Oh, Willie — Willie —

(She turns away, stricken. Suddenly appalled by his own words, STARK approaches her, trying to explain to her—to explain to himself.)

STARK. Listen, Lucy. You remember my father's house. A house set on a bare hill, on the rock chunks, and the wind beat. I lay there at night, just a boy coming on. It was night and I'd look north across that ice a thousand, five thousand, a million miles. The moon was on the snow. The wind would come riding down under that moon. I'd close my eyes, and it was like that million miles of wind was in me. Something inside me just got so big— *(Dismissing the effort to explain himself, to understand himself)* Oh, you wouldn't understand, you wouldn't understand.

LUCY. Oh, Willie, you think you are one thing, but you're another and different. But I know what you are, what you are, deep inside. I know the very bottom of your heart, what it is, Willie, what you never see anymore.

SADIE. *(Entering)* Oh, excuse me please. Tom's here. Lieutenant Boyd brought him in.

STARK. All right, bring him in.

SADIE. *(Somewhat embarrassed)* Mrs. Stark, I'm—I'm glad they found him. I mean, I'm glad he's all right.

LUCY. Yes, he's all right. And thank you, Miss Burke. *(As TOM, disheveled but cocky, enters)* Tom, Tom, are you all right?

TOM. Mom!—what are you doing here?

LUCY. *(Embracing him)* Tom, you've got to stop getting into trouble.

STARK. Tommy-Boy!

TOM. Well, Your Highness, I gotta hand it to you. Your little tin-badged highway cop tried to get rough with me. Yeah, he tried, but he didn't.

STARK. I told him to club you over the ear if he had to do it to bring you in.

TOM. Yeah, him and how many more?

STARK. Tom, four days before the Stafford game, and you break training. Miss two days' practice and get boiled.

TOM. Don't worry, Daddy dear, I'll be there Saturday to push over a few for you. *(He pours a drink.)*

STARK. Get your hands off my likker. Maybe you won't ever push over anymore. Not if you break training again. Coach Howes has just about had a bellyful of you, and he—

TOM. He wants the championship, doesn't he?

STARK. Yeah, but he'll bench you anyway. And I'll back him up.

TOM. Oh, yeah?

STARK. Yeah, I don't care how hot you are on the field. I don't care if you're a cross between Pavlova and a locomotive. I don't care if you are Napoleon at Marengo, I'll see you never get your hands on a football again.

TOM. No—no, you won't.

STARK. What do you mean I won't? You know me well enough to know—

TOM. I know you well enough to know that you want the championship worse than Howes ever did. Well enough to know you want me there to shove 'em across for you every Saturday, so you can big-shot it around. (*Seizing a cigar from* STARK's *vest pocket, setting it into a corner of his mouth in a parody of his father*) Yeah, it's my boy did it—it's my boy Tom—

LUCY. (*As* STARK *starts toward the boy*) Willie! Oh, Tom—Tom—don't—

SADIE. (*Entering*) Jack's here with a Mr. Frey.

STARK. Send 'em up.

LUCY. Come on, Tom, come with me.

JACK. (*Entering*) I'm sorry, Boss, we'll wait outside.

(*LUCY and TOM go out.*)

STARK. Come on in, Jack. It's nothing. Lucy just came to see me about Tom. Say, whoever let that get into the paper? (*Seeing the nondescript man being ushered in by* SUGAR-BOY) What does he want?

JACK. I think you'd better talk to him. His name is Frey. Governor, this is Mr. Frey.

FREY. Glad to meet you, Governor.

STARK. You want a drink?

FREY. No thank you. (*Bracing himself, with an effort at camaraderie*) Well, Governor—I am sure sorry about what happened last night. Now, I seen Tom Stark play football, and he is sure sweet. Yeah, and I made me some money betting on Tom Stark. Now, you take that Alabama game—

STARK. He was pretty good that day—

FREY. Yeah, and to see a boy like that have any trouble, you know—like last night.

STARK. Oh, hell, damned fool wouldn't give his name, so they locked him up. But that's not trouble.

FREY. But it's sort of embarrassing—

STARK. Embarrassing? Who the hell's embarrassed?

FREY. To tell the truth, Governor, yeah, to tell the truth—I'm sort of embarrassed.

STARK. What's the matter? Aren't your pants buttoned?

FREY. Ha, ha. But serious, Governor—it's sort of embarrassing—you know. It's sort of embarrassing to my little girl—my—Sibyl. (*He hands* STARK *a newspaper.*)

STARK. This Sibyl—this Sibyl Frey here—Hey, your name is Frey, isn't it?

FREY. Yeah, yeah, it's my girl. My girl Sibyl out with your boy. Got her name in the paper. It's sort of embarrassing—her name—

STARK. Congratulations, buddy, lots of girls would like to get their name in the paper with Tom Stark.

FREY. Well, Sibyl don't like it. Sibyl is sort of shy. What you might call timid —
and she —

STARK. What is this, a shake-down?

FREY. Why, no Governor, it ain't no shake-down. It ain't just what's in the paper,
Governor — it's something else — Sibyl — now she —

STARK. Mr. Frey, would you stop gargling and talk?

FREY. Sibyl — Sibyl — she's in a family way.

STARK. Oh, she's so Goddamned shy she's in a family way. Well, what am I, an
obstetrician? What the hell do you want me to do?

FREY. It's — it's — Tom. Tom Stark done it.

STARK. Why, you little bastard. It is a shake-down.

FREY. No — no, sir — Governor — it ain't no shake-down — no, sir. I'm a father —
I mean, Sibyl is my little girl — she's done give her all.

STARK. All her what, Mr. Frey?

FREY. Give her all, like they say.

STARK. (Putting his arm on FREY's shoulder, walking him out) Well, Mr. Frey, my
advice to you is to go home and tell Sibyl her all is not worth six bits.

FREY. Six bits, six bits! It ain't the money, it ain't. It's my Sibyl — I'm her father —
and she's going to have a baby — and if Tom Stark don't marry her —

STARK. (Jerking from FREY, dumbfounded) Marry! Jack, did he say "marry"? (To
FREY) Listen. I don't care if your little Sibyl is as full of squaw-fruit as a possum
is of grease. I don't care where she caught the disease. Or how. But I'm telling
you if you think some six-bit little tart can —

FREY. Tart! Tart! Sibyl ain't no tart. Ask anybody in Duboisville. Ain't no man
can say it, Governor or not —

STARK. (Seizing FREY) You'd better thank God I'm Governor. If I wasn't Governor I'd jerk your damned yellow bilious tongue out and wrap it around your
neck. I'd cut your heart out and feed it to the hogs. Now get out. (FREY,
protesting all the way, is seized by SUGAR-BOY and hustled out) God damn it.
They can't do it to Tom.

JACK. Maybe Tom did knock her up.

STARK. Hell, it's a frame-up. You can look in that guy's eyes and see it. (An idea
dawning) Duboisville. Who else is from Duboisville?

JACK. MacMurfee.

STARK. Sure, and he knows he's losing the impeachment. It's the bastard's last try.

JACK. Looks like your little boy has fixed you good.

STARK. Hell, he's just a boy.

JACK. Boy or not, he's given MacMurfee some ammunition. Well, there's always
Tiny's friend Larsen. You can always deal with Larsen.

STARK. No, by God. Deal with Larsen and he'll ask for the hospital contract.
And he won't get that, by God. (A long pause, grappling with the problem)
Jack, you remember I told you to dig on your old pal Judge Irwin?

JACK. Yeah.

STARK. Did you find the dead cat?

JACK. Yeah—what are you going to do with it?

STARK. What do you think? Put the screws on Irwin. Make him beat some sense into MacMurfee's head. MacMurfee will have to listen to him. He hasn't got many friends left. And Irwin's the biggest leg in the stool. Gimme the pussy cat.

JACK. Not yet.

STARK. What do you mean, not yet?

JACK. I mean not yet. I made a promise.

STARK. A promise to who?

JACK. To myself. Not to do anything till I saw Judge Irwin.

STARK. Hell, you go down and ask your old pal is he guilty, and sure, he'll say he is washed in the Blood of the Lamb. But he is washed in whitewash. Gimme the pussy cat.

JACK. Not yet, Boss.

STARK. What the hell do you think I'm paying you for?

JACK. Okay. I quit.

STARK. You mean it, don't you, Jack?

JACK. I mean it.

STARK. Play it your way. But take it from me—he's washed in whitewash.

(*As* STARK *turns away into the darkness* JACK *moves toward stage right, where* IRWIN *is revealed in his study, reading.* JACK *enters.*)

IRWIN. Damned glad you came by, Boy. It's a long time, isn't it?

JACK. Yes, sir, it's been a long time.

IRWIN. Let me fix you a drink—a little gin and tonic never hurt anyone—not you and me at least—we're indestructible, you and me, aren't we, Boy?

JACK. No, thanks, Judge, no drink, please.

IRWIN. Well, I'm not going to drink by myself. I'll get my stimulation from your conversation. What's on your mind?

JACK. Well, uh—nothing much.

IRWIN. There is always something.

JACK. Yes, there is always something.

IRWIN. Out with it.

JACK. You don't like Stark's methods.

IRWIN. Oh, let's not talk politics, Jack.

JACK. Let me tell you about your pal MacMurfee's methods. Miss Sibyl Frey, a little tart over in Duboisville, is knocked up, and puts the finger on Tom Stark. It's a frame-up.

IRWIN. What's this got to do with—

JACK. I know it's a frame-up, because MacMurfee offers to fix it up and call off the impeachment if Stark will make a deal.

IRWIN. That can't be true!

JACK. It's true. He wants to make a deal for the Governorship behind your back. Now, is this pretty?

IRWIN. No.

JACK. Well, you can stop it. MacMurfee will listen to you. Tell him he can't be Governor, but our organization will absorb him. Might even let him go to Congress. If he calls off Frey. Will you do it?

IRWIN. Of course not. My God, they're blackguards. Stark and MacMurfee. They're all blackguards! I won't mix in that sort of thing.

JACK. Listen, Judge, you've got to. I'm begging you, Judge.

IRWIN. No.

JACK. Judge, please. I'm not kidding.

IRWIN. Jack, I know my own mind. That's about the only thing I've learned out of life. That I know when I know my own mind.

JACK. Well, you decide tomorrow. I'll be back tomorrow.

IRWIN. I've decided tonight.

JACK. Did you ever hear of a man named Mortimer L. Littlepaugh?

IRWIN. No, I don't think so.

JACK. Did you ever hear of the American Electric Power Company?

IRWIN. Naturally, I was their counsel for ten years.

JACK. Do you remember how you got that job?

IRWIN. Yes, it was through a man named —

JACK. Judge, change your mind. Judge, I'm begging you. Judge, I'm begging you.

IRWIN. No. I told you no. (JACK *flings the documents to the desk.* IRWIN *reads, then speaks, marveling*) Littlepaugh — Littlepaugh. You know, I didn't even remember his name. I swear, I didn't even remember his name. (*Touching the papers*) It was like this never happened. Not to me. Maybe to somebody else, but not to me.

JACK. But it did.

IRWIN. Yes, Jack, it did. But it is difficult for me to believe.

JACK. It is for me, too.

IRWIN. According to these documents, my dear old friend, Governor Stanton, impaired his honor to protect me. He never told me. His failing was a defect of his virtue. The virtue of his affection for a friend.

JACK. Judge, if that's meant for me — I tell you —

IRWIN. My boy, I didn't mean that — from my heart I didn't. I just wanted you to know about Governor Stanton. That you might think well of him. (*Pause, and then a shift of tone*) I suppose your employer is trying to put the pressure on me? To blackmail me?

JACK. Pressure is a prettier word.

IRWIN. I don't care much about pretty words anymore. You live with words a long time. *(Again a shift of tone, to matter-of-factness)* Well, your employer's an attorney, and he ought to know that this stuff won't stick in a court of law.

JACK. Judge, you don't live in a court. You live in the world, and people think you are a certain kind of man. You don't want them to think different, Judge.

IRWIN. By God, they've no right to think different! By God, I've done my duty, I've done what's right—

JACK. *(Indicating the documents)* Judge—

IRWIN. Yes, I did this, too.

JACK. Yes, you did.

IRWIN. Does Stark know it?

JACK. No. I wanted you to confirm it first.

IRWIN. You have a tender sensibility for a blackmailer.

JACK. You are trying to protect a blackmailer—MacMurfee.

IRWIN. Maybe I'm trying to protect—maybe I'm trying to protect myself.

JACK. Well, you know how to do that then. By stopping MacMurfee.

IRWIN. Jack, I could do it easier than that.

JACK. How?

IRWIN. *(Coming to JACK, taking him by the shoulders)* I could just—I could just say to you—I could just tell you something—something you don't know.

JACK. What? Tell me what?

IRWIN. *(Gaily, withdrawing)* Nothing.

JACK. Tell me what, Judge?

IRWIN. Nothing. Not a damned thing. Jack— *(Turning away, listening)* You can hear the sea. There isn't any wind, but you can hear the sea rippling on the sand out there in the night. There's a half-moon, and by now it's westering across the water.

JACK. Judge, I'll be back tomorrow. You decide—tomorrow.

IRWIN. Sure, Boy, sure.

(JACK withdraws, and IRWIN, looking after him, lifts a hand in a gesture of fare-well, or benediction, as the light goes down on him.)

JACK. *(Moving to stage center)* He had not scared. The Judge had not scared. I walked through the hot night to lie on my bed in my mother's house, and then came the scream.

(His MOTHER appears, stage center rear, with a phone in her hand. She drops it, and screams. He seizes her and tries to stop her hysterics. Then she turns on him.)

MOTHER. You did it! You did it!

JACK. Did what?

MOTHER. You killed him, you killed him. Oh, I don't know how you did it — or why — but you did it — you killed him. It was you. Oh, I know it was you — you — you — you —

JACK. Shut up, Mother. Shut up.

MOTHER. You killed him!

JACK. Killed who?

MOTHER. Judge Irwin — your father — and you killed him!

(JACK jerks from her, appalled. In a desperate gesture, he presses a clenched fist against his forehead, and there is the punctuation of a muted drum-ruffle, off-stage.)

The Light Blacks Out

Act Three

(The light comes up on JACK and his MOTHER. They are standing in the same location as at the end of Act Two. JACK is looking toward the audience. His MOTHER is seated, with her eyes fixed on him.)

JACK. *(Speaking toward the audience)* So I stood here at Burden's Landing, where I had had, and lost, two fathers. A man named Burden, who had crept away somewhere to rot. And a man named Monty Irwin, who could have stopped me with four short words — "You are my son." Monty Irwin.

MOTHER. And you must love him. For remember, son, I loved him. But love is so small in the wide world. It lies in the palm of your hand like quicksilver, but it slips, it is gone, and the million glittering globules are lost. Or it is the ring you drop in the woodpath, precious and bright and small, and the leaves cover it over. You cannot find it. But, son, remember, I loved him.

JACK. *(Still facing forward, as the light is down on his MOTHER)* I will remember. I will remember as I walk in the world.

STARK. *(His voice is heard from the dark at stage left, before the light is up on him)* Jack! Jackie! Jack! *(As light goes up and JACK approaches)* So the bastard crawled out on me!

JACK. He's dead. He shot himself. If that's crawling out.

STARK. I didn't tell you to scare him to death.

JACK. *(Approaching with an air of furious assault)* All you're worried about is your Goddamned hospital. Yeah, that's all! But that's fixed. Yeah, Irwin fixed you good! *(Crowding in on STARK, his forefinger threatening him)* And there's only one thing left for you — only one thing left to turn to. You've got to go to Larsen! You've got to deal with Larsen!

(As STARK *is driven out of his office, as it were,* JACK *turns and bursts into savage laughter, which is interrupted by football music from the radio on the desk. As* JACK *turns to it, the sports announcer begins.)*

ANNOUNCER'S VOICE. This may be a black day for State — trailing Stafford at the half — but they still have spirit. The band is moving out to spell out that "S" — "S" for State. That's the school they love — listen —

(Band music.)

DUFFY. *(Enters, escorting* LARSEN*)* Mr. Larsen, this is Jack Burden. *(*JACK *is cold and perfunctory)* You got my word to tell Willie Mr. Larsen might get in this afternoon? You told him?

JACK. Yep.

DUFFY. He ain't here. His office is locked.

JACK. This is a football game. This is for the championship. This is important.

DUFFY. And Mr. Larsen here is a pretty important man, Jack.

JACK. The Boss said to be at the Mansion tonight. Eight P.M. *After* dinner.

DUFFY. Mr. Larsen, would you care to have a seat, make yourself comfortable? *(As* LARSEN *sits,* DUFFY *turns back to* JACK, *pettishly)* Mr. Larsen here is a mighty important man. Great God! Keeping Mr. Larsen waiting for a durn ball game. Looks like Stark would be here now. Looks like he —

JACK. Maybe he does wish he were here. He did not calculate on trailing Stafford University by ten points at the half. He did not calculate on the Sophomore Thunderbolt being back-broke from night life. He did not calculate on the Sophomore Thunderbolt having lead in his pants.

ANNOUNCER'S VOICE. Governor Stark is coming out of the locker room. He has been encouraging his team. With his entourage he is now moving up the sidelines to his box. *(Sound of catcalls, booing, and jeers)* This is without precedent! The Governor is being booed!

DUFFY. The Governor is being booed, right in that stadium that he built 'em. Well, I tell you, if I was Governor and I got booed in my own stadium, I would sure be here to see Mr. Larsen. If I was under impeachment, I would sure —

LARSEN. *(Calmly)* He will come, Mr. Duffy. He is in difficulties.

ANNOUNCER'S VOICE. It is the kickoff — State receives on the twenty — It is Stark — It is Tom Stark — that old Number Two — He is loose — no — no — down on the forty-five — the Stafford forty-five. There's the snap — Yes — yes — it is Stark! Old Tom is carrying the ball — it is the comeback trail — it is the old-time Tom Stark — He's loose — it is a touchdown. No — no — it is not a touchdown—four feet to go—Tom Stark was hurt on the play—Tom Stark is still down. Here comes the doctor on the field. Here is the stretcher. It appears that Tom Stark has regained consciousness.

DUFFY. Well, why don't he leave that little bastard, and come and do business?

ANNOUNCER'S VOICE. But here's the snap—it is a touchdown! These boys will not be denied. It was a straight power play. Pure power. They just boiled over the goal line. Listen to the cheers, cheers for Tom Stark. The Governor has left his box, presumably to go to his son's side.

DUFFY. Well, why don't he come on?

LARSEN. *(Calmly)* He will come, Mr. Duffy. He is under impeachment. There is even some comment to the effect that Judge Irwin did not commit suicide.

JACK. Look here—Gummy—

DUFFY. Gum—You mean Mr. Larsen, Jack.

JACK. Hell, no, I mean *Gummy*, and I will instruct Gummy that I was there.

LARSEN. Yes. I heard you were there.

JACK. Yes, by God, I was, and—*(JACK swings away, turning to speak over his shoulder)* Stark will see you at the Mansion at eight. After dinner. *(Moving to stage center, as the light is down on DUFFY and LARSEN)* Yeah, he would see Gummy Larsen. But before that he had seen his son in the hospital, with a lot of expensive medical talent spooking around the bed. Oh, yes, and the expensive medical talent said that Tom Stark—the Sophomore Thunderbolt—would be all right. Nothing really wrong, Governor. Oh, yes, Governor, we can assure you of that. So nothing was really wrong, nothing really could go wrong for Willie Stark. And the Governor was back to discharge his official function, and I came to the Mansion and it was a real party. The gang was all there.

(The light comes up on the group, and JACK moves to join it.)

STARK. *(Drinking but not yet drunk, disheveled, and bitter)* Just in time, Jackie-Boy, just in time. Mr. Larsen here is going to build the hospital for me. Tell him, Tiny, tell Jack how puking smart you feel. Tell him how Larsen is going to give you a cut for being so nice—

DUFFY. Now, Boss, that ain't the way Mr. Larsen and I—

STARK. Shut up! You're getting a rake-off and you know it.

DUFFY. Boss, I—

STARK. Shut up. Yeah, look at him. Mr. Larsen used to be a faro dealer, but now he's a big, big-time contractor. And he's just sold out his pal MacMurfee, sold him out to me. Look at that pillar of rectitude, and puke.

LARSEN. If we have arranged our business, Governor—

STARK. Oh, it's arranged, by God. But listen to me, you crook, if—

DUFFY. Boss, don't talk that way to Mr. Larsen. Mr. Larsen is a— *(STARK flings the glass of whiskey in his face, and* DUFFY *moves threateningly, then sees that* SUGAR-BOY *has his revolver half out of the holster*) Boss — Boss, what made you go and do that now?

STARK. I ought to done it long ago. I ought to done it long ago. (STARK *turns to* LARSEN, *seizing his lapel*) Yeah, it's arranged, but you — you leave one window latch off, you leave one piece of iron out of that concrete, you chip one piece of marble, and, by God — I'll rip you open — for that hospital's mine. Do you hear? Mine. Now get out.

(With perfect calm LARSEN *smiles ironically at* STARK, *and withdraws, followed by* DUFFY.)

JACK. Glad I got here for the last act. Was it fun? Well, I'll leave these papers and toddle.

STARK. Wait. *(Taking a drink from the bottle, weaving on his feet)* I told him. I told him. I said if you leave off one window latch, if you leave one iron out of that concrete, if you —

JACK. Yeah, I heard that.

STARK. I told him, I'll — I'll rip you. I told him. I said —

JACK. So you said.

STARK. I'll rip him anyway, by God! I'll do it anyway. *(With a cry of rage and pain)* They made me do it. They made me do it!

JACK. Tom Stark had something to do with it.

STARK. He's just a boy. He's just a boy. *(He sways)* He didn't mean to. He didn't know. *(He collapses on the floor.)*

SUGAR-BOY. *(Taking off his coat to spread it on* STARK) M-M-M-Might catch c-c-cold, Jack.

JACK. Yeah, he might. *(Swinging to the* PROFESSOR, *who has been watching from stage right)* Well, do you think the Boss was a scientific realist that night?

PROFESSOR. He made what arrangements were necessary. But I am not interested in the vaporings around that fact.

JACK. Well, the vaporings are the facts, and the reason —

PROFESSOR. The reason doesn't matter.

(A telephone, stage left, rings, and JACK *moves to answer it as the* PROFESSOR *withdraws.)*

JACK. Jack Burden. No, I can't disturb him. Is it important? Well, let me speak to Dr. Stanton. Adam? Yes, it's Jack. What the hell's the matter?

ADAM. *(Appearing in his office, stage right, talking into the telephone)* It's Tom Stark. I'm afraid it's very serious.

JACK. But he was all right a few hours ago.

ADAM. But he isn't all right now. They've just called me in on the case. You'd better get Stark and his wife here right away.

JACK. All right, as soon as I can. *(He hangs up. The light is down on* ADAM. JACK *turns to* SUGAR-BOY) Sugar, we've got to get the Boss up and around.

SUGAR-BOY. B-B-But J-J-Jack, he's s-s-sleeping.

JACK. But this is important. Call Sadie and tell her to bring Lucy to the hospital right away. Then bring the car around front.

SUGAR-BOY. Is it T-T-Tom?

JACK. Yeah, it's Tom, now hurry up.

SUGAR-BOY. You want I should g-g-get c-c-coffee for the B-B-Boss?

JACK. Yeah, Sugar, that's a good idea. That's a fine idea. *(The light is down on* SUGAR-BOY *and* STARK *as* JACK *moves forward toward stage left and addresses the audience)* And Tom Stark lay in the hospital that night with Dr. Stanton, the big brain surgeon, brooding over him. The Boss and I had been there a long time when Lucy arrived—and we all had a jolly little reunion in the hospital waiting room. *(Moving to join* STARK, *seated stage right.)*

LUCY. *(Entering)* How is he?

STARK. He's all right. You understand?

LUCY. How is he?

STARK. I told you. I told you, he's going to be all right.

LUCY. That's what you say. But what do the doctors say?

STARK. You wanted it this way. You said you'd rather see him dead at your feet. You wanted it. But he—he'll fool you. He's all right. He'll fool you.

LUCY. God grant it.

STARK. Grant it, grant it. That boy's tough. Tough, do you hear?

ADAM. *(Entering)* He is still unconscious, and paralyzed. The reflexes are totally gone. The x-ray shows us a dislocation of the fifth and sixth cervical vertebrae.

STARK. Where is that?

ADAM. *(Touching the back of his own neck)* Right back here.

STARK. What are you going to do?

ADAM. The decision will have to be yours. We can put the patient in traction and wait for some resolution, or we can resort to surgery. This is a technical decision. Therefore, I want you to understand it as clearly as possible. The x-ray can show the condition of the bone, but not of the spinal cord. We can learn that only by operating. If the cord is merely pressed on we can relieve the pressure, and restore some, possibly all, of the function. If the cord is not crushed. If the cord *is* crushed, the patient will remain paralyzed. Do you understand?

STARK. Yes.

ADAM. I must emphasize one other condition. The operation is very near the brain. It may be fatal. It is a radical step. It is an outside chance. It is radical.

STARK. Do it. By God, do it!

(LUCY nods.)

ADAM. I had assumed that you would make that decision. I've made all the arrangements already.

STARK. He'll be all right, do you hear?

JACK. Sure, Boss, sure.

VOICE. *(Offstage)* There is a call for Mr. Burden. There is a call for Mr. Burden.

JACK. *(As the light is down on the others)* Anne called me at the hospital. She
wanted to know. I told her. "My God, my God," she said. But God wasn't on
the other end of the phone. Only Jack Burden, and he couldn't do a thing.
And neither could Adam Stanton, that big Doc. For Tom Stark died.

*(STARK and LUCY appear at stage center, apart, he staring off into space, she
seated and speaking to him across a distance.)*

LUCY. He said Tom was an ideal. A fine, clean ideal for all the boys in this state.
Didn't he say that, Willie? Didn't the preacher say that? An ideal. An ideal for
all the years to come. Didn't he say that about Tom? *(With a burst of pain)*
And it's lies! All lies! Everything is lies, and I can't bear it. The world is lies,
and my baby is dead. *(As STARK moves to her)* Don't touch me.

STARK. Lucy, I don't know what happened, or how. But I know it happened a
long time back, and in darkness. *(Pause)* I want to come back to you, Lucy.
(Pause) You loved me once.

LUCY. *(Rising, moving away, not facing him)* I don't deny it. I loved you. But
what was once possible is not now possible, at least not now — for I have been
in the dark alone, and the dark ticked like a watch, and I remember you
laughed and said he was your son, *not* mine — *not* mine.

STARK. He's our son, Lucy. He's our son. *(As an idea comes to him)* I'll tell you
what I'm going to do. I'm going to name my new hospital after him. It'll be
the *Tom Stark Memorial Hospital and Medical Center*. It'll be —

LUCY. That's what it'll be, and the sports page and the pulpit will do what they
do. But, Willie, can't you see? Can't you see those things don't matter? Your
name in the papers. Having people cheer. Can't you see? Oh, you'll do it,
you'll name it for him, and you can have your son and use him the way you
use everybody — but you cannot have my son! Where is my son? Where is
he? And it's raining. It's raining on the ground!

STARK. Lucy, I loved you. I love you.

LUCY. If you had loved me you would have made things different. Not the way
they are — all ruined when you touch them — wherever you put your hand —

STARK. *(Shutting his eyes as though to shut the world out, and reaching a hand
toward her)* Oh, Lucy — give me your hand.

LUCY. Wherever you put your hand, it was ruin —

STARK. Lucy, give me your hand.

LUCY. If I could understand now — if it were not dark —

STARK. Oh, Lucy, give me your hand.

LUCY. (*A tentative movement toward him*) If I could only believe —

STARK. (*As her hand touches his, he swings toward her, drops to his knees before her, flings his arms around her waist*) Oh, Lucy, I have horrors in my head. They lurch and grind, like street cars.

LUCY. (*Touching his hair, looking off into the distance*) He was a good baby when he was little. He never cried.

JACK. (*Turning to the* PROFESSOR, *as the light is down on the others*) Make what you will of that, pal.

PROFESSOR. What I make of that is simply —

JACK. Wait — and see what you make of this. Next morning, in the Boss's office —

(*JACK moves to stage left and busies himself at the desk;* SADIE *sits, glumly smoking.*)

DUFFY. (*Entering*) Ain't here yet, huh?

JACK. He's coming.

DUFFY. Well, maybe he won't let it get him down.

SADIE. It's just his boy died.

DUFFY. Yeah — tough. (*Pausing ruminatively*) But you know, the Boss ain't what he used to be. Naw, he just ain't got the juice, you might say. (*Edging toward the chair at the desk —* STARK's *chair — and slipping into it*) Mr. Larsen now — I tell you, he is one sharp one. Easy to work with, too. Yeah, let me tell you —

SADIE. You know whose chair you're sitting in?

DUFFY. Huh?

SADIE. So you think it's the Boss that's dead, huh? (*STARK, wearing a hat and top coat, has appeared behind* DUFFY) Well, look over your shoulder and you'll find you're wrong.

(*DUFFY looks around, sees* STARK, *and gets out of the chair as rapidly as possible, cringing as* STARK *hands him his hat, then takes off his coat and flings it over* DUFFY's *arm.*)

DUFFY. Good morning, Boss. How you feel, Boss? We all just came in to see how you feel. Wanted you to know we was thinking about you. Like everybody in the state, Boss. Look at the telegrams there on the desk. Must be a thousand. Telegrams of sympathy and condolence. Folks love you, Boss. Yeah, and flowers at the funeral, they go to show. Them flowers from the Fifth Ward — that was a real floral tribute, Boss —

STARK. (*Ignoring* DUFFY, *stepping to the desk, giving the telegrams a contemptu-*

ous flick) Sadie, get rid of this garbage. *(As DUFFY starts out)* Tiny, you wait. *(Back to SADIE)* Call a special session of the Legislature. Get together all the stuff you have on Larsen's Construction Company, and on the Acme Electric. Anything you can on him, from my private file, and—

DUFFY. Boss—Boss—what?

STARK. You heard me.

DUFFY. Boss—you can't. Boss, you—

STARK. The hell I can't.

(STARK gestures to SADIE, who goes out to follow his instructions.)

DUFFY. Boss, not when everything is fixed with Larsen, Boss, he—

STARK. I can unfix it.

DUFFY. Boss, you can't change your mind. It wouldn't be fair. Not to Mr. Larsen, to change—

STARK. I can change a lot of things around here.

DUFFY. Boss, you call a special session, you start an investigation, you get Mr. Larsen all mad, there ain't no tellin' what'll—

STARK. Look here. Larsen may think, or you may think, that he's bought up some of my boys. Oh, I know he's tried. He may give 'em fifty bucks, but I'll give 'em galloping paralysis. They get gay and there'll be a bear market on barbers and farmhands next election, for if there's anything cheap in this state, it's sweet potatoes and statesmen. They both grow on pore ground. And as for you—

DUFFY. Boss, Boss—

STARK. —you may be wearing a hundred-dollar suit and a diamond ring, but on the hoof, you're crow-bait and, boy, I can strip you to the blast. Now get out.

JACK. *(Watching TINY's exit)* Well, you sure like to do things the hard way.

STARK. Okay, I do 'em the hard way.

JACK. I thought you had dealt with Larsen.

STARK. I have undealt.

JACK. It's none of my business. It doesn't matter if you kick Tiny around. He's built for it. But Larsen is a different kind of cookie.

STARK. You've got to start somewhere.

JACK. Start what?

STARK. Skip it, and get me the files on Acme Electric. I'm going to Sadie's office.

(The light is down on STARK.)

SADIE. *(Appearing near stage center)* He came into my office and he told me. He thought he could do it. To me. He thought he could throw me over. Me, who had made him. Sure, he'd fooled around with every little tart in the state, but he always came back. Even that Anne Stanton. He would have even come back from her. But his wife — that Lucy — throwing me over for her! Throwing me over — and trying to shake my hand. Like he was Jesus. Like he was the suffering God.

ANNE. *(Near* SADIE, *but addressing the audience)* I understand now, and would not have had it otherwise. I had loved him because I knew what he might have been, and if, in the end, he found what he might have been, why should I complain that that discovery left no place for me? But, oh, it was hard — it was hard —

PROFESSOR. *(Moving toward* ANNE *as the light is down on* SADIE*)* My dear madam, even now, when you are satisfactorily married to your early sweetheart, you can scarcely take a rational view of that old event. You had argued yourself by some peculiar, female logic into your liaison with Stark, and then, when he left you, you felt you had lost the only real man in the world. If you had had a little more experience — well, no matter. Sadie Burke, however, had a very different reaction. For when Stark threw her over, she, being a realist, knew exactly what to do.

SADIE. *(Appearing at stage left, leaning over* DUFFY, *seated)* Sure, the Boss'll ruin us. He'll ruin you. Larsen will blame you for the hospital contract falling through. And then he'll fix you.

DUFFY. You talking through your hat.

SADIE. You know what the Big Boss has done? He's throwing over that Stanton bag, the whore.

DUFFY. I'll be damned.

SADIE. She may not know it yet, but it's true.

DUFFY. Allow me to be the first to congratulate you —

SADIE. Shut up, you fool. He's going back to his wife.

DUFFY. Sweet Jesus! Haw, haw —

SADIE. Listen. Do you think Dr. Stanton knows the Boss has been rolling Little Sister in the hay?

DUFFY. Sure — don't he?

SADIE. Hell, no, he doesn't know it. Or know that that's why he got that big hospital job. And he doesn't know that the Big Boss is throwing over Little Sister because he — Dr. Stanton — killed his boy, and that's why he's being taken out of that big hospital job.

DUFFY. Is that a fact?

SADIE. Hell, no, you fool. It's not a fact. It's a lie. But Stanton will believe that lie when you tell him.

DUFFY. When I tell him?

SADIE. When you tell him.

DUFFY. Jesus—I couldn't do that, Sadie. If Stanton found that out he might—
Well—well, maybe I can get some of my boys to kind of spread the word to
Stanton—

SADIE. Sure, put it in the papers, you fool.

DUFFY. But, hell, Sadie, I couldn't tell him—

SADIE. Sure, you're afraid of what will happen when you tell Stanton that he's
no better than a pimp. I don't blame you. Not if he's what I think he is—and
pray to Christ he is. But then—then— *(Pause)* Then the Big Boss won't do
us any more harm, Duffy. And you may escape with your life. And then—

DUFFY. And then, what?

SADIE. And then— *(Drawing wearily away)* Take it or leave it. It's all your funeral
anyway.

DUFFY. All right. All right, I'll do it.

SADIE. All right.

DUFFY. Maybe you got something there. Maybe Stanton will fix the Boss.
(Dawning enthusiasm) Well, I tell you, if me and Larsen take over, Larsen'll
sure take care of you. Hell, if we take over I'll take care of you, Sadie.

(He rubs her shoulders.)

SADIE. *(With tight lips)* Get your Goddamned greasy hands off me.

(The light goes down on the scene and comes up again on JACK.)

JACK. So Duffy took his life in his hands and told Adam Stanton the big lie. And
Adam believed that lie, and I'll tell you why—

ADAM. *(Appearing stage right, toward the audience)* I'll tell you why. If you have
lived in the horrible division of self and yearn for the old integrity. If you
have been betrayed by your own father. If you have been betrayed by those
you love. If you have lived with the gnawing certainty of self-betrayal. Then
you pick each minute like a scab. You wait for the clean twitch of pain. Have
you walked a night in the dark, lost on the ground you had thought familiar?
And suddenly the lightning flash, the stabbing light on sky, sea, and wind-
heaved trees, brighter than day—and the old path clear before you. Oh, it is
sure. You run in the new dark, while the thunder rolls, and the new dark
darker than dark, but it does not matter now, for your feet know. They know
the way. At last—and I came to her and saw her face—and would I be the
happy pimp? Would I be—

ANNE. *(Suddenly appearing behind and to the right of ADAM)* No, Adam! Don't
you say it. You must understand.

ADAM. *(Turning on her)* I understand this much. I'll be no front for a scoundrel,
or a pimp to your whoring. I'll be no—

ANNE. Oh, Adam, you don't know how it was!

ADAM. I know this much. I know you — (*Pushing her away, so that she falls*) And I know him — and I know his filth. I know his face. And knowing him, at last I know myself.

(*He dashes off as the light is down on* ANNE.)

JACK. (*Appearing in a spotlight*) And that was their unreconciled parting. Anne called me to find her brother. She said I had to find him. She was wild to find him.

(*The stage blacks out for a moment as we hear* JACK's *voice and the replies:*

"*Have you seen Dr. Stanton?*"
"*No, not all day.*"
"*Has Dr. Stanton been here?*"
"*Hell, no, not today.*"
"*Have you seen Dr. Stanton?*"
"*No, not tonight.*"

Meanwhile, the light has come up on ADAM, *stage left, waiting calm and detached, as a* MAN *accosts him.*)

MAN. Howdy, Doc. My God, you been in the Legislature tonight? The Boss is sure on a tear. Maybe they won't get up the nerve to impeach him. He's given 'em heart failure. It's like a hoot owl done got in the hen house. The air is full of feathers. God-A-Mighty, the Boss is like a one-legged man tromping out a prairie fire. I'm tellin' you he sure is tearin' that Legislature apart. The things he's calling them. Things I wouldn't even call my own mule. Man, the Legislature is scared to impeach Willie, with that crowd come into town. That crowd would kill 'em if they tried to impeach Willie. (*Roar of the crowd, offstage*) By God, he's out there. He's out there on the balcony! Bet he's talking to the crowd. Man, I'm going to be there.

STARK. (*Offstage*) And my enemies say that I have done things not for the love of you, but for the love of power. Do you believe that?

CROWD. (*Offstage*) No! No! No!

STARK. (*Offstage*) What man knows the truth of his heart? But I shall look in my heart and hope to find some love for you. Some little at least.

CROWD. (*Offstage*) Willie! Willie! Willie!

STARK. My enemies say that I have used threats, deals, bribery, corruption. That I have preyed on the weakness of men. Do you believe it?

CROWD. Kill 'em! Kill 'em! Kill 'em!

STARK. What I have done, I have done. And I will not excuse myself. What I shall do I will do. I will do what I must do, but I want one thing. I want to be able in the end to look you in the eye. Listen, listen to me!

CROWD. Blood on the moon! Blood on the moon! Willie! Willie! Willie!

STARK. But listen! Listen! I want that much innocence!

CROWD. Blood on the moon!

ADAM. (*To himself*) You labor for innocence, and in the end you learn that innocence is easy. It comes as easy and unsought as a childhood recollection. It is as easy as the dearest breath. As the most casual farewell. As the sea hawk's white highest gleam in the sun. Innocence is easy.

STARK. (*Entering stage right, followed by* SUGAR *and* JACK, *stopped by several newsmen. There are flashes of camera bulbs, as* STARK *stops for a picture. Then he sees* ADAM *move to him with outstretched hand*) Well, Doc. (ADAM *presents a revolver and fires twice.* STARK *stumbles to his knees, as* SUGAR-BOY *leaps forward, firing. Even after* ADAM *is down,* SUGAR-BOY, *at a last twitch, fires again.* JACK *is leaning over* STARK. SUGAR-BOY *joins him, as the light is down on the body of* ADAM) Jack — the Doc — he — he shot me.

JACK. Oh, Boss — Boss —

STARK. Jack, Jack — why did he — do it — to me —

JACK. God damn it, I don't know!

STARK. I never did anything to him — Jack.

JACK. No — no.

STARK. Maybe he just got screwed up.

JACK. Yeah, yeah — he just got screwed up.

STARK. Maybe — I just got myself screwed up.

JACK. Boss — Boss —

STARK. It might have been different, Jack — even yet — even yet — you got to believe that, Jack.

JACK. I do, Boss, I do! I believe it! (*Rising and moving toward the audience, as the light is down on the others*) Different! It might have been different. And I must believe that. (*Swinging to the* PROFESSOR, *who has entered the area of light*) And you — you must believe that. (*To the audience*) For if we believe that, we can live, we can have a reason for living.

PROFESSOR. Mr. Burden. No, no. Those words were only the final indication of Stark's failure of nerve. For in the last phase — after his son's death — Stark became the sentimental, confused moralist, unable to deal with facts. You may think that I have no concern with morality. Oh, but I do. But the morality of an act, the means to an end, must not be confused with the end result. We can only strive to create conditions of health and well-being which will make men well adjusted and therefore able to act morally. Mr. Burden, are you too blind to see that Stark's late conversion to what you regard as a moral view accomplished nothing more than to pass on power to that — to Governor Tiny Duffy!

DUFFY. *(Revealed on the platform, addressing the audience)* — and friends, after all these years, on this memorable occasion, I can still promise you that Willie Stark's great dream will come true. I have built this hospital. I have kept faith with Willie Stark because I loved him — We all loved Willie —

SADIE. *(Appearing in a spotlight, moving toward DUFFY, accusingly)* Loved him! Loved him. My God! He killed him. *(She covers her face with her hands.)*

PROFESSOR. And when you found that out, Mr. Burden, what did you do?

JACK. *(Staring at TINY)* I did nothing. Because he is nothing, nothing. If he were something. If he were real. If he were human. I would have killed him. But he is nothing. He is the Great Twitch. He is the mob in which everything looks like everything else. He is the wind with the stink on it, and we do not know where it comes from. Unless it comes from us. From us all. For if that is the world, that is the world we made. As you say, Prof, History is blind. But Man is not!

PROFESSOR. You are only a man after all, Mr. Burden.

STARK. *(Appearing on the balcony, looking out over the heads of the audience. The other characters are revealed in various places about the stage, looking up at STARK)* I was a man, and I lived in the world of men. And being a man, I did not know what I was. But I yearned toward that definition. And all my deepest labors had not other purpose. But I was a man, among men. I say this not for forgiveness. For I have no need of that now. All I need now is truth.

PROFESSOR. *(Ironically)* Truth!

STARK. For that is the last ambition.

JACK. *(Challengingly, to the PROFESSOR)* And from that I'll make my truth.

(As ANNE joins him he puts his arm around her waist and they move toward ADAM, with a gesture of loving reconciliation. IRWIN, with an expression of warm recognition, makes a motion toward JACK and ANNE.)

LUCY. *(Lifting her arms toward STARK)* Oh, Willie, Willie!

SUGAR-BOY. It's the B-B-Big B-B-B-Boss. He can t-t-talk so good.

The Light Blacks Out

Selected Bibliography

Atkinson, Brooks. "Theatre: Stage Politics." *New York Times,* 17 October 1959, 27.

———. *New York Times,* 25 October 1959, sec. 2, 1.

Beebe, Maurice, and Leslie A. Field, eds. *Robert Penn Warren's* All the King's Men: *A Critical Handbook.* Belmont, Calif.: Wadsworth Publishing Company, 1966.

Bentley, Eric. "All the King's Men." *Theater Arts* 31 (November 1947): 72–73.

Blotner, Joseph. *Robert Penn Warren: A Biography.* New York: Random House, 1997.

Brooks, Cleanth. Papers. Yale Collection of American Literature (MSS 30). Beinecke Rare Book and Manuscript Library. Yale University, New Haven, Conn.

Brooks, Cleanth, John Thibaut Purser, and Robert Penn Warren. *An Approach to Literature.* Shorter ed. New York: F. S. Crofts & Co., 1939.

Brustein, Robert. "Robert Brustein on Theater: A Tribute to Robert Penn Warren." *New Republic,* 25 May 1987, 25–27.

Burt, John. *Robert Penn Warren and American Idealism.* New Haven: Yale University Press, 1988.

Casper, Leonard. *Robert Penn Warren: The Dark and Bloody Ground.* Seattle: University of Washington Press, 1960.

Clark, William Bedford. *The American Vision of Robert Penn Warren.* Lexington: University Press of Kentucky, 1991.

Davis, Robert Murray. "The Whole World . . . Willie Stark: Novel and Film of *All the King's Men.*" In *Film and Literature: A Comparative Approach to Adaptation,* ed. Michael Schoenecke, 33–44. Lubbock: Texas Tech University Press, 1988.

Disch, Thomas M. "All the King's Men." *Nation,* 12 December 1987, 725.

Eller, Jonathan R., and C. Jason Smith. "Robert Penn Warren: A Bibliographical Survey, 1986–1993." *Mississippi Quarterly* 48.1 (winter 1994–95): 169–94.

Ellison, Ralph, and Eugene Walter. "Warren on the Art of Fiction: 1957." In *Robert Penn Warren Talking: Interviews 1950–1978,* ed. Floyd C. Watkins and John T. Hiers, 27–53. New York: Random House, 1980.

Ferriss, Lucy. *Sleeping with the Boss: Female Subjectivity and Narrative Pattern in Robert Penn Warren.* Baton Rouge: Louisiana State University Press, 1997.

Gado, Frank. "A Conversation with Robert Penn Warren: 1966." In *Robert Penn Warren Talking: Interviews 1950–1978*, ed. Floyd C. Watkins and John T. Hiers, 70–87. New York: Random House, 1980.

Gibbs, Wolcott. "The Theater." *New Yorker*, 24 January 1948, 42–43.

Grimshaw, James A., Jr. "Biographical Trends in Warren Criticism: The 1980s." *Southern Quarterly* 31.4 (summer 1993): 51–67.

———. *Cleanth Brooks and Robert Penn Warren: A Literary Correspondence*. Columbia: University of Missouri Press, 1998.

———. *Robert Penn Warren: A Descriptive Bibliography, 1922–1979*. Charlottesville: University Press of Virginia, 1981.

———. "Strong to Stark: Deceiver, Demagogue, Dictator." *Texas College English* n.s. 23.1 (winter 1990): 17–22.

Justus, James H. *The Achievement of Robert Penn Warren*. Baton Rouge: Louisiana State University Press, 1981.

Kennedy, William. "Robert Penn Warren: Willie Stark, Politics, and the Novel." In *Riding the Yellow Trolley Car*, 165–73. New York: Viking, 1993.

Kuehl, John. "Verse Drama into Novel: Robert Penn Warren." In *Write and Rewrite: A Study of the Creative Process*, ed. John Kuehl, 234–63. New York: Meredith Press, 1967.

L.B. "'All the King's Men,' Robert P. Warren's Play, Given by the Dramatic Workshop of the New School." *New York Times* 19 January 1948, 19.

Lewis, R. W. B. "Robert Penn Warren's Canon of Precursors." In *Literary Reflections: A Shoring of Images, 1960–1993*, 259–91. Boston: Northeastern University Press, 1993.

Runyon, Randolph Paul. *The Braided Dream: Robert Penn Warren's Late Poetry*. Lexington: University Press of Kentucky, 1990.

———. *The Taciturn Text: The Fiction of Robert Penn Warren*. Columbus: Ohio State University Press, 1990.

Ruppersburg, Hugh. *Robert Penn Warren and the American Imagination*. Athens: University of Georgia Press, 1990.

Schutte, William M. "The Dramatic Versions of the Willie Stark Story." In *"All the King's Men": A Symposium*, ed. John A. Hart, 75–90. Carnegie Series in English, no. 3. Pittsburgh: Carnegie Institute of Technology, 1957.

Simpson, Lewis P. "The Loneliness Artist: Robert Penn Warren." In *The Fable of the Southern Writer*, 132–54. Baton Rouge: Louisiana State University Press, 1994.

Tanselle, G. Thomas. *A Rationale of Textual Criticism*. A Publication of the A. S. W. Rosenbach Fellowship in Bibliography. Philadelphia: University of Pennsylvania Press, 1989.

Warren, Robert Penn. *All the King's Men (A Play)*. New York: Random House, 1960.

———. "Author's Introduction." In *All the King's Men*. 35th Anniversary Edition. New York: Harcourt Brace Jovanovich, 1981.

———. *Blut auf dem Mond: Ein Schauspiel in 3 Akten*. Trans. Erwin Piscator and Hellmut Schlien. Emsdetten (Westphalia): Lechte, 1957.

———. *Brother to Dragons (A Play in Two Acts)*. *Georgia Review* 30.1 (spring 1976): 65–138.

——. *Brother to Dragons: A Tale in Verse and Voices.* New York: Random House, 1953.

——. *Brother to Dragons: A Tale in Verse and Voices (A New Version).* New York: Random House, 1979.

——. "Introduction." In *All the King's Men.* New York: Modern Library, 1953.

——. "Introduction." In *Tutti gli uomini del re.* Trans. Gerardo Guerrieri. *Sipario,* no. 127 (December 1960): 53–71.

——. "Introduction to the 1974 English Edition." In *All the King's Men.* London: Secker & Warburg, 1974.

——. "Louisiana Politics and *All the King's Men.*" In *Robert Penn Warren's "All the King's Men": A Critical Handbook,* ed. Maurice Beebe and Leslie A. Field, 23–28. Belmont, Calif.: Wadsworth, 1966.

——. Papers. Yale Collection of American Literature (MSS 51). Beinecke Rare Book and Manuscript Library. Yale University, New Haven, Conn.

——. "Proud Flesh." Robert Penn Warren Papers. Yale Collection of American Literature (MSS 51). Beinecke Rare Book and Manuscript Library. Yale University, New Haven, Conn.

——. "A Special Message to Subscribers from Robert Penn Warren." In *All the King's Men.* Signed Limited Edition. Franklin Center, Pa.: Franklin Library, 1977.

——. "Willie Stark: His Rise and Fall." Robert Penn Warren Papers. Yale Collection of American Literature (MSS 51). Beinecke Rare Book and Manuscript Library. Yale University, New Haven, Conn.

Watkins, Floyd C., and John T. Hiers, eds. *Robert Penn Warren Talking: Interviews 1950–1978.* New York: Random House, 1980.

Weales, Gerald. *American Drama since World War II.* New York: Harcourt Brace and World, 1962.

Weeks, Dennis L., ed. *"To Love So Well the World": A Festschrift in Honor of Robert Penn Warren.* New York: Peter Lang, 1992.

Wellek, René. "A Reminiscence for Cleanth Brooks." *Southern Review* 31.2 (spring 1995): 219–20.